WEYERHAEUSER ENVIRONMENTAL BOOKS

WILLIAM CRONON, EDITOR

Weyerhaeuser Environmental Books explore human relationships with natural environments in all their variety and complexity. They seek to cast new light on the ways that natural systems affect human communities, the ways that people affect the environments of which they are a part, and the ways that different cultural conceptions of nature profoundly shape our sense of the world around us. A complete listing of the books in the series appears at the end of the book.

D1617552

PLOWED UNDER

AGRICULTURE & ENVIRONMENT IN THE PALOUSE

ANDREW P. DUFFIN

FOREWORD BY WILLIAM CRONON

UNIVERSITY OF WASHINGTON PRESS SEATTLE AND LONDON

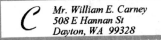
C *Mr. William E. Carney*
508 E Hannan St
Dayton, WA 99328

PLOWED UNDER: AGRICULTURE AND ENVIRONMENT IN THE PALOUSE IS PUBLISHED

WITH THE ASSISTANCE OF A GRANT FROM THE WEYERHAEUSER ENVIRONMENTAL

BOOKS ENDOWMENT, ESTABLISHED BY THE WEYERHAEUSER COMPANY FOUNDATION,

MEMBERS OF THE WEYERHAEUSER FAMILY, AND JANET AND JACK CREIGHTON.

© 2007 by the University of Washington Press
Printed in the United States of America
Designed by Pamela Canell
12 11 10 09 08 07 06   5 4 3 2 1

All rights reserved. No part of this publication may be reproduced or transmitted
in any form or by any means, electronic or mechanical, including photocopy,
recording, or any information storage or retrieval system, without permission in
writing from the publisher.

University of Washington Press
PO Box 50096, Seattle, WA 98145
www.washington.edu/uwpress

Library of Congress Cataloging-in-Publication Data
Duffin, Andrew P.
Plowed under : agriculture and environment in the Palouse /
    Andrew P. Duffin.—1st ed.
        p.   cm.—(Weyerhaeuser environmental books)
Includes bibliographical references and index.
ISBN-13: 978-0-295-98743-9 (hardback : alk. paper)
ISBN-10: 0-295-98743-x (hardback : alk. paper)
1. Agriculture—Palouse River Valley (Idaho and Wash.)   I. Title.
II. Title: Agriculture and environment in the Palouse.   III. Series:
Weyerhaeuser environmental book.
S451.W2D84   2007   630.9797'39—dc22   2007020207

The paper used in this publication is acid-free and 90 percent recycled from at least
50 percent post-consumer waste. It meets the minimum requirements of American
National Standard for Information Sciences—Permanence of Paper for Printed
Library Materials, ANSI z39.48–1984. ♾

In memory of Sarah

CONTENTS

The Wind's Gift of Wheat

WILLIAM CRONON

T HE PALOUSE COUNTRY, in east-central Washington and the western panhandle of Idaho, is not well known to those who do not live there. Back in the mid-twentieth century, travelers on a cross-country road trip would have just missed its southern margins if they chose U.S. Highway 12 through the Snake River Valley as their east-west route. Today, if they make the same kind of journey on Interstate 90 through Spokane, they sail past the northern edge of the Palouse in much the same way, never giving the Washington-Idaho borderland between these two highways a second thought. Unless they have business at one of the two state universities that lie within the boundaries of the Palouse—Washington State in Pullman and the University of Idaho in Moscow—there probably aren't many outsiders who would choose this region as a destination. The Palouse just isn't on the mental maps of most modern Americans.

This is their loss, for it is a striking landscape. Visit it during growing season, and your eyes will be met by an endless expanse of hills covered by equally endless fields of wheat. At harvest time, the visual effect is like nothing so much as a golden sea, its surface kept perennially in motion by the play of the prevailing winds upon yellowing stalks heavily laden with grain. There is little flat ground here. The hills dip and roll like waves approaching a beach, their steeper, northern slopes reaching upwards of fifty degrees—tough going even for modern agricultural machinery, and tougher still for earlier farmers relying on teams of horses to pull their plows. Yet from the evidence of these abundant fields, the potential rewards are well worth the challenges posed by the steep slopes.

Were you to conclude from this scene that it is an immensely fertile agricultural countryside, one of the most productive in the United States, you would certainly be correct. The reasons for its productivity, though hidden, are among the most interesting features of the Palouse, arising as they do from a remarkable geological history that explains both the unusual hilliness of the terrain and the cornucopian abundance of its wheat fields. If you could slice through these hills with an enormous knife, you would discover that they contain little or no bedrock. Instead, they consist of light, friable, marvelously fertile soil all the way down to the hard surface of lava on which they rest. If more ordinary landscapes have taught you to associate hills with rocks, then an underground view of *this* one would likely persuade you that the Palouse is a pretty unusual place.

How did all this rich soil come to be so copiously piled up to create these hills? The past of this place is full of geological drama that helped create its terrain. Seventeen to sixteen million years ago, eastern Washington and Oregon experienced an immense series of lava flows that laid down the hundreds of feet of basalt on which the Palouse hills now lie. Farther to the west, explosive eruptions of peaks in the Cascade range—Mount St. Helens most recently—have ejected great quantities of volcanic ash that, in drifting down from the sky, have contributed their fertility to regional soils. Thirteen thousand years ago, Glacial Lake Missoula repeatedly sent some of the most enormous floods ever seen in North America roaring across eastern Washington, scouring the landscape that lies just west of the Palouse hills and depositing fine silt in slack water pools left behind as the floods receded.

But although these cataclysmic events all made their contributions to the Palouse, its rich, rockless soils mainly arrived here via a much more commonplace route. These hills are made of *loess*, a fine, light soil blown by winds, which in this case piled up glacial flour, volcanic ash, and floodplain silt along the dry margins of the great continental ice sheets that covered the higher latitudes of North America until just over twelve thousand years ago. As the prevailing southwesterly winds carried untold millions of tons of soil particles into what is today the Palouse, they gradually built up the same kinds of dunes that one more frequently sees rising beside sandy seashores. This accounts for the patterns that make one remember the ocean when viewing this landscape from afar. It also explains why the Palouse hills more often than not have gentle southern slopes but steep northern ones: the predominant direction of the winds made them so. Because loess soils are famously fertile the world over—Iowa too is blessed with loess from the margins of the great ice sheets, as are most of the richest farmlands on the planet—the Euroamerican pioneers who first tried planting wheat here found that their farms produced uncommonly high yields. Although such settlers lacked the geological knowledge to understand the ultimate source of their prosperity, the richness of the Palouse soil—and so too of these farms—was a gift of the western wind.

This is the geological backdrop of the story Andrew Duffin tells in *Plowed Under: Agriculture and Environment in the Palouse.* At the center of his inquiry is a curious paradox. Although the farms in the Palouse have for many decades reliably produced some of the highest yields of wheat any-where in the United States, they have also, at the same time, produced some of the nation's highest rates of soil erosion. Since Euroamerican farming began here in the late nineteenth century, half or more of the region has lost somewhere between 25 to 75 percent of its topsoil. In some areas, top-soil has vanished altogether, washing down rivulets and streams to be car-ried by the Snake and the Columbia out to sea. How this could happen—and why Palouse farmers have for so long managed to flourish while remain-ing seemingly indifferent to the consequences of their own agricultural practices—is the riddle Duffin seeks to answer in this book.

At one level, the story of soil erosion in the Palouse might not seem all that surprising. The lightness of the loess particles that enabled them to blow in so easily on the back of the west wind makes them equally susceptible to being washed away by water. The steep hills enable water to gather kinetic energy as it travels down slope, carrying ever greater quantities of silt and sand as it gains momentum. By removing the cover of native bunchgrasses and other vegetation in order to plant crops, farmers left the soil open to wind and rain, far less protected than it had been when they arrived. Under such circumstances, a dramatic increase in erosion rates was almost inevitable in the absence of management techniques designed to prevent it. Unfortu-nately, such techniques were not widely adopted in the Palouse, and this is what Andrew Duffin argues is the most surprising feature of its history.

Plowed Under offers a cautionary tale for anyone who worries about the sustainability of American agriculture. Curiously, all this soil erosion has yet to destroy the region's fabled productivity. If Palouse farmers have been profligate in their use of the land, they do not appear to have paid much of a price for the vast tonnage of soil they have sent downstream to the Pacific. One reason for this no doubt has to do with the astonishing fertility bequeathed to the region by the winds that deposited the loess here in the first place. Because the original gift was so vast, it has taken longer to be used up here than in many other places. Then, too, the advent of petro-chemical fertilizers and other soil-enhancing technologies after the Second World War meant that even in places where fertility declined, farmers were able to buy back high yields by importing the very nutrients they were otherwise sending downstream.

Two other features of Palouse agriculture are central to Duffin's analysis. Like their counterparts elsewhere in the United States, Palouse farmers have come to rely on a wide array of government subsidies to support their enterprise, especially in the wake of the New Deal. Duffin provides one of the best histories anyone has yet written of the ways in which federal funds and policies helped transform regional agriculture in the twentieth century. These took the form of direct price supports for crops, of course, but also included enormous federal investments in the infrastructure that makes modern farming profitable: dams that generate electricity on the Columbia River, for instance, or highway systems that deliver crops to market—to say nothing of USDA subsidies that support agricultural research in land grant universities. But even as Palouse farmers were becoming ever more dependant on such subsidies to underwrite the profitability of their operations, they expressed fierce opposition to government regulation and to what they saw as excessive federal power. They sought quite skillfully to obtain federal funds even as they resisted federal oversight. Subsidies helped them avoid some of the economic burdens that declining soil fertility might otherwise have imposed on them, and weak regulatory oversight enabled them to avoid adopting new farming techniques that might have more successfully prevented erosion.

Whatever short-term, self-interested advantages such tactics might offer, Andrew Duffin makes clear their long-term risks. If our goal is to imagine where food will come from for the grandchildren of our grandchildren, then the paradoxical mix of private rights and public subsidies that have supported erosive soil practices on Palouse farms seems especially instructive. For just this reason, *Plowed Under* deserves to be read even by those who have never visited the curious hill country lying north of the Snake River in eastern Washington and western Idaho. Duffin would be the first to admit that his history of past Palouse land use cannot furnish a failsafe blueprint for its future. But as we struggle to define and understand the meaning of sustainable agriculture in the twenty-first century and beyond, the story of what has happened to the wind's gift of wheat in the Palouse has much to teach us all.

ACKNOWLEDGMENTS

F OR A KID born in Los Angeles and raised in rural Maine, it might seem odd that I've taken such interest in agricultural landscapes. This occurred probably because both my parents came from the Midwest and because of my many cross-country trips by car, both as a child and as an adult. Instead of seeing the Central Valley of California on US 99, the rolling prairie of eastern Colorado on Interstate 70, and the cornfields of southern Illinois on State Route 140 as drab and monotonous, I saw something else. I stared out the window at carefully manipulated agricultural systems big and small and wondered how it all *worked*. What crops grew where, why some cattle were one color or another, all that machinery, and the rhythms of farm life—I wanted to know about it all. As I got older my questions became more complex, with this book containing my most pointed questions about farming and environmental history to date. I chose to study the Palouse for the simple fact that it surrounded me while in graduate school at Washington State University; if I ever needed something to fuel my curiosity and creativity, it was right outside my window.

Paul Hirt and William Robbins gave me the tools needed to write this book. Paul forced me to hone my research, to find my audience, and to write something provocative yet not polemical. His greatest asset as an advisor was his ability to boil down my scattered thoughts and extract from them the things I really wanted to say. I met Bill while he taught as a visiting scholar at the University of Idaho. I asked him to read a first draft of a chapter, and when I got it back, I was amazed by his incisive analysis and by how freely the blue ink ran from his pen. If this book appears direct and to the point it's because of Bill's relentless editing. But more importantly, Paul and Bill are great friends and trusted supporters of my work. I can only hope that my academic future will allow me to mentor students in a similar fashion.

A host of other generous people brought this book to life. Julidta Tarver, acquisitions editor at the University of Washington Press, ushered this rookie author through the dark halls of publishing, always explaining how things got done and where I needed to be. The Press's assistant managing editor, Mary Ribesky, graciously allowed me more time to finish revisions. Copy editor Julie Van Pelt gave the manuscript a thorough going-over, clarifying weak passages and greatly improving the coherence of the notes and bibliography. And while I was teaching for a year at Western Washington University, Chris Friday vastly improved a chapter from this book that I turned into an article for *Pacific Northwest Quarterly*.

I received a summer fellowship from Washington State University's Thomas S. Foley Institute for Public Policy and Service, a grant that allowed me to work full-time on the manuscript in the summer of 2001. Thanks also to the good people at the Manuscripts, Archives, and Special Collections Library at Washington State, especially Larry Stark, and to Ed Garretson of the Whitman County Historical Society, and to the staff at the Latah County Historical Society, all of whom directed me to archived papers and photos that make this book what it is.

My WSU grad student cohorts are my trusted comrades. Jeff Crane commented on portions of the manuscript and provided me with the anecdote that begins the second chapter. He also serves as a great verbal sparring partner, while still giving his unconditional friendship. Michael Egan has been a constant source of great advice, support, and friendship. He single-handedly transformed a weak and ineffectual conference paper derived from the manuscript into my first real public success as an academic. Kevin Marsh has also been a tremendous colleague and friend, offering some much-needed help with the publishing process. And Adam Sowards, although an assistant professor at the University of Idaho, is an honorary member of our little Palouse cabal. He, too, curbed many of my literary excesses and is the kind of colleague you'd want next door to your office. All of you have helped me get through the tough times.

Special thanks goes to an anonymous reader who pored over the manuscript and called for revisions that resulted in a drastic improvement in its historical context and, indeed, its very thesis. I'm not sure if I can ever repay this debt, but I hope to have a chance to do so someday. And thanks to William Cronon, who agreed to include this work in the prestigious Weyerhaeuser Environmental Books Series at the University of Washington Press. Especially for the young scholar, it is an honor and a privilege to have one of the progenitors of environmental history evaluate and appreciate my work.

Finally, I must also thank my family. My mother, Mary Duffin, and my late father, David Duffin, developed my academic inquisitiveness from very early in my life, putting me on a path to higher education that I'm still exploring. My brother, Matt Duffin, inspired me to be at least a fraction as smart as he is, and taught me how to be a real college student. I regret that my late sister, Sarah Duffin, did not survive to see this book's completion. She was my most unflinching supporter in so many ways over the years. Her fingerprints are all over this book. Finally, the love and devotion and, above all, patience of my wife and fishing pal, Mary Jane Maxwell, made this book possible and my life full of warmth and meaning.

PLOWED UNDER

AGRICULTURE & ENVIRONMENT IN THE PALOUSE

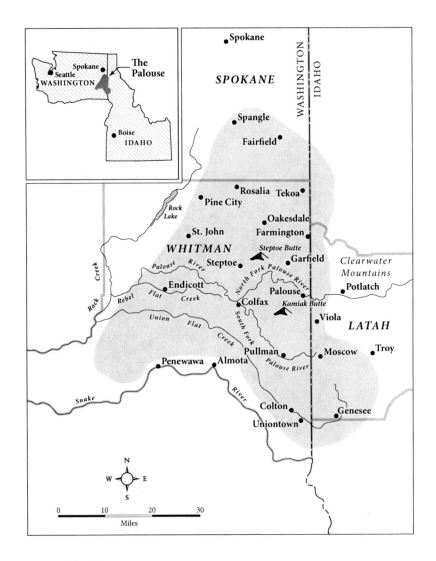

MAP 1. The Palouse

1 INTRODUCTION

A Place Called the Palouse

T RAVEL AGENTS do not steer vacationers to the Palouse. Tour buses do not stop here and few even pass through. Educated youth tend to leave for urban areas after college to escape its cultural short-comings. Compared to some other places in the West, Palouse weather is not harsh, with relatively mild winters and long, sunny summers—but there is no ocean nearby; a lazy, almost motionless Snake River suffices for seasonal watersports and undergraduate high jinks from nearby Washington State University and the University of Idaho. It has always looked rather barren and sparsely vegetated; it is not blessed with majestic mountain peaks and many of its streams are narrow, shallow, intermittent, and lack the salmon runs that have sustained other parts of the Pacific Northwest for centuries. Even local Indians used the land only sporadically, preferring the bounty of fish that the Snake and Columbia rivers provided, or the camas-filled fields near the Clearwater Mountains to the east. Towns dot the countryside, but few could be called thriving, especially in this era of strip malls and drive-through espresso. Palouse communities appear to be from another time, with dated infrastructures and an aging population. Passers-by might call parts of the landscape endearing but would likely not consider it bucolic. At first glance the Palouse fits what historian Elliott West said of the Great Plains: "The country seems to have a lot of very little."[1]

The Palouse is a sparsely populated, semiarid, hilly expanse located in

3

southeastern Washington and a thin slice of northern Idaho. While it may lack the dramatic vistas seen in other parts of the West, the place is nevertheless visually arresting.[2] The hills are what best distinguish the Palouse from neighboring zones—big, rounded mounds of loose earth formed just before, during, and after the last ice age. They are what make the region what it is. To many residents and visitors, they are beautiful, identifying a place that is quite unlike any other. Landscape artists and photographers have been drawn to the Palouse for decades, rendering what are mostly realistic impressions of this place, as though abstractions of this uncommon land would be unnecessary. But it is not an easy land to master. The Palouse is not intimidating in the manner of the giant Mount Rainier or the emptiness of the Snake River plain, but neither is it an easy place to scratch out an existence. All evidence indicates that for at least the last twelve thousand years, few people have called it home, compared to other locales in North America.[3]

One thing people *can* do here is grow crops, mostly small grains, peas, and lentils. Wheat yields in the Palouse are among the highest in the nation, and the agricultural sector has propelled regional growth since the earliest days of Euro-American settlement in the nineteenth century. Aided by improved transportation links to distant markets and continued advancements in farming technology, the natural fertility of the land produced bountiful harvests that encouraged capital investment and intensifying farming practices. By the beginning of the First World War, Palouse farming was the most important aspect of the regional economy and a key supplier of grains for the nation and the world, and Whitman County had the highest per capita income of any county in the nation.

Agricultural expansion continued and Palouse farming prospered for most of the twentieth century. But the advent of intensive agriculture in the nineteenth century required a fundamental reworking of the land and a concomitant reorientation of the Palouse ecosystem.[4] Those transformations and their accompanying social impact are the primary foci of this book. The most significant ecological change involved the soil itself. Annual crops meant repeated plowing, first by horsepower, then by tractors in the 1920s and 1930s. Once the initial layer of organic matter and native bunchgrass root systems had degraded in the early twentieth century, soil began to erode into nearby streams. The Palouse hills became less fertile. By the 1930s, scientists predicted that erosion would reduce crop yields, preliminary findings that were confirmed in the 1970s. The US Department of Agriculture (USDA) determined in 1978 that since Euro-American settlement in the late nineteenth century, erosion had stripped all of the topsoil from

10 percent of the land, and from 25 to 75 percent of the topsoil from 60 percent of the land. In addition, the US Geological Survey (USGS) found in 1994 that 87 percent of the nitrogen in regional streams and rivers came from agricultural fertilizers.[5] The combination of eroded soils and farm chemicals choked Palouse waters, making them unfit for human consumption and unsuitable as habitat for many fish species. By the late twentieth century the Palouse River system, the region's major drainage, was among the most polluted in the state of Washington.[6]

Farming activity brought physical disturbance to the Palouse, as it has in every other agricultural region. But its erosive effects were more acute here because of the unique topography and geology. The hills are everywhere, forming the most identifiable landmarks of the area. Indeed, finding suitably flat land to plat towns was a struggle for nineteenth-century settlers. From the air, the land looks like a huge expanse of ski moguls, except that they are fifty to two hundred feet high. From the ground, the hills appear as giant sand dunes—which is what they are, except that grasses, shrubby plants, and a few trees subsequently grew on and around them. These hills are central to this story. Their steep pitch and light, geologically young soil (called "loess" by geologists) meant that when people began repeatedly using steel farm implements on them, the land began to wash away.

The reactions to these conditions and the meanings behind them serve as a lens for peering into the collective actions of Palouse farmers and American agricultural society in general. On repeated occasions questions of ecological degradation and long-term agricultural sustainability confronted farmers; in most cases they continued with their traditional farming practices. The explanations for the persistence of what many considered unsustainable methods are multiple: farmers had to be concerned with immediate financial returns; sizable harvests belied the dire predictions of soil conservationists; and farmers believed that new technologies would negate future problems. Farming innovations sometimes mitigated or masked ecological harm, but plowing the steep slopes of the Palouse continued to take its toll in erosion. Technology—whether in the form of hybrid seed, machinery, herbicides, or fertilizer—increased farm yields and gave farmers a sense that they could successfully manipulate nature without negative consequences. Their practices continued to produce abundant harvests, yet ecosystems eroded.

The story of ongoing environmental damage in the Palouse also reveals how governments responded to a persistent, yet rather undramatic, agricultural problem. In short, government agencies involved in such matters (chiefly the USDA) reacted as most of their constituents wished. Although the USDA stated in 1938 that "the well-being of future generations must be secured if the nation is to continue to live. One of the great national objectives is to pass the soil on to our descendants as nearly unimpaired as possible," their actions in the Northwest reflected less urgency.[7] The Palouse erosion problem never looked like a disaster; soil was lost, but it did not resemble the Great Plains Dust Bowl of the 1930s. Palouse soil moved silently into gullies and streams and did not drift like snow, block trains, or force residents to wear masks. Erosion temporarily defaced the land in spring but was subsequently plowed out of sight or covered by sprouting crops. Because crop yields continued to increase, especially after the Second World War, few people demanded thoroughgoing change in agriculture. Volumes of scientific evidence suggested that erosion threatened future productivity, but high yields in the short term buoyed farmers' convictions that they could continue business as usual.

The Palouse soil story validates theories that Piers Blaikie spells out in *The Political Economy of Soil Erosion in Developing Countries* (1985). In this influential treatise on political economy, Blaikie argues that erosion has been and is a multicausal phenomenon of interrelated components, "the interaction between land use, the natural characteristics of that land and its vegetation, and the erosive forces of water and wind."[8] In other words, erosion and soil depletion are both dependent on and yet independent of humans, its level of intensity based on both the lay of the land and the people (and politicians) who live *on* the land. Blaikie suggests what environmental historians would later find true: people and nature both have agency, engaging in a dynamic historical relationship. Soil in the Palouse moves because it has always moved, simultaneously accumulating and receding as it has since the Miocene epoch and before. But it also moves and is replaced at rates that are a direct result of human activity.

In Blaikie's examples, which come mostly from Africa and South Asia, soil erosion is a "political-economic" issue that persists until it causes land degradation that forces regional economic change. At that point, it also becomes a "social phenomenon" that can create an enormous political stir. The discovery of environmental problems, the impetus for reform, and the development and enforcement of any land-use changes, however, come "from above." In Blaikie's framework, the grass roots are secondary in importance to those with access to political power. Moreover, once reform measures are either suggested or insisted upon, local farmers usually resist: "Soil conservation measures [are] seen by land-users to be symptoms of oppression."[9]

The confluence of Blaikie's theories and the recent history of the Palouse are striking. The federal government, not Palouse farmers, was the first to address the erosion problem, a response that came only after scientists and bureaucrats forecast dire conditions in the absence of reform. Conservationists in and out of government acted as a kind of regional intelligentsia, delivering their message to an audience that embraced only parts of the lecture. That audience—Palouse farmers—loosely resembled Blaikie's agriculturalists from the developing world, who indeed saw any government attempt at land use regulation as a "symptom of oppression."

Partly in response to local opposition, the federal government's policy aimed to reduce, not eliminate, erosion. USDA initiatives provided farmers with incentives to conserve soil, but never controlled farming practices. Federal policy acted in the short-term interests of the agricultural establishment— farmers, land-grant universities, and equipment and chemical manufacturers—who resisted strong remedies. As early as the 1930s scientists knew erosion could be controlled by eliminating annual cropping on steep hills and ending summer fallow, the practice of keeping ground bare for a year to prevent weed growth and to maintain moisture. Neither of these conservation measures were ever implemented. Instead, soil conservation programs focused on the voluntary set-aside of erodible land and the voluntary adoption of soil-conserving tillage practices. Both failed to reduce erosion to levels that scientists considered sustainable. When strict federal soil and water-quality laws emerged in the 1970s and 1980s, agricultural groups stymied corrective measures that might have improved the long-term viability of Palouse agriculture. Farmers and farm-lobby groups flexed their electoral and financial muscle and legislators and bureaucrats compromised.

Other less-noticeable environmental and cultural phenomena contributed to an ethos of ceaseless disturbance. Euro-American settlement in the Palouse occurred within a context of a wild flurry of economic activity in the United States. The late nineteenth and early twentieth centuries witnessed a flood of immigration, resource use, and capital investment—events that left indelible marks on both land and people. In the Palouse, whole communities owed their existence to the presence of inexpensive, fertile land and a willingness to use it to produce salable products. The value system that emerged in the Palouse and elsewhere centered on those things that had contributed to regional growth (i.e., intensive agriculture), producing a utilitarian landscape that its residents grew to love. As essayist William Kittredge notes in remembering his family's southern Oregon ranch, "all the work . . . was directed toward making it orderly, functional, and productive—and of course that work seemed sacred."[10] The successful commodification of the land denoted a willful dominance of nature that would imbue all future activity.

The human preoccupation with dominion over nature left little room for ideas concerning land stewardship to take hold. This should not surprise us. The idea that farmers got into farming for the singular purpose of living out some kind of Jeffersonian agrarian dream is illusory. Nationally and in the Palouse, homesteaders staked their claims and eked out a meager existence at first, but then moved as fast as transportation lines, new equipment, and easy credit would allow to become whole-heartedly enmeshed in an endless drive to accumulate wealth. Farmers have been no more exempt from the urge to increase productivity and live more comfortably than any other segment of the population. They are we, as we are they, to a great degree. The physical act of working the earth ensures neither a spiritual nor an environmental awakening. Thus, it should come as no real surprise that for most of the twentieth century Palouse farmers made decisions based predominantly on crop yields and investment returns, not on long-term environmental sustainability. From very early on, agricultural experts urged them to look, act, and think like businessmen. They did so with gusto.

But what sort of good businessman would purposely allow such a precious resource to deteriorate? And what sort of farmer would want to abandon the relative security of subsistence farming so quickly and without any obvious misgivings? The answers to these questions form the basic paradox of this narrative, and I believe they require a thorough reexamination of our ideas about American farming since the mid-nineteenth century. But solving the puzzle also involves the reworking of our current political lexicon and a willingness to see farming as the complicated social and cultural mixture of past, present, and future. We need to abandon our common use of the terms "conservative" and "liberal"—most definitely with regard to Palouse farmers, but also when it comes to describing modern farmers around the world in the context of a host of historical and contemporary environmental issues.

Consider the Palouse farmer as an amalgam of old and new, part antediluvian, part riverboat gambler, and part ward of the state—what I call an "agrarian liberal." Despite their positions on most social issues, these people were hardly conservative in terms of their relationship with the land: they took great risks in settling the land, then proceeded to plow the steep hillsides and exhaust soil nutrients until a technological fix (e.g., the farm chemicals that arrived after World War II) allowed them to continue the same practices. Then, when wheat farming nationally became perfected to the point that surpluses and low prices became a problem, farmers asked for and received an endless string of government subsidies: state college and private sector scientific research, construction of a series of dams along the Columbia and lower Snake Rivers, and generous price supports that virtually assured long-term solvency.

Palouse farmers were not conservative, in that they did not act with care, caution, or deliberation. They were eager to drink from the federal trough all the while maintaining a veneer of independence, thinking themselves immune from environmental difficulty because of technological advancements and government support. Here again Blaikie is instructive, stating that "if farms remain profitable, yield-increasing technologies tend to mask the effect of soil degradation and erosion and make up for declines in fertility that would have occurred if land had been cultivated and with a constant level of technology."[11] Farmers used their land to its limits for immediate financial gain and insisted in the 1930s and beyond that the USDA assist in the process. Indeed, farmers welcomed the expansion of twentieth-century government largesse, provided it did not dictate land-use practices in the Palouse. So in another sense, farmers also espoused the virtues of nineteenth-century liberalism: economic growth and development, publicly sponsored internal improvements, and a lack of government regulation. By the mid-twentieth century, however, these agrarian liberals were also keen on maintaining a nostalgic link with the past, one that they used to create an image of the Palouse yeoman—someone who still firmly believed in the inherent goodness of the farming life. Hence they were both *agrarian* and *liberal*—in ways and amounts that changed over time. They wanted the support of an expanding federal safety net when it served their needs *and* they clung to an outdated myth of independence.

These evolving political and commercial values, however, proved inflexible when confronted with environmental problems. A Palouse society devoted to maximizing farm profits viewed the land solely as a means of production, even when erosion, farm chemicals, and water-quality issues came to the fore. Kittredge identifies a similar problem in Warner Valley, Oregon, when describing the parallel, regrettable pasts of the American West and Jack Ray, a family ranch hand:

> Looking backward is one of our main hobbies here in the American West, as we age. And we are aging, which could mean we are growing up. Or not. It's a difficult process for a culture which has always been so insistently boyish. Jack Ray has been dead a long time now. As my father said, he drank his liver right into the ground. "But, by God," my father said, "he was something once."[12]

The Palouse also operates as if it too were "something," and unless farmers take better care they risk jeopardizing the future of farming.

Kittredge's thoughts on land ethics bring up a broader point: agriculture is audacious. It is the purposeful, repeated manipulation of the land so as to produce quantities of food.[13] That may sound like a simple endeavor, but to succeed requires a tremendous amount of human, animal, and fossil-fuel energy, centralized political authority, and luck. It is a massive undertaking to perpetually manipulate ecosystems to prevent them from returning to their former states or, more likely, to evolve into some other hybrid landscape.[14] Changing the land is easy; making those changes conform to precise human whims over decades and centuries is another matter. Agriculture entails a biotic revolution that, once begun, cannot be abandoned without serious social and ecological ramifications.[15] Nor can its imprint on the land be easily removed; areas converted to monocultural crop production only rarely can be returned to their prefarming condition. Agriculture is one of the many activities in which humans seem eager to "play God," that is, to tinker with the land and remake it according to their image.

Besides cutting and clearing trees, the most obvious physical sign of farming is seen on the ground. A variety of digging sticks and wooden, iron, and steel plows suddenly brought into plain sight what had been hidden beneath vegetation for eons. Humans now ask that the soil, the organic and inorganic skin of the planet, perform on a perennial basis. For about the last ten thousand years, humans have worked the soil to simultaneously furnish crops to feed their growing numbers, soak up rainwater, maintain soil fertility, and later to provide a source of material wealth. At times, when people have been smart and fortunate enough to enjoy these benefits, societies and nations have thrived. Take care of the soil and it will take care of you, as the Chinese could attest. For more than five thousand years their preservation of soil resources contributed to thriving, successive dynasties and the most enduring and stable government and society the world has ever known. Abuse the land, and face an uncertain future. Early agriculturalists in the Fertile Crescent (after it became infertile), the Indus River valley, and ancient cultures in much of the land adjacent to the Mediterranean Sea took more from the soil than they gave, and their political fortunes tumbled in response. These events rarely transpire quickly. Soil takes centuries to form and at least decades to destroy; thus, the historian's lens should be opened wide.

Soil erosion in the Palouse matters because it threatens the future of one of the most productive wheat-growing areas in the world. Soil loss has already reduced yields and will continue to do so if left unchecked. The Palouse earth is like Jack Ray's liver, except that a transplant is physically impossible—once lost (or jaundiced) it cannot be recovered. Erosion damages the regional economy by lowering farm profits and limiting farmers' spending power. Erosion also damages the environment by putting large amounts of soil and chemicals in streams, leading to eutrophication and habitat degradation. The economic vitality, environmental health, and aesthetic quality of the Palouse hinge on erosion control. To ignore the problem over the long haul is to court trouble. Correcting it will require political courage and a willingness to reconsider the implications of intensive agriculture, neither of which has yet occurred.

Because farming is such a fundamental expression of how humans view and use the earth, it is essential for environmental historians to evaluate this relationship over time. Indeed, to a large extent the study of agriculture initiated environmental history as a distinct field of study. Seminal works such as Donald Worster's *Dust Bowl* (1979), Richard White's *Land Use, Environment, and Social Change* (1980), and William Cronon's *Changes in the Land* (1982) all investigate the centrality of agriculture to environmental change. More recently, Mark Fiege's *Irrigated Eden* (1999) and Steven Stoll's *Larding the Lean Earth* (2002) also use agriculture as an organizing principle, but they are more apt to find instances where either the land refused to conform to human desires or where humans attempted to understand and reconcile with landscapes and natural forces. Because so much of the world's terrestrial space is in agriculture, it seems appropriate to make the study of this relationship an ongoing campaign. As Stoll insists, "farming matters." He claims that "it is the central biological and ecological relationship in any settled society and the most profound way that humans have changed the world over the last ten thousand years."[16]

The issue of sustainability runs through much of this body of work, serving as a kind of long-term litmus test for environmental ethics. In several recent monographs, scholars have gone one step further and made soil fertility the main component of their sustainability equations. Stoll's work, for example, praises early nineteenth-century American farming, boldly claiming that for at least a few decades early republic agriculturalists conserved soil and cycled nutrients in ways that could have been repeated far into the future; they were careful to preserve the soil, this "tablecloth under the banquet of civilization," making them the nation's incipient conservationists. They knew that "when it moves all the food and finery go crashing."[17] Of course this holistic attitude did not last, mostly because of demographic changes on the Eastern Seaboard and an expanding market economy, both of which put pressure on farmers to increase short-term yields and forego conservation practices. Yet Stoll describes how, for a few brief decades, an older English tradition of soil care and wisdom traveled across the ocean and allowed American farmers to prosper.

Another recent work of environmental history that links soil fertility to sustainability is Brian Donahue's *The Great Meadow* (2004), which analyzes farming practices in colonial Concord, Massachusetts. Like Stoll, Donahue wants to imagine a time when farmers were not hell-bent on exploiting their land and moving on, suggesting "the possibility that colonial farms were not extensive and exhausting." Instead, he persuades us that land use in Concord was more complicated, driven by two sets of interests and traditions. The first was the well-known, sad tale of nutrient loss and farm abandonment, while the second attempted "to cultivate nature with more understanding, skill, and restraint"—in short, to act as though one's great-grandchildren might want to plant those same plots of difficult New England soil. Although these two strands of thought have often coexisted in the minds of the American farmer, Donahue argues that in the early eighteenth century, Yankee farmers managed their resources for the future, paying attention to what they took out of the land and what they put in. Here too farmers got caught in a demographic and economic squeeze, beginning at about 1750, that led to nutrient losses and a general decline in New England agriculture. But Donahue wants to see the good side of this story, urging us to embrace the fact that these people "knew what they were doing," and that they had established "a society of freeholders who lived within exacting social and ecological limits"—even if it was all too brief.[18]

A study of an area that more closely resembles the Palouse, both temporally and spatially, is Geoff Cunfer's *On the Great Plains* (2005). Cunfer asserts that Plains agriculture *was* sustainable, and that the Dust Bowl of the 1930s came about because of normal drought cycles, not because greedy farmers tilled land that should never have seen a plow. In fact, he sees those horrible dust storms as but "a temporary disruption of a stable system." But, he is also quick to point out that over the broadest sweep of time there really is no such thing as "sustainable"—all is ultimately subject to change over time, including landscapes, and that people, "just like other species . . . work to manipulate those systems to our advantage." Thus, to expect farmers to preserve agricultural systems in perpetuity is unrealistic and unreflective of how larger ecosystems behave. Cunfer is content knowing that at least in the "medium-term"—meaning for at least several decades and up to a century—an equilibrium was attained that allowed natural systems and intensive agriculture to coexist.[19]

Those who farm in the Palouse should be held to a higher standard of sustainability. I am not content with the idea that prevailing farming practices could allow production to merely continue into the next century. Because of the meteoric rate of population growth since the Industrial Revolution and because of a belief that landscapes have inherent qualities that deserve respect, the Palouse should be treated better than it has been during the last century. Will soil erosion degrade the land to the point that it cannot be farmed, and if so, when? That is nearly impossible to answer, but we do know that erosion has caused a decline in fertility and that a small part of what makes the American West an interesting place to live, work, drive through, or think about has been diminished. Those are irrefutable historical facts that cannot be ignored, and they beg for a narrative and an analysis of that ongoing situation. Other scholars have been right to notice that human activity cannot change nature forever, or that for short historical moments people took the time to look beyond themselves, replenishing the land to serve the needs of people they would never meet. The evidence for the Palouse, however, tells a different story.

This study is not an exercise in condemning farmers. Other scholars have taken their turn at criticizing this "backbone of society," and the list of detractors is long and varied. Karl Marx, for example, in 1848 sniped at "the idiocy of rural life," and in 1852 railed against the rural "sack of potatoes" in France who had elected Louis Napoleon. Undoubtedly, the cultural conservatism that runs through most agricultural societies bedeviled Marx.[20] Historian Richard Hofstadter, another urbanite, took farmers to task in his 1955 work, *The Age of Reform*. The American farmer, in his view, behaved like a "harassed little country businessman who worked very hard, moved all too often, gambled with his land, and made his way alone." Hofstadter went to considerable lengths to downgrade the veracity and pervasiveness of the agrarian myth because he believed that cities, not the hinterland, molded the national character.[21] And Jared Diamond, author of the Pulitzer Prize–winning *Guns, Germs, and Steel*, wrote an article in 1987 about agriculture titled, "The Worst Mistake in the History of the Human Race." Recent environmental history scholarship has been pointed, but notably less cynical. Donald Worster's *Dust Bowl* (1979) examines the consequences of capitalist agriculture and the unbridled optimism of Great Plains farmers in the 1930s, and Norris Hundley Jr.'s *The Great Thirst* (1992) and Steven Stoll's first book, *The Fruits of Natural Advantage* (1999), show how the agrarian myth had absolutely nothing to do with transforming California into the nation's richest agricultural state. This list could go on considerably further, but suffice it to say that over the years, farmers have taken some jabs from scholars.

This book will be critical as well, but I also hope to contribute to a lively debate about the cultural significance of agricultural landscapes. I seek to provide a fuller understanding of the historical and environmental underpinnings of what for most is an unknown outback on a map. The Palouse is an area worthy of our attention, even if it is unfamiliar to most Americans, and even if it contains no trace of wilderness. The less spectacular, more mundane, utilitarian land that surrounds most of us ought to be studied, because, as William Cronon stated in *Uncommon Ground* (1995), "most of our most serious environmental problems start right here, at home, and if we are to solve those problems, we need an environmental ethic that will tell us as much about *using* nature as about *not* using it."[22] Although no other part of the country has the geographic qualities of the Palouse, there are innumerable other American agricultural landscapes that currently face their own unique environmental challenges. This story of the agrarian liberals of the Palouse may be useful in that it tells about the mechanisms and ideologies used to exploit the land and the concurrent environmental damage, while informing us about the extent to which farmers, governments, and society have cared about protecting middle landscapes. Farmers in other regions of the US shared the proclivities of the Palouse farmer, and along the way diminished their own disappearing, fascinating environments in New England, the Middle Atlantic states, the Great Plains, California, and many other places.[23] The study of the agricultural ecosystem of the Palouse is informative because of what it can tell us about that region and its nuances, and also because it says something about industrial agriculture everywhere.

This story is not declensionist, but rather a candid look at the land, its people, their decisions, and the repercussions of those decisions. I have attempted an honest look at the past that might in some small way guide us in charting a better, more sustainable future. The debate is not over whether or not to use the land or whether or not we should leave irreversible marks on the land—that it *will* be used in some fashion is a foregone conclusion. Instead, as Cronon suggests, "the dilemma we face is to decide what kind of marks we wish to leave."[24] However, it is unavoidable that certain groups, individuals, and ideas will face scrutiny. In a situation like the one currently facing the Palouse, where much of the topsoil has been stripped away, where native vegetation is almost nonexistent, where stream water is so dirty that it is often unfit even for livestock, and where 94 percent of the land has been converted (permanently?) to agriculture, some judgment should be passed.

Of course, the charge of presentism can easily be levied against such an approach, to which I will unapologetically plead guilty. My goal has been to write a history that takes into account the realities and mind-sets of people who lived many years ago, but which also questions some of those actions that have generated controversy as recently as last week. To my mind, having one foot in the past and one in the present is a valid means by which we can arrive at more mature, and, indeed, more *useful* interpretations of the past.

Environmental historians have struggled to pinpoint just what we do. More specifically, are we mandated to adhere to a strict, unrealistic omniscience, or can we allow some of our very current and very emotional needs guide us? To Donald Worster, who tackled this question at the opening of the 2001 American Society for Environmental History conference in Chapel Hill, North Carolina, the answer is clear: if we do not let our collective conscience be our guide then we run the risk of becoming a rather closed fraternity—one that speaks only to itself—with little impact on the nonacademic world. "The surest way to become irrelevant," he said, "is to try to repress or ignore the fact that political and moral commitments have always informed the historian's analysis of the past."[25] We need to use our heads *and* our hearts if we are to have any hope of remaining viable social critics, especially if we really want to effect change. Even the untrained eye is capable of noticing that something is not quite right with the Palouse, and with intensive agriculture generally, and it is incumbent on all of us to find out why and to figure out what to do about it.

2 THE PRECONTACT PALOUSE

A FEW YEARS AGO, my good friend and colleague Jeff Crane related a story to me about his days working the annual wheat harvest outside Pullman, Washington. Because many Palouse farms are well over one thousand acres, a considerable number of workers is needed every year to cut and bring in truckloads of soft white winter wheat (the most common of the local varieties). Usually combines plod along simultaneously with several grain trucks to move the grain from the field to nearby storage bins and elevators. Jeff drove one of the trucks. Once the harvest begins, time is of the essence: the farmer has only a small window of opportunity to get the crop in before it becomes overly ripe or is damaged by wind or rain. Work is generally done in air-conditioned comfort, but days are long and laborious. To keep the operation running smoothly, and to pass the time, drivers stay in constant communication via CB radios—their conversations running from fishing and baseball to more important discussions on how the combines and trucks can most efficiently sweep across a field. During a prolonged stretch of dead air, Jeff thought it might be fun to quiz his fellow teamsters on the origins of the earth they were all working so diligently. "Hey," he asked, "how'd all this dirt get here, anyway?" His question was greeted by a long, stony silence on the radio frequency, followed by several far-flung theories. Apparently, even for folks who had most likely lived in the Palouse for their entire lives, the natural history of the hills that surrounded them and provided at least part of their annual income remained something of a mystery.[1]

Jeff's question is a valid one for the scholar and wheat farmer alike. In order to gain an appreciation for the current environmental situation, an understanding of Palouse geology is necessary. Its hills are a unique physical feature, and their geological makeup helps explain why intensive agriculture has affected them as it has. Indeed, if we want to know how and why Palouse soils erode, we have to know their properties and how they formed in the first place. A brief trip through the eons juxtaposes the millions of years that elapsed to make the Palouse with the relatively quick spate of erosion that has reshaped the land over the last 150 years. The heavy human imprint on the land is a new phenomenon; studying geology broadens our perspective. According to historian Dan Flores, examining what he calls "deep time" is an essential part of writing environmental history: "bioregional histories should properly commence with geology and landform and then take up climate history, using an array of modern approaches from ice cores and pollen analysis to packrat middens and dendroecology."[2]

By the same reasoning, it is also important to look at other natural forces that shaped the precontact Palouse. Weather patterns (prehistoric, historic, and present-day) had a hand in shaping the hills and in determining pre- and postcontact vegetation. Data on local flora and fauna give us clues as to how many Native Americans the land could sustain, as well as information on the impact of horses and cattle. Physical geography, along with geology, say a great deal about what the land might have looked like, how it evolved over the millennia, and what types of life it might be able to support.

Understanding the land-use patterns of regional Indian groups is another key piece of the overall puzzle. The Palouse Indians, who lived mainly along the banks of the Snake River, were the primary caretakers of this area for most of the last 12,000 years. Like most North American tribes, the Palouse and others nearby exploited and altered their lands to suit their needs and wants, especially after the introduction of horses in the eighteenth century. Recent scholarly work has largely erased the notion that the precontact continent existed in a state of perpetual stasis, yet it is still crucial that this study consider the significant changes brought on by the area's first human tenants and compare them to the intense land-use practices of those who followed.

PALOUSE GEOLOGY

So where *did* all this soil come from? For a definitive answer, one first needs to consider Pacific Northwest rock formations and the parent rock of Palouse soils. Hidden beneath hundreds and thousands of feet of Columbia Basin soil and rock lies an ancient, largely unknown layer (or series of layers) of Precambrian sedimentary rock, dating back some 3.5 billion years.[3] Because most of the layers are so deeply buried, with only a handful of outcroppings for geologists to study, the exact date and composition of this formation is difficult to fix. In Washington, Kamiak and Steptoe buttes are the most prominent examples of older, Precambrian protrusions, and in Idaho, Moscow Mountain and Mason and Cottonwood buttes stand out among the younger basalt formations. The evidence of what may exist far below is scant; geologists simply do not have enough evidence to speak authoritatively about what the basin might have looked like in this era.[4]

There is, however, a great deal of evidence about more recent geologic events, the most dramatic and influential of which were the apocalyptic lava flows which began during the Miocene epoch, 23 million years ago. The lava surfaced through thousands of large cracks and fissures in the basin, which, collectively, did more to alter the landscape of the inland Northwest than any other geologic episode. By the time the flows tapered off in the early Pliocene epoch, 4.5 million years ago, forty-two thousand cubic miles of lava had been deposited in the basin. In some locations closer to the Cascades, successive lava flows reached a depth of three miles. The lava did not flow all at once, though; active volcanism was sporadic throughout the Miocene, and thousands of years could pass between eruptions. Thus, the basalt rock that formed as the lava cooled became distinct, successive layers that are relatively easy for geologists to identify and date.[5]

Lava flows are often the geologist's best friend, since they can trap great numbers of animals and plants in their molten wake and give us temporal clues about local flora and fauna. Certainly, the Palouse of the Miocene looked and felt vastly different than it does today. Fossil records of the area reveal that it was home to a variety of long-extinct creatures, including an amphibious pachyderm that resembled a rhinoceros, giant turtles, feline and canine predators, dwarfish three-toed horses, and an assortment of more familiar species that still exist, such as beaver, raccoon, and coyote. These animals thrived in a climate that would be quite unfamiliar to our contemporary inhabitants; it resembled perhaps the weather of the present-day southeastern United States, with warm, moist air, frequent rains, and mild winters. The flora of the region was a reflection of both weather and soil. Instead of the meadow-steppe vegetation that would later dominate, more humid species of plants such as bald cypress, willow, maple, and oak dotted the landscape.[6] The bunchgrasses and ponderosa pines that later inhabited the area would have to wait until the global cooling of the Pliocene epoch and the uplifting of the Cascades (which caused a rain-shadow effect to its east) to create an environment more conducive to their survival.

After the Precambrian sediments laid the foundation and the Miocene lava flows intruded, another more gradual and less cataclysmic process altered the Columbia Basin and gave the Palouse its distinctive composition and topography. From 2.4 million years ago and continuing until 12,000 years ago, prevailing winds deposited tremendous amounts of fine silt in what is today southeastern Washington and portions of northern Idaho. The beginnings of a dunelike landscape took shape—a seemingly endless expanse of hills, uniform and consistent in appearance and neither frightfully steep nor impressively high. Five major periods of glaciation and thawing provided parent material, which was deposited in up to fifty distinct sediment layers.[7]

At one time these wind-driven deposits extended far beyond their current location. Prior to the Pleistocene, hills that probably looked strikingly similar to the Palouse covered a good portion of the southern Columbia Basin, yet they would not make it past the last ice age. The hills that stood to the west of the Palouse were in fact swept away and the ground nearly stripped bare by a series of massive floods, the most spectacular of which occurred between 12,000 and 16,000 years ago. Expanding and retreating glaciers, the result of an extended period of climatic fluctuations, were the main catalysts. As any glacier grows, it also moves, and depending on what lies beneath it can move impressive amounts of rock and soil—and anything else in its path—until it encounters an immovable object or loses enough mass that it simply cannot continue. In this case, an expanding glacier managed to push enough ice and debris into the path of the Clark Fork River (in present-day northwestern Montana) to block its flow almost completely, and as the ice dam grew in size it caused the mammoth, five-hundred-cubic-mile, two-thousand-foot-deep Lake Missoula to form.[8] Similar ice dams formed on the Columbia River, causing it to change course south of its confluence with the Okanogan River, and on the Spokane River, which flooded nearby low-lying areas and created Lake Spokane.

Such a situation could not last. Sometime between 15,000 and 16,000 years ago, Lake Missoula reached its prehistoric limit and began to spill over, under, and through its saturated walls. The Columbia Basin would never be the same. While the exact sequence is unknowable, most likely a small tunnel cut into a weak side of the lake at its eastern terminus, which then developed into a more aggressive river, built up momentum and carved a deeper path, and then morphed into a raging torrent—a juggernaut of gargantuan proportions. The lake drained in about forty-eight hours. A wall of water, mud, rock, ice, and other debris tore through the Rathdrum Prairie to the southwest, then hit Lake Spokane (another, smaller prehistoric lake), where it picked up more "fuel" before continuing in a southwesterly direction. Top speeds of this glacial maelstrom are believed to have been as high as sixty miles per hour, with a flow of four hundred million cubic feet per second.[9] It carried ten times the amount of water in all the world's rivers, roughly the same volume as Lake Erie and Lake Ontario combined. The flood undid in a few days what had taken thousands and millions of years to accumulate; the light loess was no match for this kind of pounding, in which some of the land was stripped down to its basalt foundations. The visual evidence of this can be seen today in the Channeled Scablands, a broad badlands area with numerous coulees and basalt outcrops southwest of Spokane. And this was not the only catastrophic flood to hit the area. Once emptied, Lake Missoula simply filled again and flooded again—an estimated eighty-five times—as successive ice dams recreated Lake Missoula and as similar ice dams gave way. Between thirty to forty massive floods—and many smaller ones—followed over the next 2,000 years and were responsible for the further tearing up and shaping of vast areas of the ancient Northwest.[10]

To the good fortune of the Palouse (or at least to those who farm it today), the great Missoula floods roared past southeastern Washington. This geological near miss occurred simply because the Palouse is slightly higher in elevation than the land to its immediate north and west. Floodwaters followed the path of least resistance, which meant they flowed around the higher hills and gouged out innumerable coulees, ravines, and small canyons along the flow's inexorable path to the Pacific. In many places, the torrent slackened enough to allow millions of tons of silt to settle before discharging into the Columbia River. It still carried enough energy to carve out the Columbia Gorge before slowing down, temporarily inundating the Willamette Valley and finally blasting into the Pacific Ocean.[11]

The prevailing winds that blew light silts from southwest to northeast during the Miocene epoch continued to sweep newer deposits from these floods onto the Palouse even after the floods had ceased in the late Pleistocene. In fact, recent geological research suggests that extended periods of deposition continued until the end of the last glacial recession and produced most of the soils now occupying the area.[12] Water, wind, gravity, and time acted on the micas, feldspars, and quartzes of the northern Rocky Mountains, sluicing them down to Wallula Gap in south-central Washington where they were unceremoniously blown to higher ground in the eastern portion of the Columbia Basin and became loess soil. Parts of this almost circular geologic odyssey took millions of years; in others, the trip lasted but a few days.

The Palouse continued to change after the last glaciers left the scene. Because temperatures were on the rise, the glacial ice melted and plants and animals had to adapt to the new climate or be forced out of local existence. Higher temperatures and drier air meant that broadleaf plants and deciduous trees, along with the herbivores that ate them, lived on borrowed time. The cypress trees, Pleistocene sloths, and diminutive horses that once thrived soon fell victim to an evolving climate that was increasingly inhospitable.[13] Moreover, the Palouse hills continued to develop. Perennial streams acted upon the windblown loess, weaving in and around the bases of the hills, which made their slopes steeper and their elevation relative to surrounding lands appear higher. In addition, frost action and snowpack further steepened the slopes every spring, through a process called "nivation." Cold winter winds tended to push snow up over the southwestern sides of hills and left huge amounts of drifted snow on the lee side, where it would stay frozen well past winter. The ground underneath the snow, however, thawed first, causing a steady trickle of water to eat away at most north-facing hillsides, making them more sheer and more susceptible to weathering in subsequent years.[14] Travelers from Asia and later travelers from Europe encountered a Palouse that was the product of geological, biological, and climatic forces that date back more than 3 billion years. The landscape that emerged over the eons provided the first settlers, Indians, with hundreds of coulees and caves for shelter and storage sites, rivers that teemed with fish, and pasturage for horses. Later, Euro-Americans found the Wallula Gap deposits that formed Palouse soils and the semiarid climate to be ideal ingredients for dryland farming. Out of the repeated devastation of prehistoric floods and strong winds that transported billions of tons of sediment, a fertile and fragile land was born.

NATIVE FLORA AND FAUNA OF THE PALOUSE

With the deposition of the Palouse loess complete after the last glacial recession (roughly 12,000 years ago), a topography and climate emerged that were much closer to present-day conditions—an undulating dry prairie, the result of countless years of uplift, sediment accumulation, floods, and more sedimentation. Upon these hills and ravines, and in this new, warmer weather pattern, a nascent semiarid biome started to dominate the landscape.

Bunchgrasses, shrubs, and forbs took hold and provided cover for the young soil and gave sustenance and protection for a broad range of animal life. This ecosystem, a collection of plants and animals and their immediate physical surroundings, existed because of an unusual confluence of geologic and climatic factors. Neither desert nor forest, it was a kind of prairie—what biologists call "meadow-steppe." In spite of a dry climate that initially limited population, it provided Indians and white settlers with the fertile soil, water, and game necessary to create prosperous societies. Just as an appreciation of local geology is key to a fuller grasp of the more modern aspects of the Palouse environment, so too is an understanding of native flora and fauna an important touchstone to keep in mind while dissecting the intricacies and implications of settlement and agriculture in the Palouse.

It has been estimated that since Euro-American settlement, less than 1 percent of the total acreage of the Palouse remains unplowed, unpaved, ungrazed, or otherwise unaltered—thus limiting our ability to say with certainty what this place looked like or how it functioned.[15] Most of these tiny slivers of natural history are either in steep terrain or in riparian zones, neither of which is indicative of the Palouse as a whole. Although scientists have also looked to local cemeteries to determine patterns of natural flora, these areas tend to be too small to reveal a legitimate overall impression and have been subject to invasion by nonnative species. However, through the use of Indian testimony, settler histories, scientific surveys, and old photographs, we can build a tentative picture of how the hills appeared.

Colloquially, the plants that made up the Palouse are collectively known as bunchgrasses. The two most prominent and widespread of these are Idaho fescue and bluebunch wheatgrass, both of which grow in widely spaced bunches. But many more species flourished in this ecosystem as well. Shrubs such as snowberry, serviceberry, and hawthorn, wildflowers such as sego lily and native geraniums, and several legumes all called the eastern Columbia Basin home. In a 1942 study of one area, scientists identified ninety-three plant species—an indication that the Palouse contained a veritable smorgasbord of plant life sufficient to keep any botanist occupied for years. In 1961 a professor of range management at the University of Idaho compared the physical appearance and "luxuriance of growth and richness of composition" atop Palouse hills to that of the tallgrass prairies of the Great Plains. This rather arid land at one time produced an array of vegetation, one that belied the opinions of some white settlers who regarded it as an empty waste. The geographical origins of most of these plants can be traced to the south and east. The basin-and-range region of Nevada and western Utah, along with the Snake

River plain, exported much of the seeds that later became established in south-eastern Washington, and some species may have traveled from as far away as the Dakotas, the Central Valley of California, and Mexico.[16]

Though hardly ubiquitous, the presence of trees has been an important facet of the Palouse environment since the last glaciers exited. On the tops of buttes and mountains, and on some north-facing slopes, ponderosa pine dominated, accompanied by occasional Douglas fir and larch stands in higher, wetter regions to the east. Rivers and small streams, such as the Palouse River, Rock Creek, and Union Flat Creek (among many others), also became areas where large conifers could get sufficient water to grow to impressive heights. Deciduous trees also took hold in these areas. Quaking aspen, several maple species, and red alder all required more moisture than the hillsides could provide, and therefore could survive only in places close to the water table.[17] Wooded areas provided the habitat necessary for dozens of animal species that called the Palouse home and offered local Indians and the settlers who followed an essential source of fuel and shelter.

The location and seasonality of rain has contributed even more to the vegetational makeup. In eastern regions, near the Clearwater Mountains in Idaho, rainfall can be as high as twenty-four inches per year, whereas on the western edge annual totals average closer to fifteen inches. Clearly, this portion of the Northwest differs from the more lush and rainy areas west of the Cascade Range; most of the inland Northwest is semiarid or desert—a fact that surprises many who are new to the area. Moreover, because 65 to 70 percent of the precipitation falls between the beginning of October and the end of March, plants have until mid-June to take advantage of the moisture before it evaporates or percolates through to groundwater. Small grains such as wheat, barley, and oats—staples of modern agriculture—also utilize moisture mainly in the spring, when most plant growth occurs. As an adaptive measure, many native shrubs and other plants have developed very deep root systems to access moisture later in the growing season. Bluebunch wheatgrass and Sandburg bluegrass, for example, grow twice as far below ground as above. Other plants opt to spread their roots as wide as possible, both to soak up more water as soon as it is made available and to discourage competing plants from establishing themselves nearby.[18]

A wide variety of fish species have been introduced to Palouse streams and lakes since the mid-nineteenth century, including several bass species, shad, bluegill, and other spiny-ray fish, but an assortment of native cold- and warm-water fish flourished prior to white settlement. Dace, chubs, and northern pikeminnow occupied shallower, warmer creeks and intermittent streams, while cutthroat trout, steelhead, and up to a half-dozen types of salmon plied the deeper, cooler waters of larger streams and rivers. The 198–foot Palouse Falls on the Palouse River prevented anadromous fish like steelhead and salmon from entering the major river system in the area. These species existed only in waters that directly fed into the lower Snake River. Low rainfall and high summer evaporation rates, in addition to a relative dearth of streamside shade and an impassable waterfall, however, probably limited these species' ability to migrate any great distance north of the Snake.[19]

The list of native Palouse fauna is consistent with other shrub-steppe areas of the American West. Gray wolf, coyote, red fox, lynx, bobcat, and black and grizzly bear at one time roamed the Palouse and were the primary carnivores. Large ungulates—elk, white-tailed and mule deer, and pronghorn antelope—were often their intended meals. An abundance of forage in the spring and early summer (bunchgrasses, mostly) enabled herds to survive, but droughty summers precluded much growth thereafter and may have contributed to herd sizes that were considerably smaller than in the adjacent mountains. And of course, a plethora of smaller vertebrates staked their claims in the Palouse, including gophers, black-tailed jackrabbits, and Columbian ground squirrels. Most of the predators and all of the large ungulates (except the white-tailed deer) have been eliminated from the Palouse mosaic, either through hunting or habitat loss. Modern restoration projects to date have involved relatively small plots (fewer than twenty acres); it is doubtful that this component of the old Palouse can ever be recovered.[20]

Bison also once wandered here. Their numbers were probably small, but in the early 1950s, scientists discovered bison remains settlement near Othello, Washington, that predated white settlement. This location is slightly outside the Palouse, but it seems hard to believe that large herbivores such as bison would not have ambled a few miles to the east in search of food. (Indeed, central Washington is much more arid than eastern Washington and supports less vegetation.) Anthropologists think they were extirpated in the inland Northwest far earlier, but evidence also exists of a bison being killed by local Indians near Grand Coulee in 1835. The information is fragmentary and no one has suggested that bison numbers came anywhere near the vast herds of the Great Plains, but the presence of bison—along with numerous other species—contributes to an increasingly complex picture of the Palouse.[21]

The Palouse also appears to have been home to dozens of bird species that peppered the skies. At one time thousands upon thousands of sharp-tailed grouse inhabited the region. This rather tame bird, known colloquially as the "prairie chicken," lived in thickets and in hawthorn trees along streambanks and provided early white settlers with an important food source. It is now nearly extinct in the inland Northwest, with a few remnant flocks remaining in northeastern Oregon. Other native grouse species have fared better; ruffed, blue, and Franklin grouse, because of their more wary instincts, have survived the onslaught of plow and shotgun in sizable numbers. Raptors also proliferated. Red-tailed and ferruginous hawks, golden eagles, turkey vultures, American kestrels, and several types of owls found an abundance of squirrels and small gophers (and occasionally other birds). And, of course, numerous other birds—songbirds and hummingbirds, especially—rounded out avian life.[22]

This cacophony of bird life, in addition to the impressively broad range of herbivores, carnivores, and plant life, made the Palouse an alluring and distinctive place. The meadow-steppe biome that formed after glacial melting was situated in between the desert landscape of the western Columbia Basin and the foothills of the Rocky Mountains of Idaho. Though it resembled neither in climate nor habitat, it certainly borrowed from both. The result was an intriguing combination of dryland and alpine species placed atop an uneven, expansive, and peculiar-looking prairie.

INDIAN LAND USE

The complexities and cumulative effects of ecological change in the Palouse challenge any inquiry into its deep past. This includes the story of huge floods, silt deposits, soil formation, and a litany of human-induced alterations. Many of the changes brought on by the first tenants of the land, the Palouse Indians, remain partially hidden from the historian's view. In part, this is because the earliest inhabitants arrived up to 12,000 years ago. The Palouse Indians were among the oldest Native American peoples of the entire continent, thus the passage of time restricts our ability to gather data that could explain how the land was exploited.[23] Moreover, because of disease, wars, white settlement, and finally removal and tribal disintegration in the last half of the nineteenth century, living links to the Palouse tribe are few in number. By the turn of the twentieth century, most of its members had been relocated to the Yakima, Colville, Umatilla, Nez Perce, or Warm Springs reservations.[24] Genetic links to the tribe's past continue on these reservations to this day, but only a few families with pure Palouse heritage survived through the 1940s and 1950s, and the last Indians to live in the Palouse were removed in the early 1960s. Therefore, contemporary oral accounts, the standard means by which historians gather much of their information about American Indians, have to be filtered through the lenses of time and memory and must take into account the effects of the loss of tribal identity.

Several important monographs have focused on the Palouse Indians but always from the context of white settlement and eventual displacement.[25] Tribal leaders were key players in Washington territorial governor Isaac Stevens's policy of negotiation and removal in the 1850s, the skirmishes and bloody battles that followed, and in the Nez Perce War of 1877, but to date there has been no thorough look into the tribe's culture, external relations, and land-use previous to white contact. The explorers, fur trappers, and traders who occasionally passed through in the early nineteenth century mostly stayed on the periphery of the area. They tended to stay out of villages simply because they could find nothing of value to seize and because most of the Indian settlements were also concentrated along the area's southern boundary. Even though many of the trappers kept detailed journals, most were relatively uninterested in the finer points of land use or culture. One of these men, Ross Cox, who worked for both John Jacob Astor and the North West Company, wrote such fantastic stories about encounters with local Indians and animals (including a pit full of rattlesnakes) that his testimony is suspect.[26] Meriwether Lewis and William Clark would have been more than qualified to take on this task, but they failed to do anything more than look at the high prairie from their boats and remark on what fine pastureland it would make. They even misidentified the Indians they saw (as many more would do later), calling them Nez Perce instead of Palouse. In all likelihood, the steep walls of the Snake River Canyon deterred the party from an extended side trip to explore the semiarid region to their north.[27]

Other aspects of Palouse Indian society are easier to verify. It was from this tribe that the very name "Palouse" came into being. "Palus" is the Sahaptin word for a large basalt outcrop near the confluence of the Palouse and Snake rivers. Thus, the term is geographical in origin and not a name for a language or clan unit. The tribe called themselves Na-ha-um, or, "The People of the River."[28] Various scholars have mistakenly attributed the term Palouse to be of French origin, meaning "sea of grass" or "grassland plain."[29]

The ancestral territory of the Palouse tribe is also known. It overlapped the area today considered to be the geographical Palouse. On the north, Rock Lake and Rosalia formed the boundary; to the south, tribal territory extended slightly beyond the Snake River, following the drainages of the Tucannon River and Pataha Creek; on the eastern side, the Clearwater Mountains provided an obvious boundary; and to the west, the line extended as far as Washtucna Coulee, and according to some records, to the Snake and Columbia rivers' confluence.[30] These borders, however, tell only about the tribe's central homeland. Indeed, the Palouse Indians held much land in a kind of common trust with other local bands and traveled considerably to trade for tools and food and to socialize and form alliances. Their position on the Snake River made them ideally situated to exploit various salmon runs, and they shared land and netted fish with the Wanapum, Umatilla, Cayuse, Spokane, and Nez Perce Indians, among others. They also shared the verdant camas fields on the eastern edge of their domain with the Nez Perce and Coeur d'Alene tribes, where vast quantities of the root precluded serious conflict over territory. In the fall, family bands migrated to Mount Adams to pick berries, hunt, and dig for more roots. All native North Americans traveled and most relied on a seasonal strategy of resource use, but the Palouse seem to have regularly covered an inordinate amount of territory to obtain what they needed.[31]

Depending on the person and time, population estimates conflict. Lewis and Clark put Palouse population at twenty-three hundred, but their figure reflects a conflation of the Palouse and Nez Perce tribes. Protestant missionary Samuel Parker wrote that only three hundred souls inhabited the area in 1835 and 1836. Other reports conducted in the mid-nineteenth century by trappers, government survey teams, and other missionaries ranged anywhere from a low of seventy to a high of six hundred.[32]

The discrepancies can be explained in a couple of ways. One is that like all other native peoples of the continent, disease epidemics wreaked considerable havoc during the eighteenth and nineteenth centuries. Obtaining a reasonably consistent head count from these sources would be impossible if the Palouse Indians were suffering from extensive die-offs. And dying they were. In the 1850s, railroad survey doctors noted that along the Snake River smallpox had killed entire villages. In addition to the obvious personal tragedies and social dislocation caused by these ravaging illnesses, basin tribes often found it difficult just to summon the time or strength to bury their dead. Most analyses of the epidemics state that the deadly viruses traveled up the Columbia River valley and infected natives in a west-east direction starting in the late eighteenth century. Therefore, the Palouse and other inland tribes faced their first bouts with disease well before the most intense period of Euro-American settlement in the late nineteenth century.[33]

Other reasons for the fluctuating population numbers can be attributed to the Palouse's diffuse village system and migratory lifestyle. By one estimate, over forty villages dotted the landscape, with most of them adjacent to the major river arteries and a few in the region's numerous valleys and coulees.[34] Given this, it would seem nearly impossible for a transplanted nineteenth-century European or American, with only a cursory knowledge of the area, to make an intelligent guess as to the size of the tribal population. The time of year also affected village size. River communities tended to be at their largest during the winter months; in summer, the Palouse scattered in all directions to trade, dig roots, or fish. Because most whites entered the region during warmer months, their impressions of local population densities necessarily reflected a seasonal discrepancy. The resulting population counts have to be misleading.

Yet the question remains: how many people lived in the Palouse before contact? The evidence is too fragmentary and insufficient for an accurate figure. The question is a valid one, though, especially for the purposes of an environmental history investigation. If a study attempts to get at the problems associated with intensive farming and the steady shift to agribusiness, then it must make some kind of generalized estimate of aboriginal numbers. A marginalized or degraded landscape can only be considered inferior when compared to a condition that existed previously—in this case, Indian land use. This is not to suggest that the Palouse tribe lived in any kind of Neolithic paradise that purposely avoided the misappropriation of resources and abuse of their land; nor is it to imply that all changes in land use that came after the displacement of the Palouse were somehow negative. Rather, in describing what came before white settlement, using population statistics can help quantify the intensity of native land use. But because of the lack of good source material, we must be content with a vague population estimate that ranges from 300 to 2,300 people.

Documentation about the Palouse Indian diet is much more extensive. Recent ethnohistoric evidence has shown that their diet mostly consisted of roots and berries. In spite of the placement of villages along waterways, and in contrast to older scholarship, anthropologist Eugene Hunn believes that natives on the Columbia Plateau received up to 60 percent of their calories from plants—camas and biscuitroot—whereas salmon and other fish made up only about 30 percent of their caloric intake. For many years scholars assumed the Palouse and nearby tribes were piscatory in nature simply because salmon was plentiful and because the presence of deep storage bins suggested that large numbers of fish were consumed. Thanks largely to the testimonials of Indians from adjacent tribes, we know that the cornucopia of root plants that littered the northern and eastern edges of the Palouse and nearby berry fields provided most of the sustenance for native basin peoples. The land was dry and brown most of the year, but the meadow-steppe plant community fulfilled most of their nutritional needs.[35]

A long, curved digging stick with a small handle at the top was the common tool used to uproot camas bulbs. Indians used the stick to dig up a generous chunk of sod, which was then turned over to allow them to inspect the quality and quantity of roots. They collected only a portion of the exposed camas; most of the bulbs were left intact because they were considered too small and because some needed to be saved for future harvests. The Palouse clearly exhibited conservation strategies when it came to their food supplies, but one ought not to consider this tantamount to any sort of modern environmentalism. Basin tribes behaved rationally within the constraints of time (most of the roots and berries had a narrow window for optimum ripeness) and distance (especially for the Palouse).[36] For whatever reasons, they knew a good thing when they saw it. Washington Territory governor Isaac Stevens was duly impressed with the size of the Indian camas operation and the bounty of food it provided. After watching six hundred Indians (with two thousand horses accompanying them) at a camas field below Moscow Mountain, the governor remarked, "So abundant is this valuable and nutritious root, that it requires simply four days' labor for them to gather sufficient for their year's use."[37]

The use of fire was somewhat atypical in comparison to tribes from other parts of the Northwest. Due to their mostly amicable relations with neighbors and their tendency to live near rivers, the Palouse had a limited need for intentionally set fires to ward off enemies. And, as we have seen, they had little need to use fire to surround and entrap big game animals since most of their food came from either the ground or the water. Scientists have found evidence of sporadic fires in the central part of the Palouse, but nothing to suggest an ongoing fire campaign.[38] On the edges of their domain, where camas and biscuitroot thrived, fire was of great importance in generating new growth. It was in these areas to the east and north, held in common with the Nez Perce and Coeur d'Alene, where Indians aggressively used fire as a means of increasing food supplies. Many plants initiate new growth after a disturbance of any kind, with root plants faring particularly well because the bulk of their flesh stays below ground level. Fire in such areas was also beneficial because it kept unwanted woody plants from invading valuable open fields.[39] Columbia Basin peoples had little need to use fire to clear areas in the forest simply because the meadow-steppe biome had such a limited number of trees, yet the horticultural skill of the Palouse and adjoining tribes and their willingness to alter the land to suit their needs is unquestionable.

Basin tribes also altered their landscape with the introduction and pro-liferation of the horse. The precise date of the arrival of horses for the Palouse tribe is unknown. Early commentators (and later historians and ethnolo-gists) have been primarily concerned with the effects of the horse on the better-known tribes, such as the Nez Perce and Cayuse. Most reports put the horse's arrival in the early to mid-eighteenth century; Lewis and Clark believed that horses had been around for nearly a century before the explor-ers' arrival.[40] In any case, horses helped bring about substantial social and environmental change. With horses Palouse Indians could travel more quickly over greater distances and carry far more in the way of trade goods—even across the Bitterroot Mountains.

Increased trade and intensive breeding resulted in sizable horse herds. It was not unusual for prominent tribal members to own dozens and, in some cases hundreds, of horses. This animal quickly became a marker of wealth and prestige and a source of great entertainment in the form of racing and gambling.[41] So many horses lived in the basin that Indians had no choice but to let them roam free, a decision that had definite environmental conse-quences. Although the carrying capacity of the meadow-steppe was consid-erable, the constant trampling of hooves and removal of vegetation took a toll. The vulnerability of the land stemmed from the presence of only a small population of large ungulates in the prehistoric period. Deer, elk, and ante-lope inhabited the region but not in great numbers, and almost all the bison were gone by 1700.[42] Therefore, native plants evolved over the centuries with-out building up resistance or strength against constant grazing pressure.

Unlike the situation east of the Rocky Mountains, where grasslands had to weather centuries of uninterrupted bison grazing, Palouse plant life never had to endure the intense pressure of hooves and molars. Overgrazing by horses, followed by cattle a century later, opened the door for more resistant but less edible plants to invade from Europe. It did not take long for Russian knapweed, reed canary grass, Scotch broom, and countless other nonnative species to carve out a place on the prairie as the bunchgrasses were being eaten away. The introduction of large hoofed animals, first by Indians and then in vastly greater numbers by white settlers, brought irreversible ecological change to the Palouse. Bunchgrasses were eaten, trampled, crowded, and even-tually plowed out of the region and would never dominate the land again.[43]

The Palouse and other plateau tribes acted within their means to manipu-late their environment to their advantage. They did not shy away from activ-ities that left indelible marks on their homelands, yet the tribes persisted.

Some of the marks could be considered innocuous or even positive. Indians fished extensively with an array of nets, seines, and hooks, but not to the point where anadromous fish runs became depleted. And they undoubtedly took tons of root bulbs and berries every spring and summer from inland Northwest fields, but they also were keenly aware that an overabundant harvest would be harmful in the long run. How long could this situation have lasted? A very long time, indeed, according to anthropologists, who believe natives established a rational, sustainable society.

But the more deleterious aspects of native land use also cannot be ignored. Particularly after the introduction of the horse, basin Indians started down a path that, if given enough time, could well have seriously damaged their land and culture. Horses dramatically increased contact among tribes and became symbols of wealth and prestige, and their rapid proliferation did not augur well for the future. All of these changes, however, need to be kept in perspective. As powerful as Indians were at altering their surroundings, groups of invaders from the east would make all previous human-induced changes look miniscule by comparison.

3 FROM BUNCHGRASS BACKWATER

TO AGRICULTURAL EMPIRE

THEY ALL CAME CLOSE. Among Euro-Americans, Lewis and Clark were the first. While descending the Snake River on their way to the Pacific in 1805, the Corps of Discovery floated by the mouth of the Palouse River, but chose not to investigate upstream. On the return trip they passed through the Walla Walla Valley to the south, noting only that the surrounding land looked promising for grazing. David Thompson, a key player in the fur trade for the North West Company, ventured upstream on the Palouse River but stayed on the westernmost edge of the hills. In the summer of 1811 he trekked north from the river on a course for the Spokane country, a route that skirts the Palouse territory. Later that winter, Donald McKenzie and ten Astorians drifted down the Snake but left no written commentary on the area. The following summer, another contingent of Astorians traced Thompson's route almost exactly—another near miss. One member of that party, Ross Cox, may or may not have entered the Palouse proper, but his penchant for hyperbole and self-aggrandizement severely jeopardized the credibility of his testimony.[1] What all these Euro-Americans missed was an expansive tract of land that lay just outside their scope. Undoubtedly, they all gained some understanding of the area from their contacts with local Indians, but because these ventures were mostly commercial in nature and because the Palouse lacked a marketable fur-bearing animal population, they had no reason to investigate further.

As it turned out, the explorers missed a great deal. Beginning in the 1820s and extending through the 1850s, a small host of explorers, botanists, pro-moters, and government agents recognized that the prairie north of the Snake River was suitable for an assortment of agricultural purposes. Euro-Americans filtered into the Palouse when word spread and after natives had been either killed or removed, and after more attractive areas to the west and south had been claimed. Early settlers arrived in appreciable numbers in the 1870s. They put down tentative roots and quickly discovered that this land could at least sustain them in the short term. Market-oriented farm-ing dominated by the turn of the century after people discovered how well wheat performed on loess soils in a semiarid climate.

Key to development, and to this story, was the role played by a burgeoning capitalist economy, national and global market prospects, and a federal gov-ernment ready to assist private businesses such as farms. Not long after filing homestead claims, Palouse farmers gradually lost interest in mere subsis-tence agriculture and gravitated toward participation in market-based surplus production and export. They shipped their goods by way of a slow and cumbersome combination of dirt roads, steam vessels, and barges—an imperfect system, but workable. And *temporary*. A veritable explosion of rail-road building, made possible by massive government land grants in the 1880s, forever changed the picture. The construction of a cobweb of competing railroads ushered in and maintained an unprecedented amount of growth and development. The frenzy of activity cemented the ties between Palouse farmers and distant markets: the former provided staple products for export, while the latter determined how much and at what price. Unequal as it was, this relationship dictated the nature and pace of settlement. The agrarian liberal of the Palouse thus became tied to both older notions of agrarianism and nineteenth-century classical liberalism, to traditions that were centuries old and to economic systems and government-citizen rela-tions that had barely been tested.

Palouse farmers took great risks in their new ventures. Uncertainty lurked behind every loessial hill. It was no accident that the Palouse was among the last places in the West to be intensively farmed, with its dry climate and unusual landscape. But farmers gambled on this land anyway, and, for the most part, they won, as their crops and the region's small towns all sprouted nicely and kept growing. Farmers willingly accepted both the risks of plow-ing this land and the government assistance that made it even thinkable. After a few decades both farmer and government collected their winnings, successfully completing the process of transforming nature into culture.[2]

The shift from a subsistence, pastoral society to a mechanized capitalist mode of production, however, came with certain costs. Rapid population growth and the spread of farming to most of the arable land by 1900 spelled the end for much of the native flora and fauna. The monocropping of wheat, common by 1910, and the constant improvements in farm machinery contributed to ever-increasing pressures on the soil—both in terms of its fertility and its propensity to erode. But the agricultural revolution that swept over the area was so comprehensive—and welcomed—that it significantly muted any potential naysayers. By the turn of the century intensive agriculture in the Palouse was a reality that had few detractors and many proponents.

As more Euro-Americans came to the Pacific Northwest, travelers eventually encountered the heart of the Palouse. Men like John Work of the Hudson's Bay Company wandered through the area in the 1820s. In a series of rather circuitous journeys to various interior trading posts, Work stopped for a day in Almota, now a tiny hamlet, but formerly a bustling Indian village on the Snake River. There he acquired several horses from the Palouse tribe's then-considerable herd. From there, Work rode up to the confluence of the Snake and Clearwater rivers (present-day Lewiston, Idaho) for more trading and then ascended the taxing two-thousand-foot canyon slope to reenter the prairie on his way to the Spokane River and Kettle Falls areas for trade with the tribes to the north. It was on this leg of the trip that Work recorded some of the first written impressions of the hilly fields. He spoke of an area "destitute of trees," but one that was "pretty well clothed with grass," especially near the waterways, which he believed enjoyed "an uncommonly luxuriant growth."[3] Since Work was an employee of a large trading enterprise and thus primarily concerned with commercial opportunities, it is surprising to find so much ink devoted to an area basically void of furs. But it was an indication of a growing awareness of and appreciation for this previously unnoticed part of the Oregon Country.

Missionary enterprises also affected perceptions of the Palouse. A number of religious settlements, intent on bringing Christianity to Native Americans, furthered the cause of American expansion in the 1830s and 1840s. Collectively, the works of William Gray, Henry Spalding, Marcus and Narcissa Whitman, Asa Smith, Father Pierre de Smet, and others comprised the first Americans in the region who planned for settlement. In addition to their close contact with Indians, they promoted future settlement, the construction of new roads and the improvement of old ones, and the introduction of European livestock and agricultural techniques into places where neither had previously existed. Even though no missionaries established a base in the Palouse (the Nez Perce and Cayuse were considered more welcoming than the recalcitrant Palouse tribe), and in spite of the 1847 Whitman slayings, missionary activity invariably contributed to a sustained interest in the Northwest.[4]

The Oregon Trail also facilitated settlement. Though used as a fur trade route dating back to the years 1810–1920, migrants began to travel this route in earnest in the 1840s. They arrived in the Walla Walla Valley in impressive numbers; by 1880, the town of Walla Walla boasted Washington Territory's largest population. Farming in the eastern part of the Columbia Basin became a proven, viable option for Americans who wished to farm. In its capacities as a military outpost, farming and ranching community, and mining supply and trade center, this town generated and attracted capital through the mid-1880s that would later benefit the early settlers of the Palouse. For many settlers the Oregon Trail was more than a means to a metaphorical rainbow's end west of the Cascades. It also spawned hundreds of farms, small hamlets, and growing towns along the way and encouraged Americans to consider the agricultural possibilities of lands that looked and felt far different than their familiar eastern homelands.[5]

A budding professional scientific community did its share to dispel prevailing myths about the undesirability of dryland farming. British botanist Charles Geyer, for one, spent a good deal of time in the Palouse in the 1840s, and his subsequent publications alerted his readership to the very real prospects of commercial agriculture. His evaluation of plant life, climate, and soil made the Palouse sound like an awaiting Eden, not a desolate, primeval wilderness. Geyer wrote effusively about massive ponderosa pines that made for "elegant natural parks," of well-watered valleys, and of an abundance of bunchgrasses so broad and nutritious that livestock would surely proliferate. Indeed, Geyer played the part of booster and detached scientist with equal aplomb. His words seemed intended as much for a business audience as an academic one. Though he wrote about floral taxonomy and climate, his overarching goal leaned in favor of providing information that future farmers and entrepreneurs could use, not scientists.[6]

The impression that the lower Snake River area offered little but barren hills proved tough to dislodge. For every John Work or Charles Geyer there was a Lansford Hastings, a self-styled promoter, entrepreneur, and would-be politician. Hastings went to the Oregon Country in the 1840s, like countless others, to seek out personal fortune. But when he arrived in the Willamette Valley in 1842, he soon grew despondent because of the dreary winter weather and the amount of aid new settlers required from missionaries and John McLoughlin's Hudson's Bay Company. Perhaps this could explain Hastings's need to highlight the negative aspects of the Oregon Country. He decided to venture south, and after 1844 he endeavored to promote settlement from his new base of operations while simultaneously denigrating the entire Oregon Country. He wrote that the interior Columbia Basin's dearth of trees would prove to be "an insuperable barrier" to permanent occupation and that the soil was "extremely poor," covered with "burning sands and hills and mountains of unsurpassed sterility." Hastings believed that, on summer days, the hills burned to a summertime high of 180 degrees, only to drop to below minus 20 degrees at night.[7]

Although never so brazen (or unbelievable) as Hastings's prose, his maps reflected the common notion that the Palouse was a barren desert. Part of the explanation for this negative view lies in the rough proximity of the Palouse to the nineteenth-century "Great American Desert," an area (depending on the commentator) that encompassed all of the Great Basin and the western half of the Great Plains—places that were extremely dry and incapable of supporting even dryland farming. But more often, mid-nineteenth century mapmakers had so little knowledge of the eastern Oregon country that it was left rather blank. William Clark's map shows the Palouse River (under the name Drewyer's River—one of his many place names that failed to stick), but it is a crude map at best with no account of Palouse topography. Later maps sometimes failed to include the Palouse River altogether. The Topographical Engineers, a bureau of the US Army, published a map in 1838 that completely omitted this waterway, as did a later map from 1849. From his base in the Coeur d'Alene region, Father Pierre de Smet drew a map that demonstrated his knowledge of Northwest Indians, but his skill as a cartographer left something to be desired. His drawings featured the Blue Mountains extending well to the north of the Snake River and the central Palouse as the headwaters of the Spokane River.[8]

The Palouse lacked a more thorough reconnaissance. Help came in the form of Isaac Stevens, West Point graduate, Mexican War veteran, and friend of Franklin Pierce. When Pierce was elected president in 1852 he appointed his old war comrade to three concurrent government positions of tremendous significance: director of a railroad survey for a northern transcontinental route, director of Indian affairs for Washington Territory, and first territorial governor of Washington.

In performing those duties, Stevens made it a point to travel and describe the lesser-known areas of eastern Washington. He understood better than most that a rail line needed to be attractive to Congress as well as to settlers and capital. He consciously steered his energies toward proving that this part of eastern Washington was ready to be put to the plow. And unlike the trappers and missionaries, the Stevens party surveyed the outskirts and middle of the Palouse. He and his team of experts ventured from the Walla Walla River to the northeast, near what would become the Mullan Road. They also traveled north along the eastern edge of the Palouse—what is today US Highway 95. From his reconnaissance of 1853–1856 and from the several reports to Congress and speaking engagements to civic and academic groups that followed, Stevens redefined the supposed sterile backwater into an inviting agricultural opportunity. The land that had until recently been the domain of Indians and a few ranchers was about to be reinvented in the image of boosters and farmers. Looking back at this time from the vantage point of the 1930s, Genesee, Idaho, farmer George Northrup knew that a new regime was about to emerge: "Into this peaceful scene" of the past "came progress in the guise of railroad surveyors."[9]

The first comments came from J. A. Duncan, the Stevens party topographer and a man unimpressed by the Palouse. During an 1853 trip, which ran along the western edge of the region, Duncan was struck by the peculiar hills, which appeared as "an undulating stratum of basalt, which is covered with deposits of earth, sand, and gravel." He was pessimistic about farming this land, though. Besides being "destitute of timber," the soil was "light and unfit for cultivation. ... Small tracts of arable land are found near the larger lakes and the heads of the streams, but they do not exceed one or two acres in extent."[10]

Stevens, on the other hand, saw a land of unsurpassed farming potential. When he visited the heart of the Palouse, as opposed to its margins, in 1855, he was "astonished, not simply at the luxuriance of the grass, but the richness of the soil." He went on, repeating his words as if attempting to reverse all previous negative publicity about the dry country: "I will say again, we have been astonished today at the luxuriance of the grass and the richness of the soil. The whole view presents to the eye a vast bed of flowers in all their varied beauty. The country is a rolling table-land, and the soil like that of the prairies of Illinois."[11] The glowing language had the stamp of authority that others lacked. A man with his military and political résumé was far more likely to be taken seriously than a whole group of fur traders or hucksters. An air of boosterism certainly permeated Stevens's dream of a regional empire, but his brand of promotion carried far more credibility. Here was a land that could support family farming. With optimal land and favorable weather, and with pine trees that Stevens claimed were three to four feet in diameter lying in its lower reaches, settlers who had been late to claim their land in the Willamette or Walla Walla valleys could find their home just north of the Snake River.

Stevens's policy regarding Columbia Basin Indians was related to his overall plan for white occupation and prosperity. At the time he assumed his offices, hundreds of Palouse Indians still lived in their ancestral homelands, and neighboring tribes still traveled freely to dozens of villages to trade and socialize. However, that situation, if allowed to continue, threatened to short-circuit the drive for white settlement. Stevens made it his mission to subdue nearly every tribe within his jurisdiction and to place them on reservations.[12] To that end, Stevens called an assembly of inland tribes in 1855—part of an ongoing series of tribal councils held in the 1850s. The treaty that followed—and the violent confrontations that came in 1858—resulted in a defeated, demoralized, and hungry tribe that drifted away to reservations in Washington and Oregon. Palouse Indians lived on under the aegis of other Northwest reservations but without land or sovereignty.[13]

With the Indian situation apparently under control by 1858, the territorial government felt the time was ripe for an expansion of the regional transportation infrastructure. Construction on the Mullan Road, a military route between Fort Walla Walla and Fort Benton in Montana, began in 1859. It became an important mining supply line, stockman's trail, and wagon road. Another ostensible military road linked The Dalles with Salt Lake City the same year. Advances in water transportation proceeded apace as steamboats shuttled between Cascade Rapids and The Dalles in 1851, and as far as Lyon's Ferry (the Snake-Palouse confluence) in 1859. Settlers did not flood into the Palouse during this period; instead they came for gold in the Clearwater River area in the 1860s and to claim quality farmland around Walla Walla—although ranchers found the unfenced, rolling prairie to the north attractive.[14]

Palouse agriculture began with ranching. The earliest records of a year-round presence date to 1862, when a small contingent of settlers came north from the Walla Walla area to claim bottomlands along Union Flat Creek (about twenty miles west of Colfax), and records indicate that a man farmed on top of the hills overlooking present Lewiston in the same year. For the rest of the decade the area experienced steady growth, mostly made up of people devoted to grazing cattle. The first settler to make an official land claim in the Palouse was George Pangburn, who built a crude dwelling along Union Flat Creek near present-day Endicott.[15] Still, most inhabitants in the 1860s worked livestock and lived in the area only seasonally. Aided by a reduction in freight rates on the Columbia River between Portland and The Dalles, good markets in the form of Idaho and Montana mining camps, and plenty of open land, early cattle operators did well financially. News of the good profits spread, which attracted more ranchers, which led to an eventual decline in profitability. Bunchgrasses proved susceptible to overgrazing; they did not bounce back well after continued grazing and trampling, especially when sheep were added to the mix of livestock. The land simply could not absorb the added pressure.[16] Moreover, an increasing percentage of Palouse settlers began planting crops by the early 1870s. Annual crops and the fences they required to keep out cattle and sheep spelled the end of the open range, and with it came the beginning of the end to a brief but important sliver of time. Open-range cattle grazers may not have endured, but they opened the door sufficiently wide to let other agriculturalists in who would leave a more lasting impression.[17]

But ongoing inaccessibility to markets retarded the pace of development through the 1870s. Early farmers found that a variety of crops could be grown in place of native grasses, but a lack of cheap and efficient transportation lines prevented full participation in a mushrooming and increasingly interconnected national and world economy. A Walla Walla-to-Wallula railroad, completed in 1875, alleviated part of the problem, but the number of obstacles that remained was considerable.

In order for a Palouse wheat farmer to ship his harvest to market, he had to jump through an inordinate number of logistical hoops. An exclusively overland route was too expensive and required many horses and wagons and took too much time. The other option involved steamships on the Snake River, but that choice posed problems as well. First, goods had to be carted on a two- or three-day trip down to the water's edge—a dicey proposition since the steep canyon walls were nearly impassable to large horse teams and wagons. Wheat could be stored along the river for a fee of 40 cents per ton for the first month, 12.5 cents for additional months. For grains, long tubular chutes could also be used to carry goods as much as two thousand vertical feet to waiting ships, but the procedure required tedious bagging and rebagging that added time and expense. Grain agents for major wholesalers took a 2.5 percent commission on all sales. The river itself could be a problem; a low-water period from late summer through fall made shipping a seasonal business that limited a farmer's ability to sell goods when prices were high or when money was tight. Two major Columbia River portages at The Dalles and Cascades Rapids added another expense to an already costly journey before goods could finally be unloaded at the port of Portland.[18]

Poor transportation links limited agricultural growth, yet settlement continued. After the settlement of Union Flat Creek, many decided to claim land along the Washington-Idaho line near to the Clearwater Mountains, where trees were close at hand and rainfall was slightly higher. But as these lands filled up, farmers learned that the more arid western stretches of the Palouse also yielded crops of good quality and quantity. Fledgling towns sprang up in response to the influx, with the tiny communities of Farmington, Uniontown, and Pine City (all founded in the late 1870s) forming the embryonic start of an agricultural support network. These towns, along with the Snake River port towns of Penewawa, Almota, and Wawawai (all ancient Indian villages converted to ports of entry) gave outsiders the impression that the wave of the future rested on dryland farming.[19]

Even though grain crops grew well in those first years, according to one account most farmers "busied themselves with the care of their flocks and herds, giving no attention to agriculture, except that they raised a little wheat for their own consumption and some wheat hay for the horses and other stock."[20] Cattle was still important. Through most of the 1870s, wheat, the crop that became the economic lifeblood of the Palouse, was not planted from fencerow to fencerow, as far as the eye could see, as it is today. Like the prejudices held against arid grassland soils, most nineteenth-century Americans who raised crops believed that well-watered valleys offered plants the moisture and protection they needed. To William Brabyn, who raised wheat just north of Pullman, early settlers found that "the country looked too rough for farming." And to Colfax farmer Oliver Hall, "the hills were thought to be good only for cattle. A little farming was done along the flats. The hills seemed too rough and steep to even have a garden on them." Therefore, Palouse farmers tended to plant grains in between hills, not on top of them, reserving the ridgetops and exposed slopes for pasture. Looking back, Asa Short, who farmed near the town of Palouse, remarked that "the general conception that hilltops were good only for grazing," was odd, "considering the fact that stirrup-high native grasses completely covered said hilltops."[21]

That strategy began to change during the mid- to late 1870s, but perhaps as early as 1865. Through simple curiosity, because frosts affected mainly low-lying areas, and because low areas stayed wet well into the late spring, farmers adopted a trial-and-error process with hillside wheat cultivation that resulted in some sizable yields; in many cases, harvests exceeded those from adjacent lowlands. News of this exciting development spread throughout eastern Washington, and by the end of the 1870s it was common practice to till slopes as steep as the implements of the day would allow.[22] This discovery did not automatically usher in the era of wheat monocropping or the trend toward industrial agriculture, but once railroads appeared on the scene, both became far more realistic possibilities. This development also meant that hills covered with light loess soils would be regularly put to the plow—a development of vast significance for the future of Palouse erosion and water quality. No one knew it at the time, but hilltop wheat planting had far-reaching implications.

But the discovery of hilltop fertility did not alter land use instantly. In fact, as late as 1880, the Judson family farm reported that "only level tracts were under the plow as yet," and according to John Klemgard, only 10 to 15 percent of the Palouse was under cultivation in 1882. The remaining obstacle to settlement and the further use of the Palouse was poor transportation. A Colfax newspaper reported in 1878 that, "the greatest lack of the country lying east of the Cascades is the means of transporting the surplus to market." Since "wheat was an assured crop," farmer George Northrup knew that eventually "railroads would furnish the market."[23] The appearance of railroads in the Palouse in the 1880s led to an alteration of the economic and agricultural landscape unlike any other. Even prior to their operation, the mere rumor of future railroad activity often caused a stir of land speculation and capital formation that amounted to a "preemptive strike" in anticipation of profits to come. If construction was delayed, or did not come at all, farmers could quickly find themselves bankrupt. But once in place, steel rails promised to get farmers thinking beyond grain chutes and sternwheelers on the lower Snake and focusing on the new possibilities of speedy rail transportation that, in most cases, passed right through town and on to the new center of their immediate economic world—Spokane.

The Palouse benefited from a rash of construction sponsored by some of the biggest names in eastern capital. Henry Villard, who controlled both the Oregon Railroad and Navigation Corporation (ORN) and the Northern Pacific Railroad (NP), orchestrated the building of thousands of miles of tracks in the inland Northwest during the 1870s and 1880s. His NP line won the battle to be the nation's second coast-to-coast railroad, a route that roughly followed the one mapped out by Isaac Stevens. It reached Spokane in 1881 and became transcontinental in 1883. Fiscal mismanagement and supply problems delayed completion for many years, but as one commentator said, the NP would "not be suspended until the iron horse had drunk out of both Lake Superior and the Columbia River."[24] The next year it offered service to Colfax via a spur line that ran west through Washtucna and connected to Portland. It was also in 1884 that Villard's aggressiveness finally caught up with him; his empire collapsed under a mountain of debt, and the two carriers were split apart.

Financial difficulties did not translate into any sort of construction hiatus. On the contrary, in many ways it prompted wide-open competition among several carriers for the growing business in shipping agricultural goods. Over the next six years, the NP, the ORN, and the Union Pacific (which gained control of the ORN in 1887) went on an unprecedented building spree that solidified the relationship between Palouse goods and distant markets. The ORN extended its Colfax spur to Pullman and Moscow in 1885 and added another extension to Farmington the following year. The NP extended from its Spokane hub and linked the Spokane County wheat town of Spangle and the hamlet of Belmont to its regional base in 1886. When the Union Pacific (UP) entered the picture in 1887, it added another transcontinental carrier to the game and shifted the point of departure for many exports from Portland to the Puget Sound. It also directed the ORN to build new lines from Riparia (near Lyon's Ferry) to Lewiston, Idaho, from Farmington to Rockford, and from Tekoa to the Wallace mining district in northern Idaho. Nor did the NP stand still, but rather built lines from Palouse City to Genesee, Idaho, from Pullman to Moscow, and along the Clearwater River—all between the years 1888 and 1890. Other, smaller carriers joined the fray as well, including the Spokane & Palouse and the Columbia & Palouse railroads, making an already crowded playing field even more complicated.[25] Plateau farmers could then fully focus on production and export—a transition initiated by the sudden omnipresence of railroads. These events were repeated many times in the American West and gave historian Leo Marx reason to believe that "armed with this new power, mankind [was] now able, for the first time, to realize the dream of abundance."[26]

Most of these new tracks trended north and south, but did not cross the Snake River to Walla Walla, a major business center. Instead, the new focus of activity became Spokane. Platted in 1878 and chartered three years later, Spokane quickly prospered for several reasons: the presence of a large river with a waterfall for generating power; its proximity to the Palouse, Big Bend, and Spokane Valley agriculture, and to the Coeur d'Alene, Colville, and Kootenay mining districts to the north and east; and the consequent flurry of rail building in the 1880s for which Spokane served as a hub. Palouse farmers looked to Spokane for many of their durable goods needs and for the processing of certain raw materials, but it was its capacity as rail hub that drew most of their interest. Promotional literature often touted these lines as an incentive for immigration. A brochure from 1895 described the ease of shipping grain to Spokane where it could be sent to distant ports. In another pamphlet, the Pullman Chamber of Commerce published a bird's-eye drawing of the Palouse with numerous Spokane-bound rail lines featured prominently.[27] Spokane boasted five transcontinental railroads by 1910, a steel nexus that enabled Palouse wheat to land in virtually any American city. Population growth responded accordingly; from an 1880 total of just over 350 people, Spokane boomed to a population of almost 20,000 just ten years later—a growth rate that dwarfed all other urban centers in the Northwest during the same time span.[28]

The Palouse became inextricably bound to the internal logic of a mostly laissez-faire capitalist system—complete with futures markets, demand fluctuations, freight-rate discrimination, competition from other producers from the US and abroad, and an ethos that emphasized maximum production. A fair proportion of Palouse farmers entered their ventures fully aware that they were involved in a competitive business, and they were not interested in fulfilling any sort of cooperative, virtuous, Jeffersonian dream. Rather, they behaved like the prototypical nineteenth-century liberals who had taken advantage of government-subsidized internal improvements. Canadian scholar Colin Duncan has noted that federal assistance was central to creating this chaotic situation that placed so much capital in such unlikely places: "railroad investors had an incentive to facilitate the expansion of agricultural production on a scale that had no organic link to the size of the world market in agricultural produce, let alone local markets." To Northwest historians Robert Nesbit and Charles Gates, Palouse farming "was no longer a matter of homesteading small acreages and raising crops on a subsistence basis. It had become a capitalistic, commercialized business." There may not have been an "organic link" between grower and consumer, but as early as 1878 a Colfax newspaper reported San Francisco grain prices every week and claimed that Palouse wheat traveled as far as Central and South America, Russia, Japan, and Guam. With the comfort of knowing that markets were within reach, immigrants leapt at the chance to profit from the land. Railroads, not the government, sold a majority of the prime farmland in the 1880s, an indication that potential farmers sought land that would do more than just sustain them, and that 160 acres would be insufficient for their growing needs.[29]

Railroads and the revelation of loess soil fertility altered attitudes and land use. Garfield farmer Ben Manning and many others suddenly abandoned cattle operations in favor of wheat production; by 1884, twenty thousand head of cattle roamed Whitman County, down from forty-five thousand just five years before. Fences began to appear, aided by the recent invention of barbed wire. Hamlets became towns and towns became regional cultural and economic centers. A nomadic spirit inflicted some farm families as they tried to take advantage of rising land prices and the perception of greener pastures somewhere else. Stella Skinner, growing up relatively poor, had only grain sacks on her feet instead of shoes, but her family somehow managed to move from Genesee to Viola to Pullman and then to Moscow in the 1890s. Around the turn of the century, Walter Getchell moved his family seven times in thirteen years.[30] Such restlessness was notorious in the nineteenth-century US, but in the Palouse it seems to have been taken a step further.

Whitman County, with a modest population of just over nineteen thousand in 1890, had the most acres in farmland, the most improved acres, the highest value of land and buildings, and the highest value of farm products of any county in Washington. Moreover, it contained far more farms with five hundred or more acres than any other county in the state. From its beginnings with a few squatters raising cattle in the early 1870s, the land had been "pretty well taken up" by 1889, according to Pullman farmer Charles Kellogg. The data indicates that typical Palouse farmers wasted no time in acquiring the land and equipment necessary for a headfirst plunge into global agricultural markets. They would not be satisfied with small, humble homesteads that fed their families from year to year; they thirsted for something more and gobbled up nearby farm sites as soon as their neighbors went bankrupt or moved on. An article from 1878 testified that Palouse farmers wished to "give our country a wide spread reputation abroad and redound to our pecuniary advancement at home."[31] As historian William Robbins writes concerning a similar state of affairs that occurred in Oregon during the same period, there was "a growing conviction among property holders in western valleys that land should be equated with the money and profits that it would yield. In effect, the acquisition of wealth for its own sake became one end to agricultural enterprise."[32]

Money and profits were what they got. In contrast to historian David Danbom's assertion that "rural conservatism impeded greater farmer commitment to the market," the evidence suggests that Palouse farmers gladly consented to use rails to send goods to Portland and Seattle where farm products were then sent to ports as near as the growing cities, mining camps, and fisheries of the West, and as far as New York, England, and Japan. Unlike their Midwestern counterparts, Washington grain growers usually did not have to contend with middlemen; more often than not, the person buying wholesale grain also shipped goods. Thus, both parties enjoyed lower costs. However, the disparities in Northwest rail freight charges—the system that made it cheaper for goods to be shipped from Seattle to the East Coast than from inland locales—enraged farmers and damaged the bottom line.[33] The difficulties of farming for millions tried the patience and tempers of many, but if farmers wished to continue in their profession they had to accept this situation. A growing dependence on distant markets put farmers at the mercy of railroads and forced them to look at balance sheets as much as at their crops and the weather.

Farming activity between 1890 and 1914 continued along a steep trajectory, with farmers accumulating large amounts of capital (and debt) to boost productivity. In addition to land purchases, they acquired the latest farm technology to work the soil. Mechanical reapers became a common sight, as did four- to six-horse teams that pulled plows and seed drills. Hand-held implements were still used, but in decreasing numbers and usually by those just starting out. Steam-powered tractors never made much of an impact, however, due to their relatively high center of gravity and consequent inability to work the steep hills; horses and mules dominated until well into the twentieth century. Nevertheless, productivity went up at a steady clip, which helped the farmer to produce more per acre, and, according to the standards of the time, to live better.[34]

The founding of two major land grant colleges in the Palouse advanced the cause of intensive agriculture. Founded in 1891 in Pullman, Washington State Agricultural College Experiment Station and School of Science directed research projects and trained students in the latest agricultural science techniques.[35] The University of Idaho, founded in 1889 in Moscow (eight miles east of Pullman), performed basically the same functions as its neighbor—promoting innovation in agriculture and disseminating information through cooperative extension offices. Both schools offered farmers some of the first truly reliable data on climate, soil types, and fertilizers and developed hybrid varieties of wheat that were specifically suited for the Palouse. The goal of these two institutions, and of all the other land grant colleges founded under the 1862 Morrill Act, was simple: to use higher education as a means of making agricultural communities prosper. John Scobey, an agriculturist at the college in Pullman, identified the mind of the farmer precisely in 1892: "Very few people in this or any other state are farming exclusively for pleasure; nor are they engaged in that healthful occupation entirely for 'hygienic reasons.' It is principally a question of profit." The marriage of collegiate education and capitalism had been consummated.[36]

If historian Frieda Knobloch is correct, that "the distinction between primitive and advanced agriculture often hinges on the extent of 'breaking' that tillage accomplishes," then the Palouse was indeed modern.[37] Thanks largely to the $12.5 million in agricultural goods it produced, Whitman County claimed the highest per capita income of any county in the nation in 1909. Land once considered bereft of life and fertility outproduced the legendary wheatlands of the northern Great Plains on a per acre basis. The amount of land left untouched by the plow reflected this development. Although accounts vary, nearly all arable Palouse land had been put to some agricultural purpose by 1905. Not all acres supported wheat; millions of dollars of plums, peaches, cherries, and apples, in addition to other grains like oats and barley, also rolled out of the region on freight cars. Hay and alfalfa fields remained popular because of demand for dairy products and feed for draft animals. But despite this appearance of diversity, wheat monocropping gradually dominated the countryside, bringing in almost 90 percent of the total income for Whitman County in the early twentieth century. The quality and quantity of soil, climate, and transportation infrastructure all pointed toward making the Palouse the nation's number one source for wheat. Local boosters and chambers of commerce liked to refer to the inland Northwest as the "Inland Empire," a moniker that seemed increasingly appropriate given the amount of political interest and corporate capital generated by the Palouse wheat fields.[38]

However, prosperity at this time and place required an abundance of wage laborers, few of whom would ever capture and exploit the Palouse earth. Harvest workers, mostly an itinerant lot who also worked in mines, forests, and on railroads, juxtaposed the forces of an emerging landed class that dominated regional commerce, politics, and culture, with the poor working class that earned a few dollars a day toiling in the fields. Farms did not function without farm *workers*, the day laborers who literally seized the soil, but who usually did not enjoy much of its bounty.

Demographic, agricultural, and economic development brought great ecological change. A growing population had staked its claim to all but a few remote corners of the region and instituted a style of agriculture that rested on the notion that profits could be gleaned from the soil indefinitely. What people rarely considered, however, was the possibility that intensive farming practices could harm future productivity. A few voices sounded off about the loss of fish and wildlife habitat, the introduction of noxious weeds, and soil erosion, but for the majority of those involved with farming, concerns about farm productivity and profitability gained more attention. Grain prices and the weather worried Palouse residents more than ecological transformation.

Botanists at the end of the nineteenth century appreciated both the unique ecological qualities of the Palouse and the consequences of intensive agriculture before farmers or the wider public did. John Sandberg and John Leiberg, who worked for the USDA, traveled the Columbia River and Basin in 1893 and introduced the idea that trampling hooves had opened the door for a host of nonnative plant species to invade and force out bunchgrasses and shrubs. Leiberg, the team's chief writer, stated that the Palouse "does not as a whole appear to possess much resisting power and when brought into competition with eastern invaders generally succumbs." They warned that the damage caused by grazing sheep and cattle threatened to change permanently the region's ecology before a more thorough study could catalog native plants. Their findings, however, were never published. Leiberg claimed in 1897 that he needed more data before anything could be sent to press, and sometime shortly afterward he was transferred to a position in the US Geological Survey, after which the project seems to have been forgotten. Charles Piper and R. Kent Beattie, botanists from Washington State College, also studied plants in the eastern part of the state. Their 1901 book, *The Flora of the Palouse Region,* listed and classified native plants and identified habitat zones as Sandberg and Leiberg had, but the study also spoke of wheat fields that crowded out native species and encouraged the growth of nonnative plants and noxious weeds.[39] All four of these scientists noticed that grazing animals and staple crops eliminated natural flora and shrunk in size a diverse and interesting part of the Western ecological mosaic.

The business of agriculture considerably reduced mammal, bird, and fish populations but failed to cause serious alarm among residents. Predators found it especially difficult to survive under this new regime. Habitat losses that occurred during the settlement period decreased the number of prey animals available for coyote, cougar, lynx, and black bear (which mainly inhabited the wooded areas on the eastern edge of the Palouse in Latah County, Idaho). Predators that remained in their diminished habitat had to subsist on a smaller number of ungulates and rodents and whatever they could cull from farms and ranches. This brought an ongoing government eradication program. Raptors did not fare well either. Since several kinds of hawks and falcons found poultry easy prey, these avian hunters also became the targets of farmers' shotguns. Moreover, a bounty placed on ground squirrels (one animal that actually adapted well to wheat fields) limited the availability of this major food source.[40]

The demise of the sharp-tailed grouse in the Palouse counts as perhaps the most striking example in which agriculture forced the local elimination of a species. Sharp-tails declined because they relied on bunchgrasses and dense streamside vegetation, foodstuffs and habitat that were in short supply by the twentieth century. Native grasses provided plenty of seeds for food, and tightly-packed thickets served as cover and nesting sites. Intensive farming did away with both. In addition, early settlers found that grouse made a fine meal—a discovery that led to the killing of tens of thousands of birds. Moreover, for a game bird, sharp-tails are rather "dumb"—that is, they tend to land only a short distance from where they are flushed, making them easy targets for humans and other predators alike. John Klemgard bragged that in his younger days the birds were so plentiful in serviceberry bushes that he could hit "half a dozen at one shot!"[41]

A rapid decline in cold-water fish species paralleled the equally swift rise of intensive agriculture. To get the most out of their land, farmers typically uprooted trees in swampy areas and along streams. The attendant loss of vegetation removed shade from streambanks, which in turn raised water temperatures past the point at which fish such as trout can survive. Warmwater species such as chubs, dace, and pikeminnows replaced cutthroat trout and steelhead that had long been a part of the deeper waters of the Palouse. Dorothy Presby, reflecting on her family's Viola, Idaho, farmstead, wrote, "Today the timber is all gone. There is no shade for the cattle around the spring, but there are no cattle, either." Settlers noted and at times lamented the reductions in fish stocks, but like the losses of native grasses, mammals, and birds, such losses failed to inspire local residents to reexamine their relationships with the land.[42]

Numerous Palouse farmers from the nineteenth century noted how wet the land was when it was first resettled, only to see it become progressively drier. Joseph Baird, who farmed between the towns of Palouse and Pullman, remarked how large areas of the Palouse had been logged and drained to make way for the plow. "All of this," he insisted, "affects climate, rainfall, and flood conditions." The claims of weather change were dubious, but the idea that drainage patterns affected streamflow was accurate. Less water on the surface meant the water table below would also be lower. It also meant that stream volume would drop, leading to a habitat change that cold-water fish species could not withstand. Farmers David and Ann Judson noticed a definite drop in the water table on their property in Whelan, Washington (outside of Pullman). At the turn of the twentieth century, they noted, "the water was clear and never went dry as numerous springs fed the streams all summer." But by the 1930s, they noticed that "these streams only run during wet weather in the spring or are completely dry." George Northrup remembered that to the north of the Washington towns Uniontown and Colton, "even the smaller flats were dotted with lakes and ponds that sparked in the moonlight. There was plenty of small trout while it was possible in the summer to go along the tall slough grass and catch almost grown ducks in the hands." He believed mining debris from the Clearwater Mountains had despoiled this sublime environment, although that was impossible, since these mountains do not feed this part of the Palouse. In any case, Northrup observed that "grain farming and ditching the creeks finished the work," clogging local waters and ruining this placid scene. John Klemgard, who came to the Palouse in 1882 from Denmark as part of a Mormon immigration program, observed that, "Union Flat [Creek] became a muddy stream and gradually has gone dry for longer periods each summer since the land has been all under the plow." That the North Fork of the Palouse River had once been used as a splashway for pine logs also indicated a significantly higher water table in the late nineteenth century. Trees felled in the Clearwater country were once floated to mills in the towns of Palouse and Colfax—an impossible task in later years because of insufficient flow.[43]

Although no quantitative studies exist, sediment buildup in streams probably contributed to a drop in water quality. The sediment came as runoff from wheat fields, most of which had been tilled by a moldboard plow—the standard implement of turn-of-the-century western agriculture. This plow could dig rather deeply into the soil, a benefit in semiarid zones because such tilling allowed more water to penetrate the ground. But the plow also disturbed the soil more and made it prone to erosion. An expanding acreage planted to wheat also contributed. Whitman County farms planted 280,000 acres in wheat in 1899—a considerable total—and just ten years later that number climbed to nearly 350,000 acres. Wheat occupied more acres than any other crop by 1910.[44] All of those acres had to be plowed, which disturbed the soil. Erosion undoubtedly existed in the 1870s and 1880s as well, but the root remnants from native grasses and shrubs mitigated the effects. Once old root systems decayed and withered away, however, the soil was more prone to erode. Evidence of the repercussions on the Palouse River began as early as 1901, when a Whitman County antiquarian observed, "It is said that in early days its currents were clear and sparkling, but no writer with regard for the truth could describe the present stream as beautiful." A promotional brochure from 1895 called the river "much of a joke in the summertime."[45] These remarks from otherwise upbeat stories on Palouse settlement indicated the magnitude of change that swept over the region in the nineteenth and early twentieth centuries.

The first signs of soil erosion appeared just after the turn of the twentieth century. More of an annoyance than a crisis at this time, it nonetheless indicated how thoroughly the land had been altered in a single generation. William Brabyn began noticing erosion on his Pullman farm in the early 1900s, especially after heavy rains. So too did Fred Hodges, who recalled a particularly heavy rain—a "gully washer"—that brought down so much soil from the hills that it covered fences. Still, he claimed that the displaced soil did little to reduce crop yields.[46] This attitude was common, according to Washington State College agronomist Leonard Hegnauer, who began his career in the Palouse circa 1910. He wrote that when he confronted farmers about their erosion problems, "they usually explained to me that the summers were rainless and dry; that when fall came the rains were gentle and the porous soil of the dry fields drank it in like a sponge, with little or no run-off. Nearly everybody seemed to assume that the Palouse hills were indestructible and would continue forever to produce the marvelous yields for which they already were famous."[47]

A new farming regimen caused a great deal of erosion. Summer fallow, the practice of keeping a field bare for a year or more to control weeds and to conserve soil moisture, developed into a standard procedure for Palouse farmers in the 1890s and in the decades that followed. Agricultural scientists headed the list of devotees. In one of the first technical bulletins issued by the Washington State College in 1892, R. C. McCroskey urged farmers to employ summer fallow. He wrote with all the conviction of a railroad land agent that "no business that I can conceive of appears to be so free from risk as farming here by this method. The farmer is thus just as sure to realize large profits as he would be to get back his principal with interest on a time deposit in a well conducted bank." McCroskey said that it would lead to richer harvests, less expenditure on seed and equipment, and more leisure time. To those who believed that keeping fields bare seemed counterintuitive and fiscally illogical, McCroskey answered, "The farmer who is in debt says he cannot afford to lose every other crop. The fact is, he cannot afford to do otherwise." Washington State College agronomist George Severence wrote in 1908 that summer fallow "becomes necessary on account of the dryness of the climate."[48] Whether because of summer fallow or some other factor, yields did go higher. Average yields for the state of Washington went from 15 bushels per acre in 1884 to 16.5 bushels in 1894 to 19.4 bushels in 1904.[49] New wheat varieties and new fertilizers played some role, but farmers also credited the restorative powers of summer fallow with increasing their profits and making their lives easier at the same time.

Rank-and-file farmers concurred with the experts. The year 1893 was notable both because of a deep economic recession and unusually heavy rainfall. The following year weeds, especially wild oats, inundated many farms, prompting experimentation with summer fallow. The results were favorable: weeds were kept at bay and wheat crops improved. Thereafter, wheat growers increasingly used this tactic and it was applied across most of the Palouse by the years immediately following 1910.[50]

The situation seemed ideal—plant less and earn more—but it would not last. Sometime around the turn of the century soil experts began noticing a direct relationship between fallowed ground and erosion. They discovered that the removal of ground cover for an entire year left the soil vulnerable to the formation of deep lines or "rills" on many of the barren, steep slopes. William Brabyn understood the correlation: "Soon after summer fallow became common, erosion became noticeable."[51] William J. Spillman of Washington State College asked farmers to use cover crops every other year, instead of fallow, to improve the situation and to protect the valuable topsoil from eroding. Most farmers ignored his speeches and bulletins because they believed that the tremendous depth of Palouse soils would produce bountiful crops for years to come regardless of erosion. Conserving soil, they thought, was a waste of time when soil depths ran as deep as 250 feet; if soil eroded, they needed only to plow up more.[52]

A more forceful argument against summer fallow surfaced in 1912. Agriculture scientists discovered that a wheat/fallow rotation and the erosion that ensued diminished the amount of humus (organic matter) in the soil. This realization had far-reaching implications for dryland farmers everywhere. Soil chemist R. W. Thatcher pointed out that a loss of humus led to lower quantities of soil nitrogen (an essential element for plant growth), caused the ground to became more difficult to plow, and reduced the ability of topsoil to hold water. He stopped short of a general condemnation of the custom but recommended that farmers leave wheat stubble intact after harvest instead of burning it; such a practice would retain organic matter and replenish nitrogen. Thatcher also asked farmers to use more manure to build humus and to plant more alfalfa as a cover crop.[53] The subtext of his message carried greater weight than the raw data. For the first time a trained expert cautioned that new farming strategies and the level of farming intensity in the Palouse might not be sustainable in the long term. If left unchecked, losses of nitrogen, humus, and the soil itself might at some point cut into the productivity of the land and damage farm profitability. A system of farming based on maximized production, with summer fallow as a key ingredient, had already caused the soil to erode, fouled Palouse waters, and forced native animals to flee. By the early twentieth century those conditions showed no signs of changing.

On the eve of the First World War, Palouse farming appeared to be in good shape. Wheat prices from 1910 to 1914 held steady at about 75 cents per bushel, land values continued to climb, government subsidies in the form of land-grant colleges and USDA programs poured money into research, and a general optimism about the prospects for future growth buoyed the spirits of people in the farming community. It was clear that the dismissive, pessimistic early impressions of Lansford Hastings and others had been misguided. This "best poor man's land," unlike the semiarid western Great Plains, could grow a number of marketable crops, seemingly year after year without crop failure or prolonged drought. Settlers faced many problems, but the undeniable success of the Palouse wheat domain was an impressive accomplishment by most people's standards.

Upon closer inspection, however, a few cracks started to show. The meteoric growth rate that characterized late nineteenth-century farming would likely not last, if past events in other farming communities were any indication. For nearly every boom there is a bust, and Palouse farmers could not consider themselves exempt. Moreover, a progressive, export-oriented, heavily capitalized, and mechanized style of agriculture accelerated the severity of some serious environmental predicaments—chiefly soil erosion. Problems caused by this agricultural system were not inevitable, but given the economic structure that had been put in place, they were tough to avoid. When the situation grew more acute later in the twentieth century, a reliance on this agricultural and economic superstructure made a contrary response extremely difficult. Historian William Cronon noticed the same dynamic in his 1991 tome on the rise of Chicago and the commodification of the Midwestern prairies and pinelands. He noted that "where human beings organize their economy around market exchange, trade between city and country will be among the most powerful forces influencing cultural geography and environmental change."[54] To a great extent, the collective decision to mass produce a staple crop for export and an eager willingness to participate in global capitalism affected land use, habitat loss, soil loss, and water quality more than any other set of factors or variables. Concern for the environment was decades away, but the threat posed by erosion would become better known much sooner. Agriculturalists had embarked on a system that damaged the vulnerable loess soil and put their futures in jeopardy. The war years that were right around the corner only exacerbated these preexisting conditions and put this new economic engine into overdrive.

4 THE IMPLICATIONS OF PROSPERITY

T HE *WASHINGTON FARMER*, a leading weekly newspaper that catered to the agricultural community of the inland Northwest, served as a sounding board for a multitude of farming issues throughout the twentieth century. News about commodity prices, information on new equipment, and advice on wheat smut and horse colic could be found in its pages. For at least the first half of the century, it combined a homespun, commonfolk attitude with a growing awareness that being a good farmer also meant being a sharp businessman and financial tactician. The *Farmer* reflected and promoted a belief that business acumen assured farm prosperity as well as the more nebulous, yet essential, ideals of family and social stability. Palouse farming in the early twentieth century was similarly torn between the desire to maintain old habits and the urge to follow new trends. Farmers were simultaneously agrarian, concerned with growing food and providing social and financial security for their families, and liberal, which in the early twentieth century meant that they utilized new and preexisting government-sponsored research, advice, and infrastructure to systematize and expand their operations.

A quirky, whimsical editorial from late 1914 illustrates this significant paradox. The article depicts two Southern farmers contemplating the effects of the outbreak of war in Europe. "Uncle John," a youngish, progressive farmer, reasoned that after "the Kayser got a-eachin' fur a fight," and after the Tsar "started to shuckin' his coat," that the continent would be in dire need of food imports. He had planted an assortment of food crops in anticipation of shortages abroad and the attendant rise in prices, and he did well when it came time to sell his harvest. His companion, known simply as "the old man," planted cotton—a decision he dearly regretted: "I acted the fool again this year an' didn't plant much corn, thinkin' I'd strike it rich with a big crop o' cotton. I made the cotton, all right, but now I can't sell the stuff. Didn't plant much corn, an' the early drouth got it, an' now it's up to a dollar an' a quarter a bushel an' likely to go higher." To his dismay, the European cotton market dried up, since "them fool furriners was so busy a-shootin' each other that they wur a-payin' mighty little attention to whether or not they had any clothes or not, anyway."[55] The obvious message being sent to *Washington Farmer* readers was that diversification in food crops was the prudent course to follow during turbulent times.

For all the exposure, another set of the newspaper's writers had other ideas. While the *Washington Farmer* printed articles on topics such as the need to diversify and the dangers of single-crop farming, it also encouraged a shift away from diversified (or "mixed") farming toward monocropping. It called for a new breed of farmer—one who increased acreage and invested in the latest equipment in order to take advantage of the economies of scale that large farms produced. Such calls resonated with the agrarian liberals of the Palouse, the ambitious farmers who successfully combined rural life with government assistance and a market economy. An attraction to bigger farms and profits drew many operators away from diversification; the farmer of the future would be first and foremost a specialist in training, equipment, and in crops. Trade newspapers such as the *Farmer* picked up on this trend and sang its praises.

This split personality characterized the Palouse agricultural community from 1914 through the early days of the Great Depression, but it increasingly leaned in favor of intensive, specialized farming that focused solely on wheat. The high commodity prices of 1914–1919 encouraged farmers to plant every available acre in order to cash in on the misfortunes of European farmers and to contribute to the American war effort. After the war, when prices fell in the early 1920s, Palouse growers continued to work aggressively to produce higher yields to cover operating expenses and to stay in business. These actions put more pressure on land that had already started to show signs of wear and tear. The moldboard plow, summer fallow, stubble burning, and tillage on steep slopes contributed to an increase in soil erosion that alarmed a few farmers, but not enough to cause them to change their approach. Because of the emphasis on maximized production and devotion to the bottom line, farmers ignored the deepening rivulets and gullies that became a common sight in the Palouse. As long as yields improved or at least held steady, farmers saw little need for re-examining the repercussions of their actions. Ironically there was little doubt by the 1930s that Palouse farmers had sided with the old man, and not Uncle John.

National and international trends left some obvious footprints in Washington and Idaho in the late nineteenth and early twentieth centuries. External forces—westward migration, the market revolution, and the rapid expansion and improvement of transportation systems—left indelible marks on the economic and environmental makeup of the Palouse. Each shaped land-use ideas and the physical condition of the land in myriad ways that can be observed to this day. In a similar fashion, Europe's simmering feuds and dueling nationalities, once transformed into an all-out world war in 1914, dramatically affected Palouse wheat farming during and after the conflict. The assassination of Archduke Francis Ferdinand and the recoil from Gavrilo Princip's pistol were felt in Europe as well as in this distant agricultural region of the Columbia Plateau.

Farmers from all over the United States responded to the outbreak of the Great War by increasing production. The war turned many European farmlands into killing fields and millions of farmers into soldiers, effectively curtailing agricultural production for much of the continent—especially in France. Europeans harvested thirty-seven million metric tons of wheat per year from 1909 to 1913, but could only raise twenty-six million metric tons by 1919. Russia managed to keep up with production but found it nearly impossible to export its products. The loss of navigation rights to the Dardanelles in 1915 and the annual freezing of all their Pacific ports meant that Russian grains stayed in Russia.[2]

US producers willingly filled the void. A dramatic rise in commodity prices made the proposition feasible and enticing. Wheat had sold at 70 to 80 cents per bushel from 1910 to 1913, a price that allowed Palouse farmers to prosper.[3] Farmers from all over the US enjoyed this golden age of agriculture; prices on most goods increased because of faster transportation links to foreign markets, immigration, and a growing domestic population. Shortly after hostilities began in Europe in late June 1914, commodity prices went on an impressive, extended upward spiral. Whitman County wheat gained 6 cents per bushel in one week in July and continued to climb for the rest of the summer. By year's end the price reached 92 cents and less than two months later certain varieties sold for $1.40 per bushel. A 100 percent price increase in less than a year left many farmers elated (despite the dark fact that millions of dead European soldiers and civilians were the cause). The local press spoke of the "jubilant" mood in the area and reported that farmers anticipated "a still greater increase in prices as the European war cloud gains volume."[4]

The overheated market gave Palouse farmers the impetus to plant more wheat. Growers in Latah County, Idaho, planted nearly twice as much wheat during the war years as in 1909. In Whitman County, the increase was less dramatic, since "King Wheat" had already dominated the landscape for some time. Still, local growers planted 28 percent more acres in 1919 than in 1909. National trends mirrored the Palouse situation; in every year from 1915 through 1919, American wheat farmers increased production. And prices ascended even further. Strong demand boosted Northwest wheat to $2 per bushel and above from 1917 through 1920.[5] American farmers had never seen market forces work for them in such a positive way for so long a period.

Not all agricultural interests shared in this euphoria. Some believed that the sudden surge in prices and increased acreages would hurt farmers in the long run. Henry Pope, an executive from the Farmers' Union, a lobbying group, warned that "overproduction would visit upon the nation an unwarranted calamity." The editors of the Washington Farmer wrote in 1914 that in spite of high prices, "until marketing methods have been improved and readjusted more fairly, the farmer will get the short end, as usual." A year later, their defeatism tempered, the newspaper instead chose to admonish greedy farmers: "the temptation is tremendous to plant every bit of land to wheat for the sake of 'easy money.'"[6]

Harvest workers attempted, and largely failed, to use the war as a means to improve their standard of living. Many workers gravitated to the Industrial Workers of the World, better known as the Wobblies, to forcefully represent their interests. The union's goal during the war was to enlist as many men as possible, then to stage strikes during the crucial harvest weeks in August to gain wage concessions and union recognition. The Wobblies succeeded mainly in galvanizing a violent opposition, as wages did not significantly increase until a well-organized strike in 1923. But for the rest of the 1920s and in the 1930s, the number of field hands fell as quickly as farmers bought new labor-saving implements, thus reducing the need for farm union activity. For the wage workers of the Palouse, bushels per acre and dollars per bushel did not translate into dollars per day.[7]

But the overwhelming majority of voices—even from the Farmer—supported efforts to maximize production. Notions about the US farmers' responsibility to feed the world and slogans like "Wheat will win the war" resonated more than pessimism or ominous predictions about the future. The *Farmer* often cited the growers' need to look carefully at their land, because nearly every parcel contained some "waste" land: "It lies in the fence corners, along the ditches or around old buildings or barnyards. Very often it is the best land on the place, at least after having lain idle for years. It ought to be put to work. There is profit in it; there is loss if it is not utilized." More-over, at the federal level President Wilson's administration fully supported an aggressive approach, calling for farmers "to raise such big crops that cir-cumstances like the present [food shortages in Europe] can never occur." Editors in the Whitman County seat at Colfax, Washington, agreed. They wrote in 1918 that in order to satisfy European demand, "seventy-five mil-lion bushels, on the first day of this year, was needed to tide them over until July 1."[8] The Washington State Grange weighed in as well, passing a reso-lution in 1920 opposing a bill in the state legislature that proposed to estab-lish a ten-foot easement along streams in agricultural areas. The easements were intended to improve hunting habitat, but the Grange said that the tak-ing of thousands of acres of fertile land was unacceptable.[9] Warnings about overproduction and jeremiads on greed filtered through regional conver-sations, but the loudest and strongest voices were held by those who sup-ported maximized production.

In this climate of high prices and production, farmers realized they now wielded some economic leverage. For the first time, many sought to delay marketing their grain as long as possible in order to take advantage of the worldwide wheat shortage. During the first months of the war, Palouse farm-ers began "to show no disposition to sell" and saw "well-defined visions of a magnificent realization of their 1914 input." Even when wheat reached $1 per bushel later that year they delayed selling. The story was repeated each year for the duration of the war. Some of the smaller farmers were obliged to sell shortly after harvest, but medium-to-large operators often stored grain well into the fall and winter months. As farmers learned more about Europe's misfortunes and about how the international grain futures mar-ket worked, they became more financially astute and secure.[10]

Some farmers became rich during the war years, a condition that put some in the unfamiliar position of defending their newfound financial status. Farmers stressed that their profits came in the name of supplying Allied forces. A congressman from Washington asked, "Why should not the farmer of this country be prosperous when he is feeding the greatest armies that this world has ever seen?" The farm press reminded its readers that the law of supply and demand determined prices and farm income and dismissed allegations of profiteering. One commentator wrote that supply and demand was "a good law—a real one and a natural one. Man did not make it. No legislature passed it. It was not introduced by initiative, nor amended by referendum. It was right here before we came." Farmers reveled in their new economic position and hoped to perpetuate it.[11]

After the war ended and for most of the 1920s, Palouse farmers got their wish. Prices fell considerably after 1920 when Europe managed to revive its dormant agricultural sector, but the decline did not jeopardize the region's wheat farmers. Unlike those in other regions of the nation where there were widespread farm foreclosures, Palouse farmers weathered the downturn relatively well. The local press may have complained of a "ruinous slump" in 1920s wheat prices, yet prices remained well above prewar levels for most of the decade. The per bushel price in Rosalia, Washington, bottomed out at 85 cents in 1923 but remained over $1 from 1924 through 1929. The inflationary war years meant that farmers' costs were also higher, but for many the result was decreased profits, not bankruptcy.[12]

Despite this "surface" prosperity, some Palouse farmers faced hardships in the 1920s. Prices remained high, but operating expenses, especially the cost of machinery, kept many small operators struggling to stay in business. The first decades of the twentieth century saw many American farmers make the leap into mechanized farming. Both steam- and gasoline-powered tractors crawled across Palouse slopes in increasing numbers. Harvesting machines also gained in popularity; combines made the wheat harvest a far simpler and less labor-intensive chore. While these machines eliminated some of the drudgery from farming, they also necessitated high annual production. A farmer with tractor payments could ill afford more than one year of disappointing profits. And more than a few went under. The 1930 joint financial statement of the Pullman State Bank and the First National Bank of Pullman reported that "very few poor farmers have been able to survive the trying years since 1920."[13] A willingness to expand operations did not guarantee long-term solvency, but it at least made it possible.

Although large farm machinery arrived in the Palouse at roughly the same time as in other parts of the nation, it failed to create an immediate impact. Manufacturers assumed that their equipment would be used on relatively level ground—such as in the Midwest and South—and did not consider how their new devices would work on hilly terrain. The steep hills of the Palouse rendered early tractors useless, especially those with narrow front wheels or with only one front wheel. If the new tractors could not be adapted to the Palouse then neither could the combines attached to them. A mere 256 tractors worked Whitman County fields in 1920, and only 241 in 1925. This contrasted with statewide and national figures that showed tractor numbers nearly doubling in the same period.[14] Replacing teams of horses with a John Deere or a Case tractor made little sense if it wound up in a ditch or rolled down a hill.

Heavy equipment sales jumped in the latter half of the 1920s, however. Improved implements (manufacturers began making tractors with a wider wheelbase), better harvests, rising prices, and easy credit made farm mechanization the wave of the future. Although horsepower still performed most of the work in the Palouse in the 1920s, horses were no match for internal combustion in the long run. The number of tractors in Whitman County more than doubled from 1925 to 1930, and they handled nearly half of all field work. The number of combines made a similar gain, as farmers switched from horse-drawn to tractor-drawn implements. The most striking change occurred in transportation. Motorized trucks replaced horses and wagons at a startling rate—Washington farmers used more than four times as many trucks in 1930 as in 1920, and Idaho farmers used more than six times as many over the same period.[15] Farm prices dipped in the 1920s, but not deeply enough or long enough to prevent Palouse farmers from buying new equipment.

High commodity prices and farm capitalization led to an associated rise in Palouse farmland prices. Typical Palouse land sold for $35 to $50 an acre in 1900 and increased to $75 to $100 per acre just before the war, reflecting the steady progression of the wheat business. During and after the war, land prices shot up even more. An acre of Palouse land fetched upward of $200 an acre by 1923, indicating the region's prosperity and commitment to intensive agriculture.[16] But the prolonged boom carried unwanted consequences as well. Higher land values meant higher property taxes, which added to farm overhead and exacerbated the need to maximize production. Farmers certainly could have sold their estates in the 1920s and reaped a handsome reward (as many did), but at the expense of a cherished way of life.

Mechanization and high land prices led to consolidation of ownership. Economies of scale dictated that farmers best utilized expensive machinery by working it as much as possible. They derived more value from a new tractor plowing a five-hundred-acre field than one plowing a two-hundred-acre field. Likewise, grain trucks and combines only made sense if they were used often. Small operators could not use machinery for long enough periods to justify the cost. Nor could they afford such luxuries, since their limited cash flow prevented most from making the necessary loan payments. But larger operators could more easily budget for big-ticket items and pay them off—provided the weather and prices held up.

Therefore, once a farmer bought new equipment, it made sense to buy more land. The increase in the number of tractors directly related to increased farm acreage: Palouse farms averaged 403 acres in 1910, 448 in 1920, 458 in 1925, and swelled to 523 by 1930. One in ten Palouse farms topped 1,000 acres. During the same period, the number of farms went down, as some farmers either went bankrupt or chose to sell their land at inflated prices.[17] The early stages of a technological revolution changed more than just how farmers planted and harvested wheat—it also changed the financial and social structure of the Palouse.

Among the several unfortunate by-products of mechanization was an alarming rise in farm debt. Paying cash for land or equipment was not unknown but was exceedingly rare; for most wheat growers, new capital required a bank loan. As a result, when buying a new tractor or acquiring a neighbor's homestead, farmers incurred a commensurate amount of debt. Washington farmers owed banks more than $25 million in 1910, a number that ballooned to $61 million only ten years later.[18] A discernible and troubling pattern of borrowing and expanding swept over the Palouse from 1910 through the 1920s. Farmers initially felt the urge to plant more acres to exploit the high prices of an overheated market. Once they committed to this plan through capitalization, however, they were forced to ride an endless treadmill of debt and maximized production.[19] In the words of one farmer, "The Palouse farmer raises more wheat to get more money to buy more land to raise more wheat to get more money to buy more land."[20] Decisions on production, mechanization, and land purchases made in the late teens and 1920s affected the nature and pace of Palouse farming for many years. These decisions would also have a direct bearing on the physical makeup of the land that sustained them. But farmers in the early twentieth century operated with the same mentality as their parents who homesteaded in the nineteenth century: they took chances. An eagerness to accept the risks of commercial agriculture characterized the initial settlement period and the decades that followed.

The scene playing out in the Palouse closely resembled the one Deborah Fitzgerald describes in her 2003 book, *Every Farm a Factory: The Industrial Ideal in American Agriculture*. Her focus is the national trend toward the systemization of agriculture, and she argues that in the twentieth century farmers adopted industrial techniques, logic, and motivations. A comprehensive "matrix" of relationships developed—between the farmer and the land, various off-farm inputs, and financial institutions—resulting in an American farm that much more closely resembled a factory than any idyllic subsistence farm. The "agents" of this shift were everywhere, from local bankers who saw farm loans as a safe venture, to land-grant college professors working on improved seed, to implement dealers and mechanics who served farmers. All were part of Fitzgerald's described matrix and all played important roles in making Palouse farming an increasingly capitalized and complicated enterprise. A new mind-set was required, but most farmers could make the transition if given the proper training. Moreover, since Palouse farming had such an explosive start in the 1880s and 1890s, the notion that farmers had to exist in a state of perpetual reinvention was already part of the *local* matrix. To be sure, the rhetoric of agrarianism endured (as it exists today), but after World War I it must be thought of as the backdrop to commercial activity. It no longer commanded center stage. The agrarian liberal was in the process of evolving slowly away from the former and more toward the latter.[21]

The Palouse matrix of mechanization, land concentration, technical expertise, and debt impelled farmers to strive for efficiency and to make every effort to parlay new techniques and capital into profits. But in addition to adopting new technology, they also believed that certain established practices, held over from their less technocentric world, made sound economic sense. Summer fallow, the time-honored routine of keeping wheat fields bare for a year to prevent weed growth, to restore nitrogen, and to conserve soil moisture, was one such tradition. Although it left up to half of the Palouse bereft of wheat in any given year, fallowed land performed better than acres continually cropped. The practice came under fire briefly in the years immediately following 1910 because of its erosive effects, but remained a standard custom through the 1920s.

Despite the popularity of summer fallow, continuing worries about soil erosion and fertility surfaced during and after World War I. George Severence, a Washington State College scientist, wrote in 1916 that all agricultural societies go through an initial period of "soil mining," when the land is exploited with little consideration for future consequences. In this regard, the Palouse was no different. Early settlers worked the land and caused its literal decline. Severence warned that "we are not operating under any special dispensation of Providence, and this soil will, and in many cases is, already beginning to deteriorate." A few years later, he reported that the situation had local businessmen asking "whether there is any hope agriculturally for the Inland Empire." To Severence, the appearance of erosion endangered the agricultural and social viability of the region. Leonard Hegnauer, a Washington State College agronomist, shared Severence's anxiety. In the early years of a career that spanned World War I and the Cold War, Hegnauer witnessed that, "as the years passed, the waters from the fields and in the streams became darker and darker, muddier and muddier, where once they ran clear. Signs of erosion were greatly multiplied."[22]

Perhaps the strongest statement on the condition of the soil came from the USDA, the government agency Steven Stoll refers to as the "Church of Information" for American farmers.[23] In 1917, well before a concerted national effort to stop erosion gathered momentum, the department released a soil survey of Latah County. It found that "brown and yellowish-brown spots," up to an acre in size, covered the land. "These spots are due to exposures of the subsoil material, believed to be caused by continuous downhill plowing. These patches of soil are deficient in organic matter, appear to be less retentive of moisture, and are consequently less productive than the typical soil."[24] Scientists and bureaucratic experts gathered data and anecdotal evidence that suggested major environmental change was afoot in the Palouse. Transforming knowledge into policy, however, took considerable time, as the "church" struggled with its message.

As erosion became more obvious in the 1920s, Palouse farmers expressed intermittent concern. Wheat grower Joseph Baird said that there was little erosion on area farms before 1920, but that it grew worse thereafter, as old root systems broke apart. Such insight was uncommon, though. More typical was Walter Glaspey, who said that in the 1920s "there had been occasional ditches," but added, "nobody seemed concerned."[25] The disconcerting realization that local farming might be in danger came slowly. Erosion had not appeared instantly, and neither did its solutions. Uncertainty about the severity of the erosion caused some of the delay. According to some farmers, although eroding soils left gullies three feet deep and gave "the stranger a distinct shock," wheat growers had become somewhat accustomed to these conditions. A casual attitude prevailed in some circles. One reporter claimed that farmers "inured to the sight through constant association, think little of it and are inclined to regard the soil experts' warnings as the product of an excitable imagination." The writer went on to quote one farmer whose solution was simple: "I'll just run a plow up and down the ditch," he said, "and I can get over it all right."[26]

Misconceptions about Palouse geology lent credence to such an outlook. Scientists in the early twentieth century were unsure about the ancient origins of the Palouse loess; many felt that it had formed from a parental basalt that underlay the entire Columbia Basin. Time and research would invalidate this finding, but the notion that the soil came from underneath the Palouse affected the local opinion on erosion through the 1920s. A sizeable portion of the farming community believed that even if their plows caused erosion, the effects were purely aesthetic. The rivulets and gullies that appeared every year might be unattractive but need only be tilled out of sight, since a practically endless supply of soil lay just beneath their feet. They insisted that no crisis existed and that the future of local agriculture looked bright.[27]

A steadily worsening erosion problem in the 1920s legitimized the alarmists' claims and refuted the idea that the soil would last forever. Commenting with the convenience of hindsight, the Latah County Soil Conservation District reported that farmers knew something was amiss by the early 1920s. A district publication from 1950 noted that the early twentieth century "was a period of taking a good deal from the soil and putting nothing back. It resulted in rapid loss of soil organic matter, soil infertility, and very severe erosion."[28] A continuation of wheat cropping on light loess soils in conjunction with summer fallow and new and heavier machinery removed much of the organic matter from the topsoil. Once this key layer of humus was gone, the gullies—and fears—deepened. Residents became increasingly aware that their soil was being depleted and was in trouble.

Most farming experts placed the blame squarely on the practice of summer fallow. Farmers usually harrowed fields several times during the year and broke up chunks of soil and sod into a pulverized dust, which looked "clean" and well-managed but which also eroded easily. Fallowed fields may have been necessary for good yields in the short term, but the erosion it created stirred local emotions. The editors of the Washington Farmer took the lead in condemning summer fallow, attacking it as a "menace" that could eventually run hundreds of farmers out of business. The Farmer noted as early as 1919 that "it is becoming very apparent that the rich soil is getting out of condition" because of fallowing. Other articles portrayed wheat— the crop that had built the Palouse from bunchgrass backwater to agricultural empire—as a "soil robber" because it needed so much fallow time to thrive over the long term. When erosion caused "thousands of tons of the richest soils [to] wash down until the flats are covered from 1 to 12 inches deep with it," the Farmer started assessing blame. Chief among the offenders was idle, fallow land.[29]

Of the small proportion of Palouse farmers interested in preserving their soil, a growing number understood that summer fallow aggravated erosion.

After a violent rainstorm and tornado in 1921, John Klemgard noticed erosion all over his property, but "the washing on summer fallowed land was especially bad." A kind of group intuition was forming—one that told farmers that it was unnatural to see the fields run into the streams, fouling the waters and structurally changing their farmland. Second-generation farmer George Johnson knew something was wrong after another downpour in the 1920s covered his barnyard with about three feet of soil and debris from the summer fallowed field above. And when Augusta Peer began using summer fallow in 1915, he noticed that mud had "washed off the hills, covering the meadow below, in places a foot deep."[30] Although these men all knew the results of fallowing loess soil, they did not necessarily end the practice. Some felt awkward harming the ground that fed them, yet they were unable to stop because of financial imperatives.

Dormant acres were not the only cause. Many accepted and proven farming techniques aggravated the problem. The V-shaped moldboard plow, a standard implement in agriculture worldwide, gouged the soil and exposed a great deal of it to rainwater—making it more prone to erode. Mechanization had changed many facets of American farming, but basic plow technology remained the same in the years from 1910 through the 1920s. New harrows, discs, and weeders all appeared on the market in this period, but improved plows that disturbed less soil did not. In addition, after the August harvest the vast majority of operators burned off the remaining wheat stubble in order to ease plowing later that fall. The stubble, which could be a foot high, could have been returned to the soil as organic matter, thereby preventing some erosion.[31]

Professor William J. Spillman, who left Washington State College for the USDA in 1902, told farmers in 1924 that they could not continue with a wheat/fallow rotation indefinitely. He railed against monocropping and appealed for more government money to study erosion. The pleas continued in a 1927 editorial by a Whitman County farmer. The "eternal hills of scripture and poetry" of his youth were under siege from greedy opportunists who defiled the land. In spite of the erosion that grew more noticeable each year, his neighbors "tilled and tilled and tilled—wheat, wheat, wheat! Tilled till it became evident that even the deep soil of the Palouse was temporal."[32] To concerned farmers like him, a comprehensive recasting of Palouse agriculture was in order. Yields stayed high through most of the 1920s, but the visual and editorial warning signs demanded at least some experimental change.

The research arm of Washington State College believed the situation urgent enough to devote research money toward the dual ends of crop productivity and soil health. The Agricultural Experiment Station in Pullman noted in its 1919 annual report that summer fallowing "has had a very destructive effect on the organic matter which in turn has had a detrimental effect on the physical condition of the soil."[33] Even at this early date, scientists were keenly aware of the links between summer fallow, erosion, loss of humus and nitrogen, and productivity. However, they also believed that Palouse farmers were an independent, stubborn lot and that asking them to stop fallowing was unrealistic. Instead, scientists looked for other ways to improve the soil. One of those techniques involved wheat stubble. State college professors believed that returning organic matter to the soil after harvests would build humus and thwart erosion. But they also concluded that disking large amounts of stubble instead of burning it reduced yields in the short term. The remnant stalks kept soil in place but inhibited nitrification and reduced the subsequent crop. Scientists could not account for this mysterious decline in yield. They recommended further research and stopped short of calling for an abandonment of stubble burning.[34]

Several years later the experiment station offered more definitive suggestions. State college soils experts Frederick Sievers and Henry Holtz published a report in 1922 that reinforced earlier studies and local custom and featured the latest data on Palouse soil fertility. They quantified the drop in productivity from annual wheat planting and judged manure as an impractical fertilizer because it required massive doses to be effective. They also noted that in the preceding thirty years nearly 35 percent of the Palouse soil's organic matter had been lost to erosion. Although recent articles had already warned of this development, "a certain class of farmers" still believed that the soil was in excellent shape. The authors flatly stated that this opinion "is not supported by results from analyses."[35]

Sievers and Holtz also revealed new scientific information. The authors carefully dissected the arguments in favor of summer fallow and found serious shortcomings regarding soil health. They discovered, in contrast to prevailing wisdom, that fallowed land did not increase soil nitrogen levels. On the contrary, over a thirty-nine-year period, a wheat/fallow rotation lost over 22 percent of its nitrogen. The losses were even higher than those from continuous wheat cropping—a revelation to an agricultural region weaned on the benefits of fallow. Farmers believed that strong yields hinged on available soil nitrogen but were now told that this "exceedingly wasteful" tactic hindered instead of helped the production of this crucial element.[36]

The report implicated erosion as another limiting factor in nitrification. Sievers and Holtz echoed earlier sentiments that it "is becoming so severe that the resulting trenches interfere very materially with field operations and with satisfactory crop development." Their data concluded that erosion had stripped the ground of most of its microbial life during the first decades of intensive agriculture. With this key layer gone, farmers found it "more difficult to maintain the nitrogen and organic matter in the soil as the soil becomes more and more depleted of its virgin nitrogen and organic matter." Summer fallow only exacerbated this ongoing cycle. Fallowed land eroded more easily, which removed more humus and reduced nitrogen levels. If this equation proved accurate, Palouse wheat farms were on borrowed time.[37]

Farmers were stuck in a catch-22: how could they simultaneously increase production, generate nitrogen, *and* reduce erosion? To get an answer, Sievers and Holtz conducted quantitative tests of an idea that had been around for some time. They planted fields in a wheat rotation with legumes—alfalfa, clover, or peas—and found that all three led to far higher nitrogen levels and wheat totals than either continuous wheat cropping or a wheat/fallow rotation. Legumes succeeded because of their ability to fix nitrogen in soil (the plants are unique in that they have tiny nodules that can capture nitrogen from the air and transform it into a soil nutrient). Moreover, a wheat/legume rotation meant that fields could be protected during the growing season every year by plant growth, thereby reducing erosion. On a small scale, this system promised to improve fertility and help keep the hills in place. But in a larger sense, the abandonment of a wheat monocrop meant that Palouse agriculture might prosper well into the future.[38]

For all their research and evidence, Sievers and Holtz still did not advocate a comprehensive overhaul of local customs. In fact, the same bulletin that touted a wheat/legume rotation also advised farmers on "proper" fallowing methods. This may seem paradoxical, but even cutting-edge technocrats with an appreciation for sustainable agriculture could not ignore the popularity of summer fallow. The authors gave detailed information on when to plow, how frequently to harrow, and the benefits derived from leaving the ground bare. They believed that fallow reduced nitrogen and knew that it fostered erosion, but they nevertheless chose to legitimize its practice.[39] The ambivalence of these two researchers characterized the tension and indecision of the entire Palouse agricultural community in the 1920s. Scientist and farmer alike knew that farming needed new perspectives and technical expertise, but both were unwilling or unable to embrace reform that challenged basic assumptions.

Sievers and Holtz marched on with their research for the balance of the decade. A 1924 report advised farmers to increase nitrogen content by using legumes and by planting corn and potatoes in alternate years. The latter two crops did not fix nitrogen, but they used less nitrogen than wheat and could be sold at good prices for most of the 1920s. Sievers and Holtz also tentatively endorsed commercial fertilizers such as sodium nitrate, potash, and lime, although they found that difficulties in application and cost often made these inputs impractical. But contradictory advice continued to flow from the experiment station regarding summer fallow, which Sievers and Holtz also claimed would increase nitrogen and yields. How the same two men could identify summer fallow as the farmers' friend, then enemy, then friend again—all within two years—is open to speculation. What is also unknown is exactly what Palouse farmers thought about such inconsistent and vacillating advice. The resulting ambiguity must have put farmers in a quandary.[40]

The same experiment station duo published another bulletin in 1927 with similar incongruous analysis. Sievers and Holtz renewed their attack on erosion, claiming that it was "so pronounced that its control is already fast becoming the paramount agricultural problem" of the region. They were especially worried about the fate of Palouse hilltops, which had already lost most of their humus and nitrogen and were in serious decline. The report clearly stated that summer fallow had caused most of the damage. Sievers and Holtz postulated that "forty-odd years of summer fallow tillage have been directly responsible for a loss of one-third of the soil organic matter." In the opening pages of the report, they supported a thorough reevaluation of farming methods: "If the summer fallow system is responsible for erosion, then a continuance of this system of farming cannot be expected to furnish a relief."[41]

Such an interpretation, however, did not prevent them from extolling the virtues of summer fallow. The authors' research showed that a wheat/fallow rotation outperformed wheat rotations with corn, potatoes, peas, alfalfa, and alfalfa with a nitrogen fertilizer. This finding diminished the impact of their erosion message. If summer fallow made financial sense in the short term, as Sievers and Holtz claimed, then farmers invariably would be less likely to consider erosive side effects that might take years to feel. Moreover, new crops meant buying new equipment, usually on credit, which became an unavoidable obstacle to any new farming plan. The data alerted farmers to the problems associated with fallow but the scientists could not bring themselves to give an unqualified condemnation.[42]

Other university scientists in the 1920s failed to warn farmers who left fields bare. M. A. McCall and H. M. Wasner, who both worked out of the experiment station in Pullman, drafted a report in 1924 that lauded the practice. They called it a necessity and reiterated evidence that it sustained soil moisture and nitrogen. Across the state line, Ray Neidig and Robert Snyder of the University of Idaho published a bulletin in 1926 that reached a similar conclusion. They mentioned fallow as a source of erosion but also believed that it benefited soil fertility.[43] The majority of scholarly opinion sided with tradition and new research in supporting summer fallow. Scientists believed that the benefits outweighed the costs; erosion might lower yields in the future, but farmers needed to pay expenses every month and therefore looked for more immediate results.

Palouse wheat growers faced a puzzling dilemma. What advice were they to follow? The farm press agreed that a fallow-erosion link existed, as did at least part of the scientific community. But the orthodoxy of summer fallow would prove durable; the Palouse built its considerable agricultural reputation and growth on this method and any deviation from it would be slow in coming.[44] The primary alternative to the dominant paradigm was essentially a repackaging of an old idea—diversified (or "mixed") farming. From the first days of settlement through the early 1900s, many farmers grew several different crops to insulate themselves from crop failure and market swings. It was less efficient than wheat monocropping, but diversification gave farmers peace of mind and a modicum of financial security. High wheat prices and capitalization pushed this idea into retirement during World War I, but erosion and infertility in the 1920s signaled its revival.

Diversified farming in the 1920s entailed something quite different from turn-of-the-century practices. Its advocates were no longer interested in farmers tending small flocks of chickens and fruit orchards as they had in the past—this was not a plan designed to return the Palouse to a simpler bygone era. Instead, farmers were to rotate wheat with legume crops that built humus and protected the ground. Therefore, before any change could take place, a certain amount of education was in order. One reporter sent out to write on diversification commented, "Before I began to write this story, I looked in the big dictionary to see what a legume was, but I found out that I knew more about it before I looked in the dictionary than I did afterward."[45] Given this level of unfamiliarity, farmers needed to know exactly how to proceed. The local press responded by publishing numerous articles on the technical aspects of planting alfalfa, clover, and peas. Likewise, USDA extension agents traveled the Palouse to give hands-on demonstrations of proper techniques. The advice was necessary because, if improperly planted, legumes could make wheat crops suffer. Proponents of diversified farming knew that the stakes were high and that success depended on information, expertise, and results.[46]

Success also required promotion. To this end, the *Washington Farmer* ran a headline in April of 1923 that read, "WANTED: Better Slogan than 'Diversified Farming.'" The editors solicited suggestions for a catchier name to attract more adherents and offered cash prizes for the best submissions. A month later the newspaper printed 388 submissions that arrived at its Spokane offices. Some, such as "Scientific Farming" and "Balanced Farming," sounded accurate but were no less bland than the original. Others sounded awkward and boosterish. "An Egg in Every Basket Farming" and "Sure-to Win Farming" seemed unlikely to attract much of a following. "Progressive Farming" won the contest, although for some reason the *Farmer* decided against using the term in subsequent articles on diversification. The greater significance was that Palouse residents became increasingly aware of the need to plant something besides wheat. No matter what they called it, "King Wheat" was about to get a few new partners.[47]

Making the transformation to a wheat/legume system proved difficult to implement. Diversified farms cost more to run than wheat/fallow operations. Seed, new equipment, labor, and equipment depreciation costs all went up when legumes became part of the mix. Farmers lacked experience in raising these new crops and were unsure if the new practices would affect erosion or fertility. Moreover, they did not know what to do with bales and bales of alfalfa and clover and bushels of peas once harvested. Investments in a new rotation had to produce marketable goods, and it was not immediately obvious who would buy Palouse feeds.

Farmers were told that the easiest way to profit from legumes was to use them in the efficient mixed farm of the future, which would utilize its alfalfa, clover, and peas to feed new livestock herds. Here again diversified farming mimicked an older style of agriculture—one where each farm consumed more of what it grew. Herds of cattle, pigs, and sheep were not intended to eliminate wheat farming but rather to supplement it in a way that would benefit everyone. The ideal setup had about half of all land in wheat, the other half in legumes, and a small parcel of poor-yielding "waste" land set aside for livestock grazing. The return of ranching on the Palouse meant that legumes could be consumed on-site, farms could become more self-sufficient and secure, and problems with fertility and erosion would subside. It seemed like the ideal remedy for several nagging concerns.[48]

But the grand experiment never materialized. Farmers had grown accustomed to raising wheat and most resisted the call to plant legumes or raise livestock. The cost of new equipment alone deterred many from making the switch; if a farmer had borrowed heavily to expand production during World War I, an additional investment to diversify would only add to overhead and uncertainty. In addition, most agreed that fallowed acres produced good wheat yields. Legumes and artificial fertilizers showed promise but were a risky proposition to a farmer with a mortgage and an established, successful rotation. Such operations required immediate returns on their investments, and the raison d'être of diversification was based on long-term benefits. The two ideologies—and balance sheets—stood far apart. In retrospect, diversification had little chance of supplanting the wheat/fallow template.

Farmers flirted with diversification but did little more. Alfalfa production went up incrementally from 1919 to 1924 and then returned to earlier levels by 1929. Clover also saw a spike in production in the mid-1920s, but then fell far below wartime levels by decade's end. According to one soil scientist, legume crops contributed "hardly a drop in the bucket" to the overall agricultural picture. Livestock numbers paralleled statistics for legumes. They went up briefly after the war then returned to prewar levels by 1930. Wheat acreage figures indicated that farmers dabbled with other crops in the 1920s. Whitman County growers planted approximately 482,000 acres in wheat in 1919, reduced it to 377,000 acres by 1924, and then increased production to 476,000 acres by 1929. The mid-decade drop likely came from an emphasis on other crops, but it also might have resulted from a fall in wheat prices.[49] The most telling statistic from this period concerned fallow acres. Diversified-farming advocates dearly wanted this number reduced, as a drop in idle acres would indicate a retreat from the wheat/fallow rotation, an acceptance of legumes, and would hopefully put erosion into remission. A permanent reduction never occurred, as farmers reduced fallowed acres for a brief span in the mid-1920s and then gave up on the idea. By the end of the decade, nearly half of all Palouse farmland lay dormant in fallow and susceptible to erosion. Even after the enlistment of the scientific community and a thorough public relations campaign, Palouse farmers fallowed about the same number of acres in 1930 as they had in 1920. The diversification mission had failed.[50]

A clear majority of farmers believed the status quo preferable to the uncertainties and costs of diversification, even though support for summer fallow within the scientific community started to wane. Technical reports from both Washington State College and the University of Idaho written after 1927 omitted any mention of the benefits of fallow, as researchers instead focused their attention on erosion prevention and retaining soil humus. Scientists at the national level also took notice of the erosion problem. The USDA established ten erosion experiment stations in 1930—one of them just north of Pullman. The time had come to grapple with erosion, using more money and human resources. The Pullman station released some early findings on terracing, plowing techniques, and fertilizers in 1931, but conclusive results were years away. Experimental plots required years of study to bear any scientific fruit, and the Palouse hills would have to be patient.[51]

In the meantime, the practices of wheat monocropping, summer fallow, and erosion continued unabated, as structural economic forces prevailed in determining what happened to the Palouse environment. Wheat prices hovered in the neighborhood of $1.10 per bushel in the late 1920s, giving farmers decent rewards for their efforts. Yields also showed steady improvement as Whitman County growers averaged nearly thirty bushels per acre—with many farmers hitting the magical fifty bushels per acre mark. The increase can be attributed to better seed and more widespread use of fertilizer. If erosion caused yields to suffer, it was not yet apparent in the 1920s. And farms kept getting bigger. Whitman County, which already had some of the largest farms in the Northwest in the years following 1910, was home to 266 farms of six hundred or more acres in 1930.[52] For all the blustery talk about the future peril of Palouse farming, the immediate prospects looked healthy.

If farmers read newspapers and technical bulletins or if they talked to neighbors and extension agents, they knew that the future might not be so promising. Although the evidence seemed contradictory at times, some knew by the late 1920s that the gullies on their land would only get worse if they stayed with wheat/fallow farming. The photographic evidence suggested that something had to change. But change was not in the offing following World War I. As one farmer reported in 1916,

> They say that wheat is a soil robber, and persistent cropping of wheat ruins the earth and does not pay in the long run. And yet we know very well that when wheat sells for $1.50 and, maybe more, per bushel, the farmer is going to keep on raising wheat. And they know that wheat pays, and pays big, on fairly high-priced land at such figures as it brings, and has brought for the past two years. They know that, under the same conditions, they would do precisely the same thing. Urging people to drop a very profitable crop is foolishness.[53]

It *was* foolish to insist on a renovation of profitable farming methods. The agrarian liberals of the Palouse had seen their material lives improve with the odd combination of tradition and innovation. It would take either an economic collapse or government intervention to compel farmers to reconsider a comprehensive alteration. They would get both in the 1930s.

5 LESSONS LEARNED AND UNLEARNED

WILLIAM ROCKIE toiled diligently as a soils specialist for the USDA for more than two decades. His career spanned a period in American agriculture that began in the best of times—the golden age of 1910–1920—and ended in a bottomless abyss—the Great Depression of the 1930s. From his office in Pullman, he witnessed this decline in the Palouse. In Rockie's early days the region blossomed on high prices, steadily higher wheat yields, and general economic vigor. A sense of optimism prevailed in his early days, but it would not last. Uncertainty in the 1920s and then panic and dismay in the 1930s replaced the hubris that dominated the teens. Toward the end of his career Rockie must have wondered how everything had gone so wrong.

But even depressions have silver linings. Rockie and a host of other scientists and activists managed to turn a desperate situation into a call for action. In addition to the disastrous Dust Bowl of the Great Plains, the protracted economic downturn shook the very foundations of American agriculture and forced farmers to accept government assistance and to consider the long-term effects of intensive cultivation. Soil erosion, one of the primary environmental legacies of Palouse farming, received more attention in the 1930s than ever before. As markets collapsed and fears rose, people began to regard erosion as a major impediment to future prosperity. Scientists warned that erosion threatened the nation's economic security, and they seized the opportunity to put an end to years of soil depletion. In an address to the Northwest Scientific Association in 1935, Rockie noted how the Depression had made erosion a charged topic:

> My own particular field of work, that of soil studies, has for decades past been one of the most drab and least interesting of our sciences, from a popular standpoint. It has been studied in considerable detail for many years past, but until recently did not excite very general interest even among scientists, and the public none at all. Events of the past few years have, however, very materially increased the general interest in the formerly prosaic subject. We have just begun to realize that our very national prosperity is threatened by the loss of our topsoil. Yes, our national existence depends upon what we do with, to and about that resource. A few far-sighted individuals have been preaching vainly for soil conservation during the past twenty-five years, but only when measurements were obtained which portrayed the terrific rate of speed with which we were destroying this great national asset, did we sit up and take notice.[1]

Rockie and others dramatized a connection between soil loss and prosperity. From the early days of the New Deal through World War II, the federal government devoted resources to combat erosion. An entire layer of federal bureaucracy, the Soil Erosion Service (later renamed the Soil Conservation Service), was created with the sole purpose of preventing further losses. New Deal programs such as the Agricultural Adjustment Act tied relief money to acreage reduction and soil conservation. And agricultural colleges continued their work toward a better understanding of the causes of erosion and offered farmers practical alternatives to soil-depleting techniques and habits. After the federal initiatives, hundreds of regional and local conservation groups formed all around the country. The Depression had thrown the nation into an economic and social tailspin, but the ordeal also created an unprecedented opportunity to improve agricultural practices. The government insisted on a new style of agriculture—"conservation farming"—which it hoped would save farmers from environmental and financial ruin. The plan was a part of a broad-based reform movement designed to entice farmers to adopt more sustainable practices. Farm operators were in no position to quarrel over new government regulations; if they wished to receive financial assistance, they had to accept an unprecedented amount of government interdiction.

In fact, after a period of initial reluctance, farmers in the Palouse and nationally entered into a kind of partnership with the federal government and consumers. Growers of staple crops such as wheat agreed to limit production in exchange for a government check, while consumers consented to using their tax dollars to ensure both an inexpensive food supply and rural social stability. Hence, by the mid-1930s the more contemporary definition of "liberal" came to describe the agrarian liberals of the Palouse: they weathered the Great Depression storm through government assistance. Plenty of farmers foreclosed, but without government help more of them surely would have succumbed.

In many ways, Depression-era ideas and programs worked effectively in the Palouse. Farmers planted less wheat in the 1930s, which reduced erosion and nitrogen depletion. They learned and accepted new plowing techniques that partially protected the ground and used new disc plows that moved less soil. They also gained an appreciation for the tenuous nature of their business and an understanding that their land was fragile. Humility and respect replaced the dominant cavalier attitude. Yet problems with erosion still plagued the Palouse because not enough farmers embraced conservation farming on a permanent basis and because the government never forced them to adhere to a comprehensive conservation plan. Therefore, erosion continued to deplete the land. For William Rockie and dozens of local scientists, the perfect opportunity to eliminate erosion had passed. They drew attention to the need for conservation farming but could not institute sweeping reform. The agrarian liberal of the Palouse adjusted to the new paradigm of government involvement and stayed in the business of farming, and in the end they were still allowed to do as they pleased.

Palouse farmers greeted the new year in 1929 the way they had for nearly a decade—with a certain uneasiness about their crop and where wheat prices were headed. The McNary-Haugen bills, designed to have the federal government pay farmers a "fair" price for their goods and then dump surpluses abroad, finally had been laid to rest the previous year. Three sessions of Congress and one president believed such legislation would incite a trade war and create a huge paternalistic bureaucracy. The bills were defeated in 1924, 1926, 1927, and 1928. Even without an artificial boost from the government, wheat growers had reason to be optimistic at the outset of 1929. Wheat prices went on an uneven, steady ascent in the late 1920s—the kind of gradual improvement that allowed the regional economy to grow. Farmers responded by enlarging their operations in terms of land and equipment. As always, weather was a concern. The Palouse had a dry growing season in 1929, but with yields down only slightly from previous years. Farmers could rest easy in the knowledge that the Palouse had never seen a crop failure in over fifty years of continuous wheat farming. On the whole things looked good.

After the late-summer harvest, the situation changed drastically for the worse. A worldwide wheat surplus, stagnant wages, an overabundance of consumer goods, and a reliance on the gold standard spelled trouble for the Palouse. Even before the stock market crash of 29 October, wheat prices had started to slip. From a peak of $1.50 per bushel in mid-October, prices fell a few cents each day until 24 October, when wheat lost 12 cents in a single trading session. The stock market collapse the following week sent prices spiraling downward even further, but profit-seeking opportunists kept wheat afloat for the rest of the year. Wheat finished 1929 at $1.13—a dime higher than at the end of 1928. The sudden wheat sell-off and national and international panic shocked the Palouse, but most farmers entered 1930 the way they had 1929—cautiously optimistic.[2]

But optimism did not stand a chance in the face of a crippling world depression. During the next three years wheat prices (and every other agricultural commodity price) endured precipitous drops and only temporary recoveries. Wheat sank to 83 cents per bushel in August 1930, to 70 cents in November 1931, and to 50 cents in July 1932.[3] Prices for most manufactured goods fell in the early 1930s, but not as quickly or as deeply as farm commodities. As a result, farmers had less money to spend on relatively expensive necessities. Residual effects abounded. A local newspaper from Oakesdale, Washington, began accepting payments in wheat (three bushels for a one-year subscription) as a goodwill gesture and to ease financial stress. Crime and vagrancy went up as wages plummeted. The rural-to-urban migration pattern that began in the late nineteenth century nearly stopped; farm boys and girls were far less likely to seek their fortunes in western cities because urban conditions there were usually worse than on the farm. Regardless of where they were, people had less money to spend and Palouse businesses either folded or were severely handicapped by the economic malaise.[4]

Local leaders urged farmers to act cooperatively to beat low prices, promoting membership in the North Pacific Grain Growers Cooperative Association. The co-op bought, stored, and sold grain and offered farmers low-interest crop loans and more flexibility in marketing their goods. The co-op idea attracted a considerable following: in 1929 the association bought 700,000 bushels of wheat from Pullman farmers, 400,000 bushels from the Colfax area, and a whopping 3 million bushels from Latah County, Idaho.[5] Washington State Grange membership swelled during the Depression. Memberships went up across the state, but in Whitman County the number of Grangers increased fivefold between 1929 and 1934. Members marketed their crops through local chapter storage facilities in an effort to avoid middlemen and to cut shipping costs. Farmers believed that the only salvation for Palouse farming lay in collective action.[6]

The slump gave diversified farming renewed attention, because a farm built around several activities could withstand economic downturns better than monocrop operations. Farmers could plant some of their sizeable acreages in fruits and vegetables, tend livestock, and keep more of what they raised. These people were concerned but not panicked by the Depression. An editor from Sprague, Washington, wrote that even with a national crisis at hand, "securities do not have to be soaring and smokestacks belching forth smoke that people may have money. Prices of commodities may not be good but the people still have their wheat and cattle, dairy products, poultry and eggs, hay and a lot of other things on a smaller scale that bring in money." If enough of this money remained in the community and was not "sent into the cites to swell the sales of stores there or [to] bolster up businesses there," then towns in the inland Northwest might be spared.[7] But with so few dollars chasing so many goods, it probably mattered little where the money was spent. The Depression was a global event that transcended local interests, and emotional appeals to protect hearth and home could not overcome an international capitalist economy gone haywire. The pandemic nature of the crisis underscored the need for federal solutions.

Although frequently chided for inaction, President Herbert Hoover and Congress attacked parts of the farm problem before the Depression started. To alleviate chronic surpluses, Congress passed and Hoover signed the Agricultural Marketing Act in June 1929. The law allocated $500 million for loans to regional marketing cooperatives (such as the North Pacific Grain Growers) with the hope that large co-ops would market commodities better than individual farmers. Co-ops could also issue more crop loans, which allowed farmers to pay expenses before their harvest actually reached the market. The act did not placate Western and Midwestern farm constituents who still pined for the more generous McNary-Haugen bill, but it did extend the ideological limits of a conservative president who firmly adhered to laissez-faire values. Hoover sympathized with farmers and was sensitive to their predicament; his agricultural policy demonstrated a measure of flexibility and compassion.[8]

The marketing act also established a new federal agency, the Federal Farm Board, to oversee implementation, setting lending rules and assisting local co-ops in buying and selling goods. Its secretary, Alex Legge, was committed to helping farmers through cooperative action, but stayed true to Republican macroeconomic ideas, insisting that government money for co-ops should be a temporary measure—and that his job and his agency should be shut down when the crisis had passed. The long-term answer to the farm problem, as Legge saw it, was a simple readjustment of supply and demand. Because prices were low and wheat surpluses high, Legge bluntly told farmers in August 1930, "don't plant so much." If they planted fewer acres, supplies would fall and prices would rise, giving farmers the income they desired. This simplistic prescription did not consider complications such as farm debt or the trend toward mechanization, but it was consistent with a Republican faith in the efficacy of market forces. Legge understood that the proposal would be criticized but argued that farmers were "fed up on patent medicine stuff and want the straight dope. It may taste bad at the time, but it's better to know the real facts." Legge thought that farmers should act like businessmen, not helpless dependents. Cutting production made sense because "that's what industry does. Henry Ford disagrees with the theory of restricted production for agriculture, yet he closes down his plant when the flivver supply gets beyond the demand—and so does every other business, for that matter."[9]

Neither the rhetoric nor the policy reduced supplies. The Farm Board and local co-ops attracted many customers but did not prevent farmers from growing more wheat. National acreage figures for many goods remained constant from 1929 through 1932, but wheat production went up sharply. American farmers in 1930 harvested 823 million bushels, 886 million the next year, and 942 million in 1932. The amount of wheat stored in silos and elevators went up even more, from 112 million bushels in 1929 to an alarming 375 million in 1933. Wheat production worldwide saw more modest increases—4.3 billion bushels in 1929 to 4.8 billion in 1933—but the upward trend did not bode well. Washington farmers planted and harvested nearly the same amount of wheat in 1932 as they had in 1929. Latah County farmers planted slightly less over the same period, but their impact on international supply was negligible. Any local production cut was likely to have little impact on national or international prices because the Palouse constituted only a fraction of the world's wheat supply.[10] And Legge's words were indeed prophetic—the board *was* temporary; it had spent nearly all its $500 million by the end of 1931 and had nothing to show for it. Hoover retired the plan early in 1933. The Farm Board and the cooperative movement succeeded only in providing a more efficient means of grain storage; both failed to reduce the national surplus that drove prices down. Hoover and Legge lacked the foresight and political will necessary to mandate a short- or long-term solution. Too many farmers were growing too much food, and until this trend changed wheat prices were bound to continue their descent.

Farmers could have taken Legge's advice and planted less, but that would have cut profits and increased losses. The sensible reaction to low prices was to plant *more*, because a combination of smaller harvests and low prices would prove instantly fatal. Agricultural economists at Washington State College understood this and recommended that Palouse farmers continue with a normal planting regimen, even though "if no more than one-half as much wheat were to be produced in 1932 as in 1931 there would still be sufficient supplies of wheat to meet the requirements in the United States."[11] Farmers might cut production to reduce some of their costs (seed, feed, and fuel), but fixed costs dominated their balance sheet, especially loan payments. They needed as much income as possible to keep the cash flowing and to hold creditors at bay. Even at deflated prices they were better served by planting as much as possible.

It should have surprised no one that prices tumbled. Wheat prices fell through most of 1932 as elevators filled and the Depression tightened its grip on the industrialized world. The late July price of 50 cents—already abysmally low—fell to 38 cents by year's end. It was the lowest price ever recorded for this bellwether of the inland Northwest economy.[12] Farm families such as the Comstocks took in boarders to stave off creditors, even though it seemed "nobody was making money in those ten years." Pullman farmer Vincent Higgins had to borrow $800 from a local bank just to stay in business; he was fortunate to be able to pay off $150 of this balance by late 1933. John Jacob Bauer, who had farmed in Uniontown since the turn of the century, helped his own cause in these tough times by continuing to sell bacon, eggs, chickens, and lard.[13] Banks fared no better. Pullman State Bank, which had $948,000 in assets in 1929, saw that figure shrink to $655,000 in 1932. Its chief competitor, the First National Bank of Pullman, lost more than $400,000 in assets over the same period. But at least these two lenders stayed afloat; roughly half of all banks based in the Palouse went under during the Depression.[14]

Desperation replaced hope and confidence as the prevailing mood. In the summer, farmers in Genesee, Idaho, and in the Pullman area attempted to push prices higher by withholding their harvest from the market. Forty-two farmers promised to store their grain for sixty days or until wheat reached 75 cents per bushel.[15] This "wheat holiday" idea emulated the Farmers Holiday movements in Louisiana, North Dakota, and Iowa in 1930–1931, where farmers tried to coerce their neighbors to refrain from selling. But in each case the plan fizzled because most could ill afford to store crops and risk prices falling even more. The economic downturn hobbled all efforts at revival and left people searching for answers.

A potential savior came to the White House in 1933. Franklin Roosevelt arrived in Washington DC with a mandate for change, a willingness to experiment, and a desire to right the economic ship.[16] His campaign speeches stressed the vital role of agriculture in the national economy, and he displayed a genuine affection for farmers and rural America. Roosevelt liked to refer to his sprawling, pastoral estate in Hyde Park, New York, as his "farm," even though he raised no crops and kept no livestock. He was about as much a farmer as his cousin Theodore was a cowboy, but that did not prevent him from implementing some of the most important farming legislation in US history. Through his actions and the efforts of a talented cabinet and federal bureaucrats, Roosevelt fundamentally changed the way American farms operated. The federal government was about to become a permanent factor in determining the size and shape of farms all over the country. This shift would have a profound influence on both the economics of farming and on the environment, and would bring Palouse farmers closer to being "liberal" in a contemporary understanding of the term.

After a meeting with farm leaders in March 1933, Roosevelt wasted little time putting a plan in motion. The Agricultural Adjustment Act (AAA), signed on 12 May, targeted surpluses as the leading cause of low commodity prices.[17] The act encouraged farmers to sign three-year contracts with the USDA to reduce acreage by up to 20 percent. Participating wheat farmers received an extra 29 cents per bushel for their crops (financed through a new tax on processors). The government's financial commitment was massive; American farmers received over $1 billion in the first two years, with Washington wheat growers collecting $6.5 million in the first year alone. Palouse farmers greeted the plan with enthusiasm. Of the 2,837 farmers in Whitman County, 2,667 agreed to reduce their production by a total of 404,500 acres. They received $1.4 million for their efforts, most of which the USDA delivered by late October. Local and national surpluses finally began to dry up, both because of the AAA and because the Great Plains' Dust Bowl rendered entire counties agriculturally useless. This stop-gap measure made voluntary crop reductions feasible and gave farmers what they needed most—more income. The laissez-faire approach to American agriculture had come to a close, and in its place a new government-brokered system emerged.[18]

The AAA improved the farmer's balance sheet, but aggravated the erosion problem, because the removal of acres from production usually

A Soil Erosion Service crew harvesting bunchgrass seeds in southern Spokane County, 1934. This photo gives some idea of the look of a pre-contact bunchgrass plain. (Photo courtesy Washington State University, Manuscripts, Archives, and Special Collections)

Wheat harvest, c. 1904. Even with combined harvesters and threshers, this was a labor-intensive task that took weeks. A close inspection of this photo reveals at least twenty workers. (Photo courtesy Whitman County Historical Association)

(*Facing page, top*) Sternwheeler docked at Wawawai, on the Snake River, c. 1902. Goods bound for the Palouse then met the two-thousand-foot hills almost immediately at the water's edge. (Photo courtesy Whitman County Historical Association)

(*Facing page, bottom*) Palouse farm, c. 1910. Note the indications of diversified agriculture—animal pens and barns, a fruit orchard in the background, and pasture in the foreground. (Photo courtesy Whitman County Historical Association)

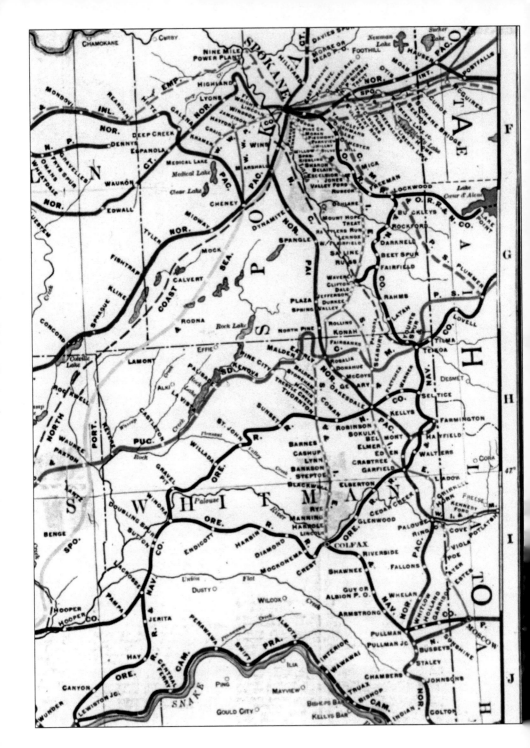

Sacked grain on wagons awaiting transport on the electrified Spokane and Inland Empire Railroad, 1913. (Photo courtesy Whitman County Historical Association)

(Facing page) Railroad map of the inland Northwest, 1910. This tangle of rails reflected the needs of current farmers and expressed an optimism for future growth. (Photo courtesy Washington State University, Manuscripts, Archives, and Special Collections)

Wheat harvesting team and crew, 1931. (Photo courtesy Whitman County Historical Association)

(Facing page, top) Not all Palouse wheat farmers had money to spend or borrow for the newest implements. This undated photo is of a Ford Model T pulling a plow through the soil. (Photo courtesy Whitman County Historical Association)

(Facing page, bottom) Grain truck with sacks of wheat on a steep Palouse hillside, 1917. (Photo courtesy Whitman County Historical Association)

Soil Conservation Service staffer in an eroded ditch, 1934. (Photo courtesy Washington State University, Manuscripts, Archives, and Special Collections)

C. J. Bauer farm near Moscow, Idaho, 1934. The rill erosion in the background washed into the deepening gully in the foreground. (Photo courtesy Washington State University, Manuscripts, Archives, and Special Collections)

(Facing page, bottom) Soil Conservation Service supervisor Earl A. Victor's caption to this 1934 photo states that this gully is so large, "it will soon destroy the road." (Photo courtesy Washington State University, Manuscripts, Archives, and Special Collections)

6 - 4

This photo exhibits two important soil conservation techniques popularized in the 1930s. First, it shows contour plowing—planting and cultivating along a line perpendicular to the slope of a hill; second, strip cropping—alternating two or more crops (or wheat and summer fallow, in this case) in a field, which helps reduce erosion. (Photo courtesy Washington State University, Manuscripts, Archives, and Special Collections)

(Facing page, top) The Soil Erosion Service stated that after a year of summer fallow in 1933, this farm near Palouse, Washington, lost fifty to seventy-five tons of soil per acre in 1934. Such losses were common in this era. (Photo courtesy Washington State University, Manuscripts, Archives, and Special Collections)

(Facing page, bottom) Massive sheet erosion on summer-fallowed land, southwest of Colfax, Washington, 1936. (Photo courtesy Washington State University, Manuscripts, Archives, and Special Collections)

The Civilian Conservation Corps was also active in the Palouse erosion control effort, as this 1934 photo east of Moscow, Idaho, shows. This dam is made out of stone, but other, more crude structures were built of straw or wood—or a combination of both. (Photo courtesy Washington State University, Manuscripts, Archives, and Special Collections)

(Facing page) This Soil Conservation Service cartoon, which appeared in a Palouse, Washington, newspaper in 1957, depicts three eras in American farming: the "Pioneer Age," with a humble farmer toiling behind two oxen; the "Destructive Age," when a greedy farmer exchanges precious soil for monetary gain (which goes to a nameless fat cat); then, the "Age of Reason," where the farmer allows the guiding hand of the professional, college-educated technocrat to establish proper strip-cropping and contour-plowing methods. The propaganda was at once critical and optimistic. (Photo courtesy Whitman County Historical Association)

Devastating erosion ate away at still more land in the 1960s. This 1968 photo, taken in northern Whitman County, shows rill erosion that took away an estimated 150 tons per acre in one winter. (Photo courtesy Washington State University, Manuscripts, Archives, and Special Collections)

(Facing page, top) This field in Thornton, Washington, lost an astounding three hundred to five hundred tons of topsoil in the winter of 1967–1968. (Photo courtesy Washington State University, Manuscripts, Archives, and Special Collections)

(Facing page, bottom) Instead of just showing eroding soils on bare hillsides, this 1976 photo from north of Plaza, Washington, by Soil Conservation Service mainstay Verle Kaiser, dramatizes how erosion can lower crop performance. (Photo courtesy Washington State University, Manuscripts, Archives, and Special Collections)

This Verle Kaiser photo from east of Spangle, Washington, also shows a field that will produce less wheat because of a bad erosion problem. The rills on the hillside have deposited their loads on top of the young wheat in the foreground, effectively ruining that part of the field. (Photo courtesy Washington State University, Manuscripts, Archives, and Special Collections)

resulted in more summer fallow. The USDA gave farmers the option of substituting legumes and perennial grasses for wheat, but most chose to keep fields bare for the duration of their contracts. In Whitman County, fallow acres increased from 387,806 acres in 1929, to 451,712 in 1934; in Latah County, the number of fallow acres rose from 36,168 to 42,542 over the same span. Legume production showed only slight gains in both counties.[19] In a series of articles published in 1933, William Rockie pleaded with farmers to plant cover crops on retired land. "Forage crops," he wrote, "have a feed value without handicapping the erosion control work and without violating federal regulations." The message went unheeded, and a clearly discouraged Rockie feared that "ultimate impoverishment" lay ahead.[20]

Farmers certainly had the information necessary to make better choices. The federal government raised awareness during the 1920s through the funding of university experiment stations, but in 1930 it became far more active when Congress authorized the formation of ten new experiment stations specifically devoted to erosion research. These stations were a boon to those who took advantage of them, and they clearly indicated the government's level of commitment to farming and to the notion that farmers needed more subsidized research than they were already receiving. The idea was hatched primarily to combat erosion in the South and in the Great Plains, but after several members of the House Appropriations Committee for Agriculture toured the inland Northwest, Congress tabbed Pullman as a station site. Station director William Rockie led the first set of comprehensive, long-term investigations on Palouse erosion, although farmers had to wait several years for the research to produce definitive results and recommendations.[21]

In its first years of operation the Pullman erosion station reiterated the findings of earlier studies and offered concrete suggestions. It asked farmers to eliminate summer fallow, to plant cover crops in its stead, and called for an end to stubble burning. The station advised against plowing up and down the ubiquitous hills in straight lines and instead advocated contour-plowing around them. This was old advice but not all of it was derivative; the station also developed and promoted new ideas and tactics. Rockie and his staff worked with new disc plows that left plant residues on the surface and stemmed erosion. They experimented with reshaping the hills into terraces, in hopes of preventing soil from settling in low-lying swales and nearby streams. They planted trees on hilltops to see if the small amount of remaining topsoil in these problem areas could be preserved. The station also tried to save the hills by removing soil from low areas and transporting it back to eroded hilltops and steep slopes. This last measure—a massive soil relocation project—was unrealistic and perhaps even ludicrous if intended for the entire region, but scientists eagerly considered all options to combat erosion. Collectively, these innovations became known as "conservation farming," and were considered the foundation of progressive agriculture in the Palouse.[22]

Scientific explanations and remedies for erosion were only part of the mission. The Pullman station attempted to prove that controlling erosion made sound financial sense. It determined that if farmers were going to accept the tenets of conservation farming, they needed an economic incentive. During the first fifty years of Palouse agriculture, farmers made decisions based on profitability—from the earliest days of settlement when hilltops were initially planted to the adoption of hybrid seed to the decision to forego diversification in the 1920s. The erosion station realized this and crafted a message to satisfy farmers' interests. It postulated that farmers who tilled eroded fields spent more money per acre on equipment and maintenance, since tractors and combines crawling through deep eroded troughs used more fuel and were more prone to break down. The station calculated that eroded fields cost an average-sized farm (approximately five hundred acres) an additional $250 per farm per year—a considerable sum in the Depression years of the early 1930s. The station's studies did not consider the added costs of erosion control, but as the decade proceeded conservation advocates became convinced that appeals to the bottom line were the best way to sell erosion-control ideas.[23]

The station also realized that it needed to dramatize and publicize the erosion problem. A devastating rainstorm in July 1931 gave Rockie and his colleague, Paul McGrew, an opportunity to plead their case. Midsummer downpours are rare but not unknown in the Palouse. When the heavens opened up on July 30, one rain gauge near the erosion station recorded one and a half inches in only twenty minutes, and another about a mile away registered three inches during the brief, intense storm. In the days that followed, scientists scurried about the Palouse to track the amount of soil lost during this event and came to some disturbing conclusions. At the bottom of a fallowed, steep slope at the erosion station a new layer of soil and debris eighteen to twenty-seven inches deep covered the ground. Station personnel estimated that on fallowed land throughout the region, erosion removed an average of two inches of topsoil (about 275 tons per acre), with some areas losing up to six inches of soil. For the roughly twenty thousand Palouse acres in summer fallow in 1931, about 5.5 million tons of soil were removed in one torrential downpour. The crew also noted that on fields covered by wheat or grasses, almost no erosion occurred. Rockie and McGrew had proof that summer fallow was the silent villain in Palouse agriculture, and they did their best to spread the word.[24]

Erosion stations were just the beginning of a sustained federal initiative to improve the nation's soil resources. While the Depression dragged on and the New Deal took shape, politicians attempted to grapple with the Dust Bowl, which had moved rapidly from an annual annoyance to a nightmarish apocalypse in the early 1930s. President Roosevelt, Secretary of Interior Harold Ickes, and Secretary of Agriculture Henry A. Wallace decided early in their tenure to create a federal agency dedicated to erosion control, and in September 1933, the Soil Erosion Service (SES) was born. The service's primary task was to fix the disaster on the Plains, but it also worked to preserve soil resources in other threatened areas, including the Palouse.

The first director of the SES, Hugh Hammond Bennett, was eminently qualified to lead the new agency. His work in the Bureau of Soils and in the Bureau of Chemistry, dating to 1903, left no doubts as to his scientific and technical expertise. But of greater significance for this new appointment was Bennett's single-minded devotion to erosion issues and his nonpareil abilities as an orator and promoter, a talent he used to whip up support during several speaking tours in 1933 and 1934. His lectures packed all the emotion of a tent revival as he implored audiences—in rural and urban settings—to make soil conservation a national priority. He tried to "convert" citizens into believing that the nation's food supply and economic well-being hinged on soil conservation. A self-styled conservation messiah, Bennett blended well with an administration that valued charisma and guile as much as intellect.[25]

In its first two years the SES operated in the US Department of Interior. The decision to locate the agency in Interior instead of Agriculture raised a number of eyebrows in many parts of rural America. In terms of erosion and soils knowledge, the USDA had amassed a considerable body of expertise and experience that no other department could match, working closely with land-grant colleges for decades and producing its own passel of extension agents who were familiar with soil conservation and local conditions. But after numerous consultations with assistant agriculture secretary Rexford Tugwell, the mercurial Columbia economist who doubled as a board member for the Public Works Administration, Bennett agreed to work under the Department of Interior. Tugwell reasoned that in order for the SES to obtain sufficient funding from Congress it should focus on soil conservation and employment. Since Ickes ran both the Public Works Administration and Interior, it made sense to put the SES in his charge. Disgruntled

USDA employees criticized the move as purely political, yet most of the department's seasoned soils experts (William Rockie included) made the move to the SES and the Department of Interior.[26]

Many aspects of the erosion problem involved farming techniques, but because several of the proposed solutions required a sizable workforce, a public works approach seemed appropriate. The Civilian Conservation Corps (CCC), working under the aegis of the SES in the Palouse, became the labor source for much of the heavy lifting in the fight against Palouse erosion. More than just a tree-planting outfit, the CCC moved tons of earth in the mid-1930s. From their base camp in Moscow, Idaho, crews of twelve to twenty men traveled the area to repair gullies, dig out fences that had been covered in silt, build small wooden check dams (which fell apart), and build small masonry dams (which worked better). They planted trees along ridgetops and on hills, but most of their work involved putting soil back where it belonged or devising ways to prevent soil from moving in the first place. Some of the labor was local, but most workers came from rural Kentucky and Tennessee, where the Depression had exacted a far worse toll than in the Palouse. The influx of Southerners made for interesting cultural exchanges. According to one local SES scientist, the Southern transplants "talked in a language that only boys from the backwoods could understand." Dialects aside, the importation of labor reflected the national scope of both the Depression and the erosion problem. Like many New Deal programs, the CCC attempted to correct several predicaments simultaneously; the Roosevelt administration made sure the CCC addressed social concerns as well as agricultural and economic issues. This attempt, however, was too small and short-lived to fix the erosion problem for good. It put some of the soil back to where it had been but did not seek comprehensive reform.[27]

Local and national leaders also needed to broadcast their ideas and promote soil conservation. While CCC crews repaired the physical damage caused by erosion, SES and USDA representatives went on an educational campaign to change attitudes and to gently scold farmers for years of abuse. When it became apparent that farmers had replaced wheat with summer fallow under the AAA, scientists from around the region begged them to reconsider. Dozens of university professors, CCC officials, SES employees, and extension agents crisscrossed the Palouse in 1934 and 1935 delivering speeches in churches, court houses, lodge halls, wheat fields, and even in private homes. They wrote letters to the editors of local papers, spoke to school children, and sponsored erosion demonstrations at state and county fairs. For each presentation and publication the basic message was the same: discontinue summer fallow and plant legumes, and your soil can be saved.[28] Secretary of Agriculture Wallace became an active participant as well when he paid a visit to the Moscow CCC camp in July 1935 to inspect the progress made to date. His visit was more symbolic and promotional than substantive but suggested the federal government's commitment to improving farming methods and the erosion situation.[29]

Wallace's junket also hinted that as late as 1935 most farmers did not consider erosion a serious problem. The SES and CCC did their best to discourage summer fallow and promote better methods, but it was easier for farmers to leave fields idle and collect AAA money than to plant, maintain, harvest, and market other crops at deflated prices and collect the same amount. Farmers had been encouraged for years to become more financially astute, and they acted logically, given the available options. Being an agrarian liberal in the 1930s meant that a farmer embraced some crop reductions and payments; buying into all that came from a government agency was never these farmers' intention. The SES and experiment station scientists understood that economics dictated farmer behavior and began quantifying soil losses, but their research could not relate erosion to crop performance. In the short term, it seemed to make no difference if violent storms occasionally washed away millions of tons of soil, because per acre wheat harvests climbed steadily through the early 1930s.[30] Soil conservation advocates needed more time to gather data and a better argument to reeducate farmers.

To many farmers, erosion was an inevitable part of doing business in the Palouse, at once regrettable and unavoidable. George Johnson, whose career working the land began in the 1880s, had been on a summer fallow regimen for years despite knowing it caused erosion. In the early 1930s a strong downpour took tons of soil from a field and deposited it—about three feet in depth—in his front yard. He was "at a loss to set up a better system for wheat farming." A similar downpour hit the Judson farm in 1933. David Judson, who had been an advocate of conservation farming, seemed to throw his hands in the air in an act of resignation: "It is difficult to plan a way to combat such erosion as that. Ordinary measures would be futile." Charles Kellogg, like many other wheat growers, filled erosion gullies with straw as a means of preventing further damage. But after heavy rains, he too noticed that the soil—with the straw in tow—often ended up at the bottom of a hill. All he could offer was that "it seems to rain harder than it used to." Christian Naffziger perhaps said it best. He hardly expected the scientists and government agents to end erosion on his farm "unless they can stop the rain falling."[31]

One way to counter such negativity and strengthen the long-term viability of soil conservation was to relocate erosion specialists back where they belonged—in the USDA. The Department of Interior had been useful insofar as it had effectively initiated corrective measures and put thousands of unemployed people to work, but even Ickes acknowledged late in 1934 that the future of erosion research and development lay elsewhere. Erosion was first and foremost a farming problem. Therefore, at the behest of Wallace and Bennett, the Roosevelt administration decided to transfer the SES to the USDA in March 1935. Wallace ushered through Congress a bill designed to perpetuate government assistance for conservation. The Soil Erosion Act, signed into law a month later, officially recognized erosion as a national menace and authorized the agriculture secretary to oversee all aspects of federal erosion work. The Soil Erosion Service also received a new name—the Soil Conservation Service (SCS)—to denote the change in departments and to give the agency a more upbeat and positive moniker. Local CCC erosion work tapered off that summer as public works projects were deemphasized, but in its place a more focused effort emerged in a more appropriate department.[32]

Bennett soon realized that he needed more than a change of address and official congressional sanction for the SCS to work efficiently. One of the problems that had continually dogged soil conservationists was poor communication. Many farmers had read about conservation practices, but they needed more hands-on help in implementing new techniques. Extension agents worked well but lacked the manpower to cover the Palouse thoroughly. The SCS had a field office in Pullman but was similarly hamstrung. University scientists published in research station bulletins and released similar information to newspapers but could not work closely with individual farmers. Bennett surmised that the SCS needed to break up its operations into smaller components in order to disseminate erosion information, demonstrate proper techniques, and loan equipment. He drafted a model law in October 1935 to establish regional conservation districts. Roosevelt agreed and in February 1937 he urged all state legislatures to adopt Bennett's idea.[33]

Twenty-two state legislatures, mostly in the West, authorized the formation of local soil conservation districts by the end of 1937. Washington did not approve local districts until 1939. The reasons for the delay are unclear, but one possible explanation is that in the most erosion-prone parts of the state—the Palouse—farmers and activists formed their own conservation districts well before any official endorsement. Civic leaders, farmers, and

Grange members from a broad area around the North Fork of the Palouse River organized a conservation district in late 1936. The group did not aspire to impose any regulations, but offered farmers grass seed, advice, and labor to help build small dams and demonstrate contour plowing. Similar districts soon formed in the towns of Garfield, Washington, Genesee, Idaho, and the Moscow-Pullman area—all in advance of Bennett's decree. Through local donations and with a small amount of equipment donated by the USDA, the districts aimed to improve farming practices by encouraging and especially by showing that conservation farming could be easy and inexpensive.[34]

Conservation advocates received another boost from the US Supreme Court. It gave soil conservation new vigor when it struck down the Agricultural Adjustment Act in *US v. Butler* in the first week of January 1936.[35] Secretary Wallace immediately drafted and gained passage of a new plan— the Soil Conservation and Domestic Allotment Act of 1936 (DAA). The new law divided crops into two basic categories: "soil depleting crops" (row crops and grains that drained the soil of nutrients and/or encouraged erosion) and "soil conserving crops" (legumes and grasses that replenished the ground and held soil in place). Farmers could receive money for converting up to 15 percent of their soil depleting crop acres into soil conserving crops. The amount of money received depended on local conditions and on national supply levels (which were still high, for wheat); in Whitman County, farmers received an average of $16.60 per acre converted. Moreover, they could earn additional payments by starting "soil building" practices such as tree planting, stubble mulching, and contour plowing. The program was instantly popular, as six million farmers made the switch from the AAA to the DAA and collected nearly a half billion dollars in the first year alone. In its attempt to subvert Roosevelt's heavy regulatory hand, the Supreme Court actually made it stronger.[36]

The DAA looked like the perfect solution: it encouraged Palouse farmers to plant less wheat, which would hopefully raise prices; it avoided a direct tax on producers, marketers, or consumers; and it promoted soil conservation in a voluntary manner that rewarded farmers with a cash subsidy. Wallace and Roosevelt intended the law to be a temporary relief measure, but conservation proponents hoped that the erosion control methods adopted under the plan would be repeated for years to come. SCS and extension agents believed that this new federal law lacked a forceful regulatory stick, but it undeniably contained several very attractive carrots.

It is impossible to know precisely if Palouse conservation districts and the DAA helped farmers to take better care of the land. The USDA kept statistics on summer fallow and wheat and grassland acres, but only at five-year intervals. The agency conducted an agricultural census in 1934 and again in 1939. Other evidence suggests that some farmers became more interested in soil stewardship in the mid-1930s. With increasing frequency, inland Northwesterners spoke of a genuine affection for farms and of the farmer's unique responsibilities for keeping lands fertile, productive, and attractive. In some cases, sons challenged fathers to see who could grow more wheat while using various soil-conserving methods. It is entirely possible that such actions spoke of lasting agrarian ideals held over from the nineteenth century and before, times when nutrient cycling, sustainability, and above all caution informed farming decisions. A Washington state school superintendent wrote that it was every citizen's responsibility to appreciate "the true heritage which Mother Earth has bound up in her soil for the benefit of mankind." Another Palouse agriculture leader insisted that "to husband the land is not to extract all or to mine or to exploit or to tear down the very structure upon which we attempt to build. To husband is to manage with frugality, to replenish as well as to take from, to build as well as to tear down."[37] A sentimental appreciation for the Palouse as a place that should be handled with care emerged in the mid-1930s that competed with the prevailing commercial, profit-driven attitude on which the region was founded. A more balanced and respectful mind-set appeared possible.

Many farmers proudly proclaimed their newfound interest in conservation. Colfax farmer Oliver Hall bragged in 1934 that he could grow a good crop of wheat on hilltops that had had exposed "clay points"—places with no topsoil—only a few years prior. Specialized training had made this possible, as Hall's words contained all the hallmarks of a Progressive Era reformer: "Farming is no longer the career for the dummy of the family while the bright boys are educated for Law, Medicine, or other Professions. Farming is the job that requires the best brains, the most careful training of any." And Walter Fiscus, who farmed in northern Latah County, also took better care of his land than many of his peers. In particular, he avoided summer fallow and began contour plowing when soil experts told him it was a good idea. But in the 1930s he also expressed disappointment that large portions of the Palouse that had been covered in trees were now gone. This longtime farmer wished that, at the time of settlement, Palouse settlers—himself included—had taken a more careful, thoughtful look around them and decided *not* to remove these divine creations: "Americans have it bred into them to hate trees on their land. The toil of grubbing and clearing that has been the lot of our ancestors who would not know how to use a grub hoe or briar scythe will be brought up to appreciate trees. Let us teach them that; farms are cleared by fools like me, but only God can make a tree."[38] The act of conservation—whether of soil, trees, or any other resource—required that producers and consumers repeatedly say "no." No to the immediate demands of the market and of creditors, and no to the most innate tendencies of American farmers. It came naturally to a few, and to others only after they had seen the effects of intensive agriculture.

Even detached and emotionally removed soil scientists, trained to ignore the emotional tug associated with agrarianism, began to write sentimentally about the Palouse. Earl Victor, CCC camp superintendent and local SCS official, wrote an article in 1935 that accused early settlers of "destroying" native vegetation, which resulted in erosion and the despoiling of numerous picturesque valleys. William Rockie told an audience of scientists in the same year that the Pacific Northwest enjoyed "a larger percentage of crystal clear streams and lakes . . . than any other particular section of the United States." He aimed to keep it that way, even though he knew that Palouse waters were already heavy with silt runoff. Rockie published an article several years later that targeted the "checkerboard of wheat and fallow" on the Palouse that left a "greasy semifluid mass" running in streams. He openly hoped for a return to presettlement days, to a time before moldboard plows, harrows, and tractors: "Channels now dry except during the flood season were occupied by small but permanent running streams, in which trout could be caught at any time." Victor and Rockie helped spawn a new scientific outlook that considered aesthetics and ethical issues of land stewardship.[39]

Soil experts in Washington DC also developed a deeper appreciation for the natural systems of the Palouse. *To Hold This Soil*, a 1938 USDA publication on erosion, examined the progress of New Deal conservation initiatives in several case studies. Like Rockie's works, it criticized the typical early Palouse settler who possessed "an enmity toward trees" and who "never realized that he was skinning his land by pushing it too hard with hoof and tooth and steel implements." These farmers plowed and fallowed for years until the South Fork of the Palouse River became "an ugly sluice, a gash, a river in name only." But with the advent of conservation farming, the USDA contended that Palouse wheat growers had mended their ways and were beginning to farm differently: "Older people around Pullman, Washington, say that for the past few years the river has certainly become more as it was at the beginning of the century, when it flowed all year 'round and was clear enough to be full of trout. . . . Now it seems to be coming back. Trout from the better watered reaches of the stream or from the North Palouse reappears in its waters. Pullman fishermen are catching them."[40] The department desperately wanted to show that its efforts had been worthwhile even though it could only offer anecdotal evidence of improvement. A quantitative erosion study was not completed until 1939 and water quality data was decades away. But New Deal programs succeeded in broadening the perspective of the USDA to include issues that were merely tangential to the original conservation message. Soil scientists, like many Palouse residents, wished for the return of at least some aspects of their simpler, cleaner past. They may have developed a veneration for the former natural beauty of the Palouse only when it became apparent that it could not easily be resurrected.

Walter Lowdermilk, associate chief of the SCS, had an even more creative way to promote stewardship. During a trip to the Middle East in 1939 and a tour of ancient cities and civilizations that had decayed and fallen because of poor land-use practices, he wondered what Moses might say if the prophet returned to this once-fertile area. Lowdermilk thought Moses would be aghast at the barren wasteland that Palestine had become and would add an "Eleventh Commandment" to his previous ten. This contrived proclamation, first delivered as a radio address in Jerusalem and subsequently circulated through the SCS (often in an Old English typeface), called on farmers and ranchers to treat their land with more reverence:

Thou shalt inherit the Holy Earth as a faithful steward, conserving its resources and productivity from generation to generation. Thou shalt safeguard thy fields from soil erosion, thy living waters from drying up, thy forests from desolation, and protect thy hills from overgrazing by thy herds, that thy descendants may have abundance forever. If any shall fail in this stewardship of the land, thy fruitful fields shall become sterile, stony ground and wasting gullies, and thy descendants shall decrease and live in poverty or perish from off the face of the earth.[41]

Ambivalence in the Judeo-Christian tradition regarding land use has existed for centuries. For some, Christian duty included "subduing" the land and extracting its riches for the cities of God; for others, the land itself as a divine creation demanded respect and proper care. Lowdermilk and the SCS definitely favored the second interpretation, in which farmers used their land but not to the detriment of future generations.[42]

Other trends in the 1930s left a decidedly mixed legacy. Farm mechanization, which began in the 1920s, expanded rapidly during the Depression and gave soil conservationists reason to jeer and cheer. Improved tractor technology spawned part of the expansion, as diesel engines replaced gasoline-powered machines and horses. Better reliability and fuel economy, cheaper fuel, and more low-end torque made them an attractive alternative and a cost-effective means for plowing and harrowing fields efficiently. The Caterpillar crawler, the implement of choice in the Palouse because of its width and low center of gravity, could plow thirty acres in a day and did not need to be constantly watered and fed. Moreover, farmers who mechanized no longer had to set aside acres for pasturage or corrals and could use more land for marketable crops.[43]

The move away from horsepower denoted a higher level of expertise and success; the truly progressive farmer hailed mechanization because it increased long-term profitability and afforded farmers more leisure time. As Ray White, editor of the *Latah Citizen*, wrote, "Progress in civilization—in intellectual attainment, in personal welfare, in human happiness—is dependent in no small measure upon quantity production, and that upon the use of labor-saving machines in the production of commodities to meet human demands." Statistics on tractor use confirmed the shift: the number of tractors on Washington and Idaho farms more than doubled from 1930 to 1940 and eclipsed the national trend by a wide margin.[44] The figures are startling, especially since the Northwest and the nation were suffering from a debilitating economic slump. Wheat farmers could not resist the lure of profits and the labor-saving attributes of tractors and other new implements.

Because of their size and expense, tractors aggravated Palouse erosion. Although better for soil than conventional tractor tires, the weight and the metal treads of Caterpillar crawlers compacted the ground more than horse hooves. When winter and early spring rains hit the hardened ground, water tended to run along the surface, transporting topsoil as it moved along. The increased power of these machines allowed them to pull heavier plows and harrows at greater depths, techniques that exposed more soil to the ravages of rain and gravity. In addition, the cost of tractors (about $2,000) necessitated frequent use. Since an idle implement made for a poor investment, it behooved farmers to use their machines as much as possible to extract the maximum benefit. Modern tractors transformed the sight, sound, and even the smell of local wheat farming while simultaneously exacerbating the erosion problem. Scientists and soil advocates may have succeeded in improving tilling practices and in promoting the need for conservation, but new tractors counteracted some of those benefits.[45]

Other innovations made meaningful contributions to soil conservation. In particular, the one-way disc plow, developed in the mid-1930s, allowed farmers to prepare seedbeds and displace far less soil than the old mold-board plow. The device consisted of rows of metal discs that cut into the ground at an angle in order to turn over remnant wheat plants. The discs were a vast improvement over the V-shaped moldboard, which completely inverted the soil and old root systems. SCS officials advised farmers to use the new device to till-under old wheat stalks in order to increase soil humus and check erosion. Farmers also began using the stubble puncher after harvests to prepare fields for the coming winter. Developed in 1938 by a farmer in Waterville, Washington (in the Big Bend area, near the Columbia River), this contraption used foot-long metal rods to poke holes in the ground, which allowed moisture to enter. A spring plowing was required to ready the ground for seeding, but the puncher left more organic matter (or "trash," as it was commonly called) on the ground during the wet winter months. Conservationists also praised the straw spreader, another tool in the battle against erosion. This device was specifically designed to improve soil quality by chopping up and distributing wheat stalks left behind after harvesting. The resulting mulch protected the ground in winter and decomposed faster than large pieces of straw. As older implements wore out and conservation farming gained a modicum of acceptance, some farmers invested in such soil-saving equipment. Erosion became the mother of necessity; when the demand for better farming practices arose, more appropriate machinery appeared.[46]

In the wake of nearly a decade's worth of soil conservation activity—from massive government initiatives and the formation of a small army of national and regional soil experts, to the local promotion of land steward-ship, to the manufacture and sale of improved implements—it is safe to say that erosion continued to plague the Palouse in 1940. The SCS finally completed a thorough study of more than five hundred Palouse farms in 1939–1940 and found that *an average of 11.5 tons of soil was lost from every acre that year.*[47] That startling total was probably an improvement over the past but was still unacceptable to scientists in the long term. Farming could not last with erosion of that magnitude no matter how deep the loess. If national and local conservation leaders wanted better results they would have to consider more drastic steps, such as the abolition of annual cropping on steep hills. But because of financial pressures that demanded high output and opposition to federal land-use regulations, Palouse farmers resisted cutting production, which limited the possible scope of New Deal reform. Roosevelt and Wallace did well, given these constraints.

Several key indicators explain the situation, the most glaring of which was summer fallow (see table 1). Palouse growers idled 423,974 acres in 1929,

TABLE 1. Depression-Era Land Use in Whitman and Latah Counties (in acres)

Land Use	1929	1934	1939
Cropland harvested	758,786	682,679	703,577
Summer fallow	423,974	494,254	452,478
Hay	83,716	95,494	79,467
Alfalfa	N/A	37,854	47,940
Clover and timothy	N/A	5,219	4,034
Wheat	574,492	431,274	421,168

SOURCE: U.S. Census Bureau

or over half of all cropland. That figure jumped to 494,254 in 1934 largely because the AAA rewarded farmers for reducing the size of their wheat crops. The number of fallowed acres dropped to 452,478 by 1939, but the amount of fallow compared to the amount of cropland actually increased during the decade; for most of the 1930s, farmers devoted more acres to fallow than to wheat. The AAA and the DAA helped bring down wheat totals from 1929 levels but failed miserably as a means of eliminating the leading cause of Palouse erosion.[48]

Under the generous terms of the DAA, the USDA did not compel farmers to replace wheat with conservation crops like alfalfa. Operators had the option of using grasses and legumes to make a profit on lands that formerly produced wheat, but most farmers decided against this conservation tactic. Census numbers show that hay production in the Palouse went up sharply in the early 1930s but then fell below 1929 levels by the end of the decade. Alfalfa, which doubled as a soil saver and a nitrogen booster, showed impressive gains, but clover and timothy acreage remained negligible. Wheat acres declined over this period, but Palouse farmers did not seize the opportunity to use this land to conserve soil or to market new crops. Other small grains—barley, oats, and flax—were planted on most the remaining arable land. Acreages for all three went up in the 1930s because the USDA did not list them as "soil depleting" crops in the DAA, even though farmers usually rotated them with summer fallow.[49] In a separate study, the state of Washington revealed that from 1936 through 1938, soil-conserving crops made up a mere 8.2 percent of all Whitman County cropland.[50] The empirical evidence suggests that even after passage of the DAA, most farmers did not deviate from the standard grain/fallow rotation.

A Washington State College survey confirmed the veracity of those figures. The college's Agricultural Experiment Station questioned eighty Palouse farmers in 1936 about their crop selections and tillage practices and found barely a trace of conservation farming. Of the eighty, only seven grew any cover crops and only eleven had planted perennial grasses in erosion-prone areas. The report mentioned that several farmers tilled excessively—ten times per year, to be precise—to prevent weed growth and to obtain the "dust mulch" that was still popular. The station intended to use the study as a way to promote an "equilibrium" in Palouse farming that favored forage crops over wheat, new tillage practices over old, and a return to livestock grazing. From the evidence gathered, it had a considerable amount of work to do.[51]

What discouraged or prevented farmers from embracing soil conservation? Why did they continue using methods that were harmful and might eventually put them out of business? One reason was that the Roosevelt administration made most New Deal agriculture plans voluntary. It used cash subsidies to induce farmers to plant less wheat and more forage crops, but neither Congress nor the executive branch ever forced farmers to switch. Asking farmers to limit acreage was a huge leap in itself; most found it counterintuitive to plant on 70 or 80 percent of their land and accepted reductions only out of financial need. Farmers surely would have resisted had either branch demanded compliance, but the paradoxical desire to get federal help and resist regulatory compliance was perhaps the most basic component of the twentieth-century agrarian liberal. The voluntary nature of New Deal agricultural policy assured that soil conservation would not be fully implemented.

The SCS did everything in its powers to encourage conservation but often had to rely on moral suasion to accomplish its goals. This involved a delicate balancing act. The agency had to frighten farmers into believing that erosion could destroy their livelihoods, but it could not be unduly harsh or critical of past mistakes lest the audience become alienated. The SCS outlined the proper way to deal with individual farmers in a 1939 handbook. "Above all," it stated, agents must "avoid contention. An ounce of diplomacy may be more useful than a pound of argument."[52]

Local conservation districts faced a similar predicament. Membership was strictly voluntary and nonmembers had the right to ignore conservation suggestions, practices that undermined what could have been a strong layer of local government. After the Washington and Idaho state legislatures officially approved the formation of local conservation districts in 1939, both states began receiving federal money and leftover CCC equipment, but the districts wielded very little authority. The laws stated that district supervisors had the right to impose land-use regulations, yet supervisors never exercised such authority for fear of negative backlash. The state of Washington finally rescinded this bylaw in 1948. An overweening respect for private property rights and a tradition of independence prevented rules that could have slowed chronic erosion. The districts were weak and ineffectual, despite all their hard work and blustery prose about the benefits of "self-government" and "local control."[53]

Soil conservation also suffered because the New Deal narrowly focused on reducing wheat acreage and supplies to raise prices. Instead of using the shell game of shifting acres from wheat and fallow to other crops, the USDA could have attacked surpluses and erosion with one simple stroke: the permanent retirement of highly erodible land. Scientists knew by the mid-1930s that most of the soil lost each year came from the steepest hills and slopes— about 10 percent of the land—but this land was never taken out of production for more than a few years. During the entire run of the New Deal, the USDA never ordered the retirement of any Palouse land, even in small parcels on vulnerable hilltops, in spite of the wishes of soil experts.[54] Quite the opposite occurred—the Palouse actually had more land under cultivation in 1944 than in 1929, and average farm size continued to grow in response to mechanization and capital-intensive production.[55] The USDA failed to use agricultural surpluses and data on erosion patterns as justification to install long-term solutions.

Had the USDA and SCS taken stronger action to correct a wider assortment of the known causes of erosion, a great deal of time, effort, and money could have been saved. According to Verle Kaiser, a local SCS expert whose career spanned more than forty years, individual soil-building techniques were easy to apply. "Sure, it is relatively a simple matter to get a good stand of sweet clover. Stubble can be plowed under, too." But Kaiser insisted that "one or two simple practices will never do the job. It is going to take a complete program using many practices and systematically repeating their use every year that the land is farmed. There are no short cuts!"[56] Hugh Hammond Bennett and Henry Wallace, who believed that poor farming practices caused most of the ecological damage on American farms, were unwilling and unable to summon the necessary money and authority to instill a different set of priorities in the mind of the Palouse farmer.

Besides all the troubling policy issues and entrenched attitudes, soil conservationists had to contend with certain agricultural and economic forces that undermined their message. Although scientists speculated that erosion would eventually lead to lower wheat yields, none could offer a conclusive link. Washington State College experts began studying the relationship in the 1930s, but their results were years away, and as late as 1944 the SCS still could not offer proof that soil loss led to a drop in yields. What people did know was that per acre wheat yields increased in the 1930s. Whitman County growers hauled in more than thirty bushels per acre in 1939, while their neighbors in Idaho tallied nearly twenty-seven bushels per acre—an appreciable increase over 1920s harvest totals that had averaged about twenty-three bushels an acre.[57] If erosion threatened the future of Palouse agriculture, it was not apparent from these figures. Moreover, the cycle of farm growth, mechanization, debt, and maximized output that operated in the 1920s carried over to the following decade. New Deal programs could not change the fact that farmers had to extract as much as possible from their land if they hoped to remain solvent. Farmers were reluctant to reduce tilling operations or otherwise change tactics at a time when economic uncertainty ruled the day. In this case and during the trying days of the Depression, caution erred on the side of the tried-and-true, not the experimental.

Beginning in 1939, conservationists faced their biggest challenge to date. Germany invaded Poland in September of that year, dragging almost all of the developed world into the Second World War. The most horrifying aspect of this global disaster was that it left over 50 million people dead. It also left indelible marks on American agriculture. In the inland Northwest, soil conservationists wondered if the small amount of progress made in the 1930s would all go to waste. They worried that the mistakes made during the First World War—overproduction and excessive soil depletion— would be repeated under the pressure of worldwide demand for wheat. Given the track record of farmers in the preceding years, they had good reason to be concerned.

In the first two years of the war, economic forecasters urged farmers to proceed with caution. Confronted with record wheat surpluses and wary of repeating the World War I scenario, farm experts warned against increasing production. At first, European nations did not import large quantities of American wheat; instead they bought more fresh fruit and tobacco. These factors, and the still-sluggish domestic market, signaled farmers to remain conservative. But Washington State College agricultural economists predicted that if the war intensified, Europeans "will before long be desperately in need of certain supplies," including wheat.[58]

Calls for imported American wheat increased toward the end of 1941. The killing fields of Europe had again embroiled much of the continent, making it nearly impossible to grow or harvest food at prewar levels. The war in the Pacific eliminated access to the Asian market, but by 1942 world demand had driven wheat prices above the $1 per bushel level for the first time since 1929. In response to inflation fears, Congress passed the Emergency Price Control Act of 1942, establishing price ceilings on staple goods. Even with the new law, the price of wheat climbed to over $1.30 per bushel in 1944 and exceeded the parity price (the "fair" price farmers received for their goods) for the first time since 1929. In addition, the federal government removed much of the risk from wheat farming in 1938 when it instituted a crop insurance program that insulated growers against crop failure. All signs pointed to a steep rise in production in response to supply and demand forces as well as government action.[59]

Conservationists went on the offensive to avoid a repeat of the World War I experience. The experiment station at the University of Idaho promised that agriculture would put defense first, but added, "There is need for agriculture to keep its condition healthy, also. By continuing the emphasis on soil conservation, farmers can meet the demand made on them without waste of soil resources."[60] The *Washington Farmer* regarded conservation as essential whether the nation was at peace or war. Its managing editor asked readers, "Can we afford to practice soil conservation during the war emergency when maximum crop production is so essential? My feeling is that we cannot afford not to. If the war ends quickly we can produce enough foodstuffs to meet requirements without jeopardizing the soil. If it continues over a long period of years we cannot produce enough unless we do take good care of it."[61] The SCS also continued to publish articles and counsel farmers on the benefits of conservation. The agency operated under several new departments in the 1940s because of the war, yet remained committed to the cause of conservation. Its advice in the 1940s sounded much like that given in the 1930s—end summer fallow, plant grasses and legumes, and stop burning crop residues.[62] If farmers ignored the experts again, it would not be for lack of effort.

Perhaps some of the conservation message got through. Palouse farmers planted only slightly more wheat during World War II (see table 2). Wheat acreage went up by 12,446 acres from 1939 to 1944—a paltry 3 percent increase. The rewards for their efforts increased dramatically; higher prices pushed gross sales to $19.3 million in 1944, compared to just under $8 million in 1939. Even more striking was the precipitous drop in summer fallow acreage

TABLE 2. Wartime Land Use in Whitman and Latah Counties (in acres)

Land Use	1939	1944
Cropland harvested	703,577	913,937
Summer fallow	452,478	295,577
Hay	79,467	64,333
Alfalfa	47,940	45,154
Clover and timothy	4,034	3,938
Wheat	421,168	433,614
Peas	69,271	288,338

SOURCE: U.S. Census Bureau

from 452,478 acres in 1939 to 295,577 in 1944—a 44 percent decline in five years. Conservationists were disappointed by a slight-to-moderate drop in acreage for most grasses and legumes but could take heart that substantial progress had been made with summer fallow.[63]

The statistics beg two important questions: what happened to acres formerly devoted to summer fallow, and what did farmers do with the extra 210,360 acres put into production from 1939 to 1944? The answer to both was a surge in acres planted to peas. This leguminous plant, which had been in use since the early 1900s, became a popular replacement for summer fallow because it restores nitrogen better than most other legumes and contains high levels of protein, which made it an ideal livestock feed. Because of inflated wartime prices, peas also brought farmers generous financial rewards; Palouse growers earned $18.5 million from field peas in 1944, a profit that rivaled receipts from wheat. These factors caused pea production to balloon from 69,271 acres in 1939 to 288,338 acres in 1944, proving that farmers seemed willing to adopt a conservation tactic when it proved cost-effective.[64]

But not all conservation methods were equally effective, and a jump in peas did not automatically translate into an end to erosion. Fewer acres in fallow certainly helped, but grasses and other legumes did a better job of holding the soil in place, because peas encouraged weed growth and required more intensive cultivation than other cover crops. In addition, the heavy pea plant residues left behind after harvest made fall plowing difficult and led to increased burning and loss of humus. Peas became a feasible, profitable way for farmers to increase soil fertility and conserve soil, but they were no panacea for erosion.[65]

Observers found evidence to suggest that the erosion menace confounded farmers through the early 1940s. One farmer opined that erosion in the spring of 1942 left "tracks that are deeper and longer than they have been for many years," because too many had "worked the land until the soil was so finely pulverized it was unable to resist erosion." An article from the *Washington Farmer* in 1943 praised a group of farmers from Fairfield, Washington, who helped an injured neighbor summer-fallow 130 acres in only five hours. The reporter neglected to mention the irony that this act of community spirit actually harmed their agricultural futures and their most important natural resource. Two years later another reporter grieved over the general lack of conservation ethics in the Palouse, complaining that "less than one farm in 10 is following a definite, year-in-and-year-out program of soil maintenance and building" and that "less than one out of 30 is participating in the organized program of the Soil Conservation Service."[66] Many outward signs pointed to a return to the reckless days of the preceding war, when Palouse farmers saw their chance to cash in—while ignoring the future consequences.

The Latah Soil Conservation District, still in its infancy during the war, gave the perfect description of the ambivalent mood. As a voluntary association, it could not be overly critical of either its membership or the farming community at large. Yet on the other hand it could not ignore what it saw—the relatively speedy dismissal of conservation farming. With the convenience of hindsight, the district's 1950 report commented on the conflicted state of affairs in the early 1940s:

> There soon developed two kinds of farmers among those who had already established conservation practices. Those who believed that they could keep up the program of conservation and still produce an abundance of badly needed food crops, and those who thought that the needs of the nation and world were so great, that they should throw every good practice out in order to produce more, and then the prices began to climb a little and so with prices up and the demand great, the latter became the most popular method.[67]

The raw data reinforced the notion that conservation farming had not taken hold. In its ongoing annual survey of over five hundred Palouse farms, the

SCS determined that each acre of land lost twenty tons of soil during the 1941–1942 season. That total fell sharply during the next three years but only because of below-normal rainfall. Soil losses went up again thereafter.[68] To a variety of onlookers in the 1940s—SCS scientists, university researchers, journalists, and farmers alike—it was clear that a majority of farmers did not consider soil loss to be serious enough to warrant reform. By any reasonable yardstick, the New Deal conservation plan did not measure up to expectations.

Old habits die hard, and that cliché was especially true of Palouse farmers. In spite of a generous support network and constant warnings about soil loss, they never abandoned old practices en masse, nor did they enthusiastically support comprehensive change. Farmers were not allergic to change altogether (e.g., the shift to tractor power and the surge in pea production), but the agrarian liberal was predisposed to continue practices that had been profitable in the short-term—even when these methods appeared unwise in the long run. Farmers made decisions based on immediate concerns such as loan payments, weather, and international markets. The dangers posed by erosion could not be felt in the 1930s, and it made little economic sense to reorient Palouse farming for what *might* happen in the future. Stewardship never filtered into the hearts and minds of Palouse farmers during settlement days and it never generated much attention between the 1920s and the 1940s. Farmers had no ideological impetus to conserve soil in part because stewardship had been lacking all along. To expect them to suddenly conjure a new land ethic during the Depression was quixotic at best. A conservation ethic required less concern with next year's harvest and more concern with the yields hauled in by the next generation of Palouse farmers—a real land ethic would take into account profitability *and* responsibility. Convincing farmers to shift to such an outlook had already proven difficult to accomplish, and with the advent of agricultural chemicals looming in the future it would become even more complicated.

One massive change during the 1930s was the level of government intervention in American farming. The Depression and the Dust Bowl spurred the USDA to reevaluate how it perceived market agriculture and the ecological impact of intensive farming. The government could no longer consider farmers to be helpless victims of economic forces beyond their comprehension or control; the government took an active role in protecting this important interest group by offering financial assistance tied to responsible farming practices. Although some of these policies were popular and others were unpopular in the Palouse, and some government ideas about land ethics went unheard, the economic collapse of the 1930s forever linked the government and the farmer in a relationship that continues to the present day.

6 BETTER FARMING THROUGH CHEMISTRY

F ROM GEORGE PANGBURN'S rustic homestead in 1869 to the mul-
timillion dollar farms of today, Palouse farmers have constantly sought
to enhance their productivity. Though often chided as being conservative and inflexible, Palouse and most other American farmers have been
quick to use new products and methods when convinced they can reduce
manual labor or make their operations more efficient and profitable. In the
Palouse the first Euro-American agrarians abandoned mixed agriculture
when it became obvious that wheat could grow throughout the region's hilly
terrain. They increased wheat production during World War I in response
to rising demand in Europe. They purchased new implements when manufacturers produced equipment that suited the terrain. And when the federal government made reducing wheat acreage a financially attractive
option in the 1930s, farmers temporarily made such reductions, thus
embracing important liberal concepts of the New Deal. Market revolutions,
production innovations, and technological change, so often associated with
the manufacturing sectors of the Western world, should also be understood
as rural, agricultural phenomena. The American farmer offered numerous
and illuminating examples of how thoroughly one socioeconomic group
could comprehend and seize technological opportunities.[1]

In the years following World War II, several technological breakthroughs
promised to transform Palouse agriculture more than any previous innovation or event. New chemical herbicides, especially 2,4–D (2,4–dichlorophe-

noxyacetic acid), killed broadleaf weeds effectively and became an instant commercial success. New fertilizers such as anhydrous ammonia enabled farmers to restore soil fertility, and researchers developed hybrid wheat varieties that resisted fungi and produced higher yields. Insecticides such as DDT killed insects indiscriminately, which helped farmers reduce crop losses. The effects of these and allied developments were spectacular; yields for all farm products soared from the 1940s through the 1960s.[2] The USDA, the scientific community, chemical manufacturers, and individual farmers were elated that modern science had made Palouse farming even more profitable. After years of depression and war it appeared that Palouse farmers could once again enjoy a taste of the good life, giving them a chance to pass along this altered agrarian dream to another generation.

The ecological costs of prosperity put a damper on some of the enthusiasm. A litany of side effects from agricultural chemicals surfaced in the 1940s and intensified through the 1960s. Lax government regulations and uncertainty about proper quantities led to occasional overuse and damage to crops and animals. The opposition to chemicals before 1962 was somewhat muted compared to later years, but the early debates on the role of agricultural chemicals revealed an undercurrent of anxiety and were a harbinger of things to come.

The most troubling development of this period was the persistence of the soil erosion problem. The federal government and local soil conservationists conducted an ongoing campaign to rectify the matter using tactics from the 1930s—providing subsidies that rewarded conservation farming, publishing promotional articles and giving public demonstrations, and conducting constant research. In short, successive postwar administrations entrenched liberal New Deal policies. But that effort failed for many of the same reasons it had before: the government did not force farmers to adopt conservation measures; soil conservation districts lacked money and regulatory power; and a stewardship ethic was sorely lacking. The postwar Palouse story was much like its earlier prewar version.

But chemical farming significantly changed the erosion dynamic. When farmers understood how well new fertilizers and herbicides worked, they saw bigger harvests and very little incentive to conserve soil. Although Palouse fields continued to lose millions of tons of soil each year, production per acre in the 1950s and 1960s eclipsed previous levels by wide margins. The idea that erosion would lead to reduced yields and impoverishment sounded alarmist and inaccurate, especially after farmers had access to a cornucopia of powerful chemicals that made many of their weed, insect, and fertility problems disappear. Farmers did not innovate further because they felt there was no compelling reason to do so. The midcentury production boom made many farmers rich and silently encouraged them to use more chemicals and to ignore the persisting erosion problem. Full of optimism and pride, Palouse farmers witnessed something of a return to the halcyon days of the years immediately following 1910. But despite the benefits of the post–World War II surge, the land continued to suffer from old farming methods and was threatened by a host of potentially disastrous new ones.

Before World War II farmers had several methods at their disposal to control weeds. Summer fallow was the most popular means, since farmers believed it simultaneously eliminated some weeds and retained soil moisture. Early chemical agents, including petroleum products, salt, copper sulfate, iron sulfate, sulfuric acid, and carbolic acid, had been in use since the early 1900s. These chemicals never attracted a large following because weeds could withstand these products in small amounts and they killed both weeds and crops when applied too freely. To obtain any benefits and to avoid a chemical disaster, farmers had to use the proper amount—a task made more difficult because of variations in local conditions and a lack of good information from manufacturers or retailers. Most farmers avoided these products, used summer fallow, and grudgingly accepted weedy fields.[3]

Farmers began winning the war on weeds in the mid-1940s. The herbicide 2,4–D, first synthesized at the University of Chicago in 1941 and patented by the DuPont corporation in 1943, signaled the dawn of the chemical farming era.[4] This potent new weapon used hormones to disrupt the food-making process early in the life cycle of certain plants, and it killed weeds before they had the chance to mature and produce seeds. Moreover, 2,4–D was a selective killer because it affected only broadleaf plants and left grains and grasses largely intact, making it the perfect choice for Palouse wheat fields. Hundreds of other herbicides flooded the market in subsequent years, but 2,4–D remained the single most effective and popular weed killer in the Palouse for decades.[5]

The response to 2,4–D was overwhelmingly positive. *Agricultural Chemicals* magazine reported in 1946 that "the general public appears willing and anxious to believe that this new weed killer, 2,4–D, will turn out to be a final cure-all for all weed problems." It added that, "within certain limitations, these ideas may be well-founded," because the chemical eliminated "certain noxious plants while not harming the metabolism of their good neighbors."[6] In the same year an Oregon State College researcher predicted that "within three or four years farmers here in the Northwest will be treating not a few thousand acres but in the hundreds of thousands. The program [of 2,4–D use] has almost unlimited possibilities in Oregon, Washington, Idaho, and Montana." That opinion seemed accurate, because 2,4–D production in the US swelled from 631,000 pounds in 1945 to 5.3 million the following year.[7] Farmers bought the chemical in such quantities because it performed as advertised—weeds died and grains thrived. Fewer weeds meant less competition for moisture and nutrients and a reduced tilling regimen that would cut costs. In addition, 2,4–D was relatively inexpensive to purchase and apply after an initial investment in new equipment. Farmers had plenty of good reasons to spray every available acre, and the use of the chemical increased every year during the late 1940s and 1950s.[8]

The development of the chemical fertilizer anhydrous ammonia followed a trajectory similar to its herbicidal cousin. The Shell Oil Corporation first concocted this agent in the 1930s and introduced it to consumers in Southern states on a trial basis in 1947 and 1948. Anhydrous ammonia is a liquefied gas derived from nitrogen and hydrogen that supplies soil with a jolt of nitrogen that is soluble to growing plants. In undisturbed ground this task is performed by blue-green algae and bacteria and microbes that convert nitrogen in the air into nutrients that plants can use. But in areas where intensive agriculture has caused erosion (as in the Palouse), much of this vital microscopic component had been washed away. Nitrogen fertilizers had been in use for decades, but this new formulation contained 82 percent nitrogen—far higher than any other substance. Anhydrous offered Palouse farmers a cheap and efficient way to reverse the continuous depletion of nitrogen.[9]

Soil scientists wrote effusively about the restorative powers of anhydrous. A team of Washington State College agronomists published a report in 1946, claiming it would increase nitrogen levels in Palouse soil that had been degraded by years of tilling. USDA extension agronomist C. B. Harston insisted in a 1949 article that "nitrogen is nearly always required for maximum production," and he called for heavy use of anhydrous and all other fertilizers. The presence of "bald knobs" atop many hills—places where erosion had removed all the topsoil—put an even greater premium on artificial fertilizers in the 1950s, because anecdotal evidence suggested that these areas had been producing far less wheat than adjacent lowlands for many years. Infertile hills should have been the canary in the coal mine, a warning to farmers to modify their behavior or stop the annual cropping of these areas. Nevertheless, Palouse farmers who used anhydrous quickly saw healthier and bigger grain crops in low areas and on hilltops and it soon became the region's leading fertilizer.[10]

Although insects troubled farmers less than weeds, certain pests had a negative impact on crops. In particular, the number of aphids in the Palouse fluctuated greatly, but they periodically became a serious nuisance in pea and spring wheat fields. A new insecticide, DDT, came on the market in 1945 and gave farmers new hope in the battle against bugs. Although first synthesized in Germany in 1874, the insecticidal qualities of DDT were not known until 1939—a discovery that led to its use by Allied forces in World War II. Military officials were duly impressed with the chemical's ability to kill insects, mitigate tropical diseases, and eliminate body lice from soldiers in Europe; in 1945 the USDA made it available for American consumers. The popularity of DDT soared in the late 1940s and 1950s as rural and urban dwellers alike discovered its effectiveness. US production exceeded 84 million pounds in 1953, the vast majority of it used on farms to combat insect pests. Palouse farmers applied insecticides to more than 110,000 acres in 1964—less than herbicide and fertilizer use, but nevertheless a substantial amount.[11]

With the initial success of 2,4–D, anhydrous ammonia, and DDT, farmers showed greater interest in using other kinds of chemicals. Some products had been in production for years, such as sulfuric acid, potash, and lime, while others, like the herbicide 2,4,5–T and the insecticide benzene hexachloride, appeared on the market for the first time in the 1940s. Farmers also applied more trace elements to their fields. Elements such as magnesium, zinc, boron, and molybdenum constitute only a small part of the chemical makeup of Palouse soils, but they can be used to adjust pH levels or to increase fertility. A belief in the curative powers of agricultural chemicals created a steady demand for an array of products designed to increase output and profits.[12]

Research scientists also produced new and improved varieties of wheat. Intensive laboratory work on wheat hybridization dated back to the late nineteenth century, but the new varieties introduced in the post–World War II era resisted disease and produced far better yields than older strains. Scientists were particularly interested in breeding wheats that could resist fungi, since most chemical treatments had proven unsatisfactory or worked only on grasses.[13] Laboratories developed two new varieties in 1949, Elmar and Brevor, strains that the Washington State College experiment station believed would reduce fungal growth. But field testing revealed that both wheats were susceptible to infection, leaving farmers and scientists looking for more answers. Temporary help arrived in 1955 with the introduction of Omar, a wheat that seemed to prevent most fungal outbreaks. After several years, a rare type of rust fungus infected Palouse wheat, Omar included, and scientists returned to the drawing board. They developed a new variety in 1961, Gaines, that resisted fungi and produced a much shorter stalk that resisted "lodging"—the flattening of ripe grain by wind and rain. This "semidwarf" wheat became an overnight sensation in the Palouse and elsewhere in the Northwest because it avoided fungal outbreaks and was easier to handle in the field. All these varieties shared one key characteristic: more bushels per acre. Elmar, Brevor, Omar, and especially Gaines raised harvest totals throughout the inland Northwest and contributed to the region's postwar economic resurgence. The symbiotic state, scientist, farmer, chemical manufacturer relationship had once again proven to be a valuable and lasting union.[14]

The combination of these four innovations—chemical herbicides, fertilizers, pesticides, and new wheat varieties—culminated in an astonishing rise in crop yields in the 1950s (see table 3). Barley, a grain that became an important part of the grain/fallow rotation in the 1940s, showed considerable improvement; yields per acre went up 76 percent from 1949 to 1954. Wheat crops benefited even more from new technology, with per acre yields increasing 85 percent from 1949 to 1959; pea yields also went up 72 percent over the same span. Every crop witnessed gains, with most experiencing meteoric growth rates. Palouse farmers had become accustomed to moderate improvements through most of the twentieth century, but the postwar rate of increase made previous gains look minuscule. The value of all Palouse farm products sold in 1959 topped $60 million and continued to climb through the 1960s.[15] The possibilities for continued improvement seemed unlimited, thanks to the marvels of modern science, and there was no mistaking the key sources of this newfound bounty. As one entomologist asked in 1952, "Is it any wonder that our (US) food production far outweighs other nations on a comparative basis, and that we have been called upon to aid the starving peoples of many lands? The great production of food and fiber crops is largely attributed to the scientific use of chemicals." John Boyd Orr, a British social scientist, raved in 1953 that "with modern engineering and chemical science, the only practical limit to food production is the amount of capital, labor, and research we are willing to devote to it."[16] American farmers had plenty of capital, labor, and research at their disposal in the mid-twentieth century, and their future indeed looked bright.

The amount of machinery on Palouse farms changed in proportion to the rise in production. Record yields and economies of scale led to a continuation of the process that had begun in the 1920s and 1930s. After World

TABLE 3. Palouse Crop Yields, 1949–59

Year	1949	1954	1959
Wheat acres	562,570	422,480	460,833
Wheat yield (bushels)	14,977,113	18,484,811	19,797,507
Pea acres	158,027	103,820	149,566
Pea yield (pounds)	131,074,577	140,978,664	213,573,329
Barley acres	52,875	171,763	182,418
Barley yield (bushels)	1,405,150	8,027,733	8,116,503
Alfalfa acres	28,801	40,192	35,307
Alfalfa yield (tons)	42,827	71,400	69,043
Commercial fertilizer (acres)	N/A	351,856	531,876

SOURCE: U.S. Census Bureau

War II manufacturers developed faster, larger tractors and self-propelled combines that were also better equipped to stay upright on steep hills. As older machines depreciated and wore out and as the pressure on farmers to produce more goods increased, the amount of new equipment also increased. The number of tractors in Whitman and Latah counties grew from 3,287 in 1944 to 5,208 in 1959—a 58 percent gain. The number of combines, farm trucks, and baling machines also grew at a brisk pace, indicating the degree to which farmers had completely eliminated horsepower from their operations. The only real need for horses after World War II was for county fairs and 4–H shows.[17]

The boom in chemicals, hybrid seed, productivity, and machinery contributed to an amazing increase in farm size. Whitman County farms averaged 610 acres in 1944 (already well above the national average) and continued to grow in the ensuing years. A decade later that figure reached 724 acres, and in 1964 it hit an astounding 862 acres.[18] Thousand-acre spreads were no longer considered atypical; rather, they became quite commonplace. Farming in the Palouse was now big business, relying on modern technology to supply new goods and higher crop yields. The leap in farm size merely reflected the comprehensive changes elicited by improvements in the means of production.

In any radical change to the means of production, unintended consequences are bound to occur. Whether the industry is labor intensive, heavily mechanized, or technology driven, when major alterations affect how goods are produced, an uncomfortable adjustment period is nearly inevitable. Such was the case with chemical farming in the Palouse. Anhydrous ammonia, 2,4–D, and higher crop yields thrilled the local agricultural sector, but problems associated with this new style of farming also arose. In the years prior to the publication of Rachel Carson's *Silent Spring* (1962) and before the modern environmental movement gathered momentum, a relatively light but steady drumbeat of discontent reminded farmers of the dangers associated with chemical use. In most cases farmers and their allies successfully countered their critics and staved off regulations, yet they were forced to address some very pointed questions on the harmful effects of their technologies.

A basic question farmers asked regarding chemicals involved quantity. How much was enough and how much was too much? Manufacturers had only educated guesses in the late 1940s. For 2,4–D, the chemical industry recommended between one-half and two pounds per acre, but one spokesman added, "It may be that after experimental trials it will be necessary to raise or lower our recommendations; we are not sure."[19] At times the industry urged caution and warned farmers that too much spraying could cause crop failure. Lambert Erickson of the University of Idaho experiment station did not agree. He wrote in 1950 that cutting back on 2,4–D use "is a short-sighted and mighty expensive way of saving money." Lambert reasoned that if only small doses were applied, certain strong weeds would develop a tolerance to herbicidal treatment and would become an even greater problem in the future. He stopped short of prescribing actual amounts, but stated that farmers needed "the dosage high enough to kill the sensitive weeds for the benefit of this year's crop. But more important, we also need a rate high enough so that it will stop seed production of the more resistant weeds or we will inherit it and its kind for our battle in years to come."[20] The American Chemical Paint Company, an early manufacturer of 2,4–D, also recommended that farmers use as much as possible to control noxious weeds. Company president Franklin Jones stated in 1950, "There is no upper limit to concentration, except that dictated by economy."[21] In the early years of chemical farming, more was clearly thought to be better. A subsequent study by the University of Idaho confirmed that the one-half-to-two-pound range per acre would suffice, with annual weeds receiving more and perennial weeds less.[22] But a good deal of confusion plagued farmers, and as late as 1960 they were still unsure about quantity. In a weekly newspaper column in Tekoa, Washington, an extension agent wrote that "if you're not sure how the chemicals will fit your conditions you scout around and find out the history on some of the neighbors' places."[23] This kind of advice was at best vague and at worst an open invitation to overuse agricultural chemicals.

The advice for anhydrous ammonia use was equally haphazard, with suggested dosages increasing steadily during the 1950s. Washington State College issued a bulletin in 1950 urging farmers to use twenty pounds of anhydrous per acre. In field tests in Moscow the following year, researchers obtained maximum results from applications in the twenty-to-forty-pound range. By the end of the decade the University of Idaho was advising dosages of up to fifty pounds per acre. The upper limit on anhydrous had not yet been detrimental, and this caused some farmers to inject massive amounts into their land. According to D. F. Franklin, a University of Idaho experiment station superintendent, "In their enthusiasm over nitrogen dividends, some farmers have been pouring on twice and occasionally three times what would be a conservative rate for their locality."[24] Like 2,4–D, the sudden success of anhydrous ammonia led farmers to believe that if a little was good, a lot was better.

Not surprisingly, with the scientific community either unsure about proper quantities or willing to suggest greater amounts, farm chemicals created some unwanted side effects. Through the 1950s and early 1960s people in and out of agriculture blamed 2,4–D for damaging clover fields, for contaminating irrigation systems and milk supplies, and for killing honeybees. Both the liquid and dust forms of the chemical were prone to drift in high winds, which made it difficult to pinpoint the offending farmer. Moreover, the use of airplanes to apply chemicals, though faster and less expensive than ground equipment, often resulted in misapplications because of pilot error and wind.[25]

Public outcry over anhydrous ammonia was considerably less intense, in part because Washington State College offered seminars to farmers on proper application techniques, and also because the liquefied gas was injected directly into the soil and was thus less likely to drift. The *Organic Farmer*, a Pennsylvania-based magazine that was highly critical of corporate agriculture, pointed out that heavy anhydrous use reduced the number of earthworms in the ground, but no one in the Palouse seemed to notice or care.[26] Concerns about human health did not generate much attention, either. One county extension agent asked, "Can we continue to pour chemicals into the ground and produce health-giving crops for human consumption? The most concentrated use of commercial fertilizers in the world is in Holland. The Hollanders have a life expectancy of 72 years, compared to the average life expectancy in the United States of 70 years. This indicates that food grown with commercial fertilizer cannot be very unhealthful."[27]

False syllogism aside, there were no reports of any ill effects to humans from anhydrous. The real problem with anhydrous was that farmers needed it in the first place; the depletion of nitrogen caused by years of intensive cropping made it an essential ingredient for long-term soil fertility. The ability of this new chemical wonder to reinvigorate the soil made people forget or ignore that most of the microbiotic and animal life in the soil was already long gone.

An all-or-nothing mentality pervaded the agricultural industry. The literature is filled with hypothetical scenarios depicting the barren wastelands that would result from an overbearing bureaucracy that had banned all synthesized products and from lackadaisical industry leaders who failed to adequately inform the public about the absolute necessity of agricultural chemicals. "There are no harmful products," wrote Walter Weber in the magazine *Agricultural Chemicals* in 1971, adding, "this includes toothpicks. I mention toothpicks because one was responsible for the death of an Indiana man last summer." Gordon Berg, editor of *Farm Chemicals* magazine, wrote in 1968 that Americans needed to "return to reason" when it came to environmental questions. In making his point, he cited a line from the film *African Queen*, where the prim Audrey Hepburn told a typically disheveled Humphrey Bogart, "Nature, Mr. Alnutt, is what we are put on this world to rise above." Indeed, the chemical industry had risen above nature, and it intended to stay there.[28]

Yet other industry outlets sounded a conciliatory note, acknowledging causes of general environmental damage, specific harmful chemical agents, and particular environmental issues brought on by the quest for progress. One company, Phillips Petroleum, understood before any of their competitors that their agricultural chemical products could be deadly, and that good public relations and dependable market share relied in part on accepting responsibility for the negative side of industrial agriculture. A 1956 fertilizer brochure opened with a quote from the nineteenth-century Kansas senator John James Ingalls about the importance of grasslands: "Forests decay, harvests perish, flowers vanish, but grass is immortal. It yields no fruit in earth or air, and yet, should its harvest fail for a single year, famine would depopulate the earth." The passage was intended to rationalize the use of powerful fertilizers and to acknowledge the effects of nutrient losses caused by intensive cattle grazing. "As the white man's herds displaced the buffalo," the brochure continued, "our prairies began to decline. Every ton of grass-fed beef took 50 pounds of nitrogen from the range. Wind and water erosion removed additional fertility." The most responsible way to compensate for nutrient loss, Phillips Petroleum reasoned, was to implement "intelligent management"—the use of ammonia-based fertilizers—which would "improve our grassland vegetation which in some way supports the health and welfare of every one of us." The rhetoric, while self-serving, bucked the more prevalent trend of an industry geared toward an unyielding support for growth and development. In this case, a manufacturer factored stewardship and responsibility into their business plan.[29]

Opposition to DDT formed shortly after its introduction, none of which emanated from the Palouse. The USDA reported in 1945 that DDT killed honeybees—a revelation that had obvious negative implications for farmers. The *New Republic* warned a year later that DDT indiscriminately killed birds and beneficial insects. Charles Hovey, an entomologist working in Maine, conducted a study in the same year that showed livestock exposed to DDT suffered a loss of appetite and developed tumors. The *Organic Farmer*, the *Cleveland Plain Dealer*, and the *New York Times* voiced misgivings in 1949, insisting that the new insecticide caused fish and birds to die, made soils toxic, tainted the milk supply, and accumulated in animal tissue cells. The popularity of DDT continued to climb during the 1940s and 1950s but so too did the level of discontent.[30]

Despite the protests generated by DDT, Palouse farmers continued to use it in large quantities. This can be attributed in part to the voluminous amount of contrary evidence supplied by academic sources as well as by the farm press and chemical companies. A technical bulletin published by Washington State College in 1951 attempted to debunk various claims made against DDT. R. L. Webster, chair of the university's entomology department, denied that the substance caused lung problems in humans and accused the *New York Times* of using sensationalism to scare the public. But while Webster insisted that "there is no evidence that the use of DDT has ever caused human sickness," he also urged users of the pesticide to avoid skin contact, to wear gloves and a mask, and to wash thoroughly any clothing worn during an application. Webster conceded that farmers could experience coughing, tightness in the chest, and headaches, and he noted cases of dizziness experienced by crop-duster pilots. Still, the overall tone of the bulletin reinforced the notion that DDT was safe. In addition, the very fact that this proclamation came from an agricultural college lent it an air of authority that its detractors could not match.[31]

In the regional media, the *Washington Farmer* sang the loudest praise for DDT. In dozens of articles and editorials from the 1940s through the 1970s, the weekly touted DDT's insect-killing prowess and economic benefit. It warned farmers not to believe the organic farmers and "food faddists" who began advocating for a chemical-free food supply as early as the late 1940s. Instead, the *Farmer* argued that chemical farming made for a prosperous agricultural sector at home and a better-fed population abroad. Some Palouse farmers may have been in a quandary as to which side to believe, but the people who best served their immediate interests—university researchers and the farm press—clearly favored chemical use.[32]

Besides health risks to people, animals, and crops, farmers worried about the long-term effectiveness of herbicides and insecticides. Weeds and insects gradually developed a tolerance to some chemical treatments, a trend that threatened to diminish or reverse the midcentury production boom. According to L. C. Terriere, an Oregon State College entomologist, "a fraction of a microgram" of DDT killed most pests in the mid-1940s, but after a short time, "300 times that much will do no more than make it dizzy. This requires several generations and several months, but the transformation from weakling to superfly is steady and sure."[33] Here again was another opportunity for farmers to reconsider how they operated and to deemphasize or discontinue a potentially unsustainable practice. Here again another opportunity slipped away. Manufacturers began producing an ever-expanding smorgasbord of new chemicals that could improve upon the diminishing returns of older products. If DDT could no longer do the job, then newer pesticides such as parathion or tetraethyl pyrophosphate (TEPP) might be tried; likewise, if weeds persisted after several years of 2,4–D applications, a farmer might try 2,4–DB or MCPB. Or they might find that some combination of two or more chemicals worked better, although farmer experimentations with mixing volatile agents often ended in disaster. Farmers had difficulty keeping up with the most recent agricultural chemicals, a problem that one writer likened to changes in women's fashions. But they continued to ask for an ongoing supply of new products designed to keep them one step ahead of weeds and insects.[34]

Because of safety questions and the proliferation of hundreds of new chemicals, Congress became interested in more stringent industry regulation. Before World War II the key law governing agricultural chemicals was the 1938 Federal Food, Drug, and Cosmetic Act. This law forced manufacturers to prove to the USDA—usually through industry-sponsored university research—that a given chemical performed as advertised and was not a risk to human health. Gaining approval was normally a simple task, and the law did not seriously impede manufacturers. After the war and as the number of chemicals in use grew exponentially, Congress attempted to secure a stronger grip on the certification process with the Federal Insecticide, Fungicide, and Rodenticide Act of 1947 (FIFRA). FIFRA kept the truth-in-advertising and safety components of the 1938 law intact, but also required manufacturers to display adequate warning labels on containers and to register their products through the USDA. The law also contained a gaping loophole—if the USDA denied approval of any chemical on safety grounds, a manufacturer had the right to protest the decision and sell the product during an appeals process. Because appeals could take years to adjudicate, chemical companies could legally continue to market potentially hazardous goods.[35]

Congress frequently amended FIFRA. In response to questions about pesticide residues on crops, Congress passed the Miller Amendment in 1954, which established maximum residue levels on raw goods. Four years later it added the Food Additives Amendment and the Delaney Amendment, which put processed foods under the same residue scrutiny as raw goods and ordered a ban on any known carcinogenic chemical. Congress again amended FIFRA in 1964 and several more times in the 1970s and 1980s, all in an effort to guarantee the safety of the nation's food supply.[36]

On the heels of federal action, states and counties enacted chemical laws of their own. Both Washington and Idaho passed laws in the 1950s governing agricultural chemical labeling and registration. They were essentially the same as the original FIFRA law, in that chemicals had to perform as promised and had to contain all the elements that the manufacturer claimed. State laws also allowed counties to prescribe limitations on certain agents (like 2,4–D) that might harm crops. Whitman and Latah counties both issued ordinances in the 1950s that limited herbicide application to the early evening hours, when winds tended to subside, and Latah County forbade the use of 2,4–D, 2,4,5–T, and MCP in oil-based forms from the middle of May to September.[37]

Some people balked at any attempt to regulate chemicals. A vocal contingent feared that restrictions on some products would ultimately lead to a prohibition on all chemicals. In a 1961 article, the *Washington Farmer* warned that "only a small spark is needed to set off a reaction leading to legislative action banning all chemicals" and urged farmers to become more politically active. The chemical revolution had allowed them to achieve unprecedented affluence and many were distressed at the prospects of working without herbicides, pesticides, and fertilizers. The article downplayed the dangers of chemicals and defiantly insisted, "We cannot and we will not stop or abandon progress."[38] This alarmism was largely unfounded; the regulation of some chemicals did not inexorably lead to an outright ban on all products, and US production of most farm chemicals climbed steadily higher through the 1950s and early 1960s.[39]

Some farmers regarded these new products as a godsend and as a business necessity. Others sounded a more triumphant note, confident in their ability to use science to confront and subdue nature and to make it operate according to their needs. In either case, it was apparent that modern technology had aided their cause by permanently altering natural systems. But Palouse agriculture continued to suffer from an affliction for which science had only imperfect solutions—soil erosion. Improved farming implements and techniques ameliorated but did not solve this serious agricultural problem. After the Second World War, conservation advocates and the USDA again tried to coax farmers into adopting soil-saving practices and again were met with indifference.

Statistical evidence indicated the severity of the erosion problem in the late 1940s and 1950s. The annual comprehensive SCS erosion survey of 1945–1946 indicated that Palouse fields lost an average of 20 tons of soil in this one year alone. Dry conditions the following year reduced that number to a meager 1 ton per acre, but when the rains returned in 1947–1948, so did erosion. Farmers lost an average of 16 tons per acre that year, and in the succeeding three years erosion took an average of 8 tons of soil from every acre of farmland.[40] The SCS estimated that in a rainy year on steep summer-fallowed land a farmer could lose up to 130 tons of soil per acre. One scientist working on the 1948 study quipped, "If that ground still manages to grow 30 bushels of wheat an acre, it will be at a cost of five tons of topsoil per bushel—a poor trade."[41]

Numbers like these were particularly galling to Verle Kaiser, an SCS soil scientist from Spokane. In an internal memo in 1946, Kaiser described a ground and aerial tour of eastern Washington farms that he and several other SCS employees had recently made. He could hardly contain his disappointment. Kaiser griped that a small stream on one farm was "thick as gravy with 15% silt," the result of a nearby field so eroded that it looked like "a giant hand squeezing putty which was oozing out from between the fingers." "Everywhere you look, you see erosion," Kaiser wrote, and as their plane passed over Palouse Falls, a dramatic two-hundred-foot cascade in western Whitman County, he bemoaned the "muddy flood of water" that flowed beneath them. He estimated that "every 30 seconds for the past two weeks, that river has been hauling away a freight carload of some of the best of our soil." Toward the end of the outing and after seeing a day's worth of destruction, a clearly dejected Kaiser lamented, "About that time a person commences to feel a little sick."[42]

Again, the question must be asked: How could this situation persist? How could farmers knowingly behave in a manner that led to the scene that Kaiser saw? Some of the reasons for this disturbing trend in the late 1940s sound similar to those in the 1930s. For one, Palouse farmers still lacked a strong stewardship ethic. Only on rare occasions did local farm leaders speak of the need to protect the land for any reason other than its potential to affect future output; "healthy" land meant "productive" land. Farmers failed to understand the significance of losing topsoil and organic matter—the living skin of the land that had taken thousands of years to accumulate and which intensive farming had largely eliminated in a few short decades. Too few farmers appreciated the inherent natural beauty of the Palouse or questioned the total commodification of the land as acceptable, inevitable, or desirable. Second- and third-generation farmers lived their entire lives without seeing a single clump of bunchgrass or a cool, clear stream on their property. The irony for farmers was that in order to keep their operations productive it would have been helpful to consider the Palouse in ecological terms.

Such events on the Palouse would not surprise historian Colin Duncan. In *The Centrality of Agriculture* (1996), he theorizes that in spite of the obvious improvements that chemicals bring to crop yields in the short term, there are numerous less quantifiable losses associated with soil degradation. In any area that adopts intensive agriculture, Duncan states clearly that the most serious loss, soil erosion, persists precisely because chemicals delude farmers and governments into believing the soil is still fertile, when in fact it often becomes "merely a physical support system for the roots." And once started, the process of degradation is difficult to reverse, as a kind of "fertilizer treadmill" develops—not unlike the treadmill of farm capitalization that economist Willard Cochrane defines—that puts more chemicals into the ground, which allows the soil to be depleted, and forces even more chemicals to be used. Piers Blaikie would agree, having stated that "yield-increasing technologies tend to mask the effect of soil degradation and erosion and make up for declines in fertility that would have occurred if land had been cultivated with a constant level of technology." Indeed, erosion would have been a problem even without chemicals, but scholars who study soil on a global scale contend that new technologies tend to distance the farmer from the land, a disconnect that leads to erosion and the eventual decline of agricultural societies. Soil scientists Daniel Richter and Daniel Markewitz concur, likening yield-maximization tactics to a simplistic "dose-response relationship" of chemical use and high yields that produces unrealistic expectations for future productivity.[43]

A small contingent within American agriculture confronted problems such as this and developed a deeper stewardship ethic in the 1940s. The genesis of this ethic began as a reaction against mechanized industrial agriculture and its tendencies toward land ownership concentration and maximized output. The proponents of the new land ethic were in part a nostalgic lot who yearned for simpler times, when farmers ate more of what they grew and cared less about material progress or the latest consumer goods. Land ethicists also understood the complexities of the twentieth-century world and promoted agricultural systems that were at once ecologically responsible and profitable. They demanded that all land—farmland included—be recognized as possessing unique biological characteristics that deserved the respect of its caretaker. The land was a precious resource that contained living and nonliving things and that had a right to exist beyond its utility to humans.[44]

One of the primary driving forces of the new land ethic was Aldo Leopold, the renowned naturalist, Forest Service supervisor, writer, founding member of the Wilderness Society, part-time farmer, and full-time exponent of better land use. In dozens of department memos, articles, and books directed at both professional and lay audiences, Leopold dramatized the repercussions of irresponsible land owners and users. He made a few people think about the interconnected qualities of natural systems and about how extractive industries can affect land and water resources over great distances.

In his most famous work, *A Sand County Almanac*, published posthumously in 1949, Leopold took aim at the abuses committed by farmers in northern Wisconsin. He criticized intensive agriculture but was also a great believer in the beauty and value of rural living. Leopold owned a small pastoral farmstead and was adamant about the social and emotional benefits of small-scale agriculture. He wrote, "There are two spiritual dangers in not owning a farm. One is the danger of supposing that breakfast comes from the grocery, and the other that heat comes from the furnace." Leopold was among the first to mourn the loss of native vegetation—"the funeral of native flora"—and the overall biological devastation caused by profit-driven farming. He questioned "whether we cannot have both progress and plants" and spoke of the need to cherish the land and see it as something more than a means to an economic end.[45]

Although not on a scale approaching either the Great Plains or the Palouse, erosion also marred the area around Leopold's Wisconsin farm in the 1930s. He watched as CCC crews planted trees and as some farmers began to farm more responsibly because of government incentives. But he saw fundamental flaws in the New Deal agricultural policy of subsidizing practices that should have been standard procedure all along. With land ownership comes responsibility, and Leopold believed that financial incentives were a poor way to educate farmers and inculcate stewardship. Conservation, to Leopold, meant an emotional bond, "a state of harmony between men and land," not a federal policy. Local soil conservation districts should have worked better than federal legislation at promoting stewardship, but they too fell short of his expectations. He scoffed, "The District is a beautiful piece of social machinery, but it is coughing along on two cylinders because we have been too timid, and too anxious for quick success, to tell the farmer the true magnitude of his obligations." Leopold wanted farmers to behave according to what he believed was right, not what was expedient, but found that they instead "selected those remedial practices which were profitable anyhow, and ignored those which were profitable to the community, but not clearly profitable to themselves."[46]

Other writers joined Leopold in castigating American farmers. Ward Shepard, a friend and colleague of Leopold, wrote *Food or Famine* in 1945 to highlight the pitfalls of industrial agriculture. He blamed farmers' penchant for "conquering" nature for a string of agricultural and social woes, including soil erosion (and its attending siltation of rivers) and Third World hunger. Shepard, like Leopold, pushed for stronger local soil conservation districts that could make and enforce laws and become "efficient as an army corps" in stopping soil loss. He also understood the difficulties in making this wish a reality, because "the naïve belief that any kind of organized social action is a wicked restraint of inborn liberties" infected most rural communities.[47]

Two other works, Karl Mickey's *Man and the Soil* (1945) and Fairfield Osborn's *Our Plundered Planet* (1948), echoed the sentiments of Leopold and Shepard. Mickey cautioned readers against viewing nature as a mere commodity to exploit and advised that "the man who would gain nature's rewards must first learn her laws and obey them implicitly." Osborn, director of the New York Zoological Society, challenged the notion that technology could cure all agricultural and societal ills. Through historical examples that spanned three millennia and numerous economic systems, he demonstrated the need for small farms and sustainable agriculture. In each example, Osborn critiqued the incompatibility of profit-driven farming with agricultural sustainability: "Nature gives no blank endorsement to the profit motive."[48] Despite their acknowledged inability to reverse its course, Mickey and Osborn shared a contempt for the mechanized leviathan that American agriculture had become.

A small band of activists was more eager to offer a viable alternative. The organic farming movement began in the late 1930s and 1940s as a reaction against the ecological harm caused by industrial agriculture and the use of chemicals. In their 2001 book, *A Green and Permanent Land*, Randal Beeman and James Pritchard define this movement as a "farming philosophy" that attempted "to see the topsoil and crops from the viewpoint of ecological interrelatedness, which would allow the organic farmer to emulate the natural growing conditions and fertility creation of nature."[49] In general, organic farmers eschewed all pesticides, herbicides, and commercial fertilizers; they relied on animal and green manures and compost for fertilizer, and espoused family-run, small-scale agriculture. Pennsylvanian J. I. Rodale, who published the *Organic Farmer*, and the group Friends of the Land, publishers of a quarterly journal from Ohio, led the way in teaching farmers how to substitute unhealthy, unethical methods with a simpler brand of agriculture that was ecologically responsible *and* profitable.[50]

The stewardship sermons preached by these neophytes went largely unheard in the Palouse, where farmers demonstrated indifference to adopting a new land ethic or organic farming. The local record in the 1940s and 1950s is silent on these issues, suggesting that Palouse farmers were reasonably content with their land-use practices. The rank and file gravitated toward ideas that favored maximized output and judged the land based on its ability to produce. Moreover, most land ethicists and organic farmers came from the East Coast and were likely regarded as ignorant of agricultural realities in the West. In this small corner of the American West, the most remarkable thing about the new land ethic was its conspicuous absence.

The federal government exhibited little interest in alternative agriculture after the war. Although organic farmers and their ideological kin wanted to be profitable, maximized returns on investments were not their primary concern, and they did not draw much attention from the USDA. On one key issue—soil erosion—stewardship advocates and federal agencies shared a common interest, but they differed on how to achieve lasting results. For people like Leopold, Osborn, and Shepard, improvement would come from a heartfelt, emotional, and empathetic relationship with the land and from active local conservation districts. The USDA, on the other hand, essentially recycled New Deal policies to promote conservation. The department used financial incentives to make conservation attractive and profitable. The problem with this policy in the past was that it had been only marginally successful in changing attitudes and creating awareness. With the Depression over and with both yields and the economy booming in the postwar era, an economic answer for chronic erosion seemed unlikely to interest Palouse farmers. Moreover, in the mid-1950s Congress set out to expand foreign markets to alleviate surpluses, an initiative that further hindered conservation efforts. The USDA trotted out old ideas, ignored stewardship as a top priority, and stood by as its plans were greeted with lukewarm enthusiasm.

Absent from the discussion on Palouse erosion were proposals to dictate land use. By the 1940s scientists knew that erosion could be drastically reduced with one simple step: the elimination of annual cropping on the steepest hills and on hilltops. This measure did not require government incentives or subsidies, nor did it involve the adoption of a new land ethic or organic farming. It did, however, demand political courage to stand up to the inevitable backlash that Palouse farmers would have generated. Ever since the New Deal the federal government had taken an active role in regulating countless aspects of the American economy, including agriculture. The time had come to take this a step further and insist that these lands be protected by instituting a known remedy.

Instead, the federal government promoted soil conservation in the 1940s by extending the New Deal policy of rewarding farmers for soil-saving practices. Farmers received cash payments for cover crops, contour plowing, tree planting, and for planting legumes as they had in the past, and by 1947 they also earned federal dollars for stubble mulching and using nitrogen fertilizers. Such programs did not bring about systemic change during the Depression and were even less effective after the war. The return of higher prices in the 1940s and an inability to attract farmer participation contributed to lackluster results. Wheat prices had again topped the $2 per bushel plateau late in the decade, a fact that discouraged conservation. In addition, USDA money was inadequate; Whitman County growers received an average of $255,000 annually for soil conservation—a reasonable sum for a modest plan but insufficient for an ambitious campaign.[51]

Policy makers in Washington DC again resurrected the spirit of the New Deal in 1956. As part of the Agriculture Act of that year, Congress created the Soil Bank as a means of reducing surpluses of staple crops and for retiring erosion-prone land. In the acreage reduction plan (ARP), farmers signed annual contracts with the USDA and promised to replace staple crops (in the case of the Palouse, wheat) with grasses. They received payments based on a percentage of the average yield for the diverted land. Another more significant component, the conservation reserve program (CRP), paid farmers to remove land from production for three to ten years and put it into a soil-saving use—usually perennial grasses. Retired land was thus "banked," or saved from further deterioration but could be put back into production at a later date if supplies dropped. Although the economic situation in the 1950s was not nearly as perilous as in the 1930s, chronic surpluses and continued soil erosion prompted Congress to reinstitute the basic ingredients of the Agricultural Adjustment Act of 1933 and the Soil Conservation and Domestic Allotment Act of 1936.[52]

The Soil Bank plan was never attractive in the inland Northwest and probably had little impact on Palouse erosion. It foundered in part because of an earlier bill—the Agricultural Trade Development and Assistance Act of 1954 (also known as Public Law 480 and the Food for Peace bill). This law attempted to relieve surpluses in the US and to enlist Cold War allies by selling commodities to developing countries in their own currency. Instead of reducing commodity supplies it served as an inducement to increase production because of the expanded market base; as a consequence it negated the appeal of taking land out of production for the Soil Bank. Acreage reduction plans also suffered because of the perception that soil conservation would not generate immediate, sizable financial returns. Many farmers wanted proof that retired or diverted acres would be more profitable than their standard rotations.

In some regions of the country, particularly in the Southwest, diverting acres did pay; some farmers put all of their land in the CRP because it made sound financial sense. But in the Palouse, small grains, legumes, and grasses were still more profitable and most farmers retired only small parcels of poor land—if any. The number of acres under contract grew every year in the 1950s, but the overall acreage remained small in the Northwest. In the peak year of participation, 1960, farmers in all of Washington set aside only 340,000 acres in the CRP; Idaho farmers banked just over 294,000 acres.[53] Whitman County growers never exceeded 2,200 acres in CRP cover crops. In a climate of escalating yields and expanding foreign markets, it made little sense to farm conservatively. Congress rescinded the ARP in 1959 and the CRP in 1965 when it became apparent that the Soil Bank idea would not reduce supplies or save soil.[54]

Government soil conservation programs may have been a low priority for Palouse growers, but scientists and local soil conservation districts gave conservation farming their full attention. Washington State College researchers devoted time to studying the causes of erosion and experimented with crop rotations that produced good yields and held the soil. Reports from the 1940s and 1950s reiterated what had become the mantra of conservation farming—plant cover crops, plow on the contour, and avoid summer fallow. But the scientists could not prove the existence of the one relationship that might have sparked interest in soil conservation: that erosion led to lower crop yields. Scientists offered proof that a plan of continuous conservation farming did not harm profits, but they could not show that its *absence* reduced yields. Instead they relied on vague assertions: "the loss of soil by erosion tends eventually to lower soil productivity and reduce crop yields," and "continued soil losses ... will eventually reduce the fertile topsoil to a point where production will decline." Nowhere could agricultural officials provide hard evidence that erosion would cut profits. As long as the statistical evidence was lacking, conservation advocates and legislators faced an uphill battle in winning the support of farmers or in crafting strong regulations.[55]

Despite their best efforts, Palouse soil conservation districts were not able to prove the economic benefits of conservation farming. District officials often cited the bumper crops of responsible, conservation-minded farmers as evidence that conservation farming made sense. On one farm in northern Whitman County, "an island in a sea of erosion," the North Palouse Soil Conservation District noted that better care of the land made it far more profitable than eroded neighboring farms. A Latah County district reported in 1949 that after participating farmers adopted conservation practices, grain yields went up an average of 21.8 percent. And in Genesee, Idaho, district farmers attributed a 47 percent gain from 1929 to 1947 to improved tillage methods that saved precious topsoil. The problem with these interpretations and dozens of similar stories was that they were anecdotal and inconclusive; they did not factor in the myriad of other inputs that can affect output. Yields went up or down based on many factors, and to attribute the gains solely to conservation bordered on the irresponsible. These anecdotal analyses did little to bolster the arguments in favor of conservation and may have compromised the scientific credibility of regional soil conservation districts.[56]

Like the USDA, university soil agronomists and local conservation districts couched their messages in strictly economic terms. This in itself should not be surprising because all three groups were created with a single goal in mind: to make farms more profitable. They worked to satisfy the wants and needs of farmers and used generous government support to ensure a stable agricultural sector. In many respects, farm leaders and scientists performed admirably, as evinced by the postwar production explosion and growing international trade network. But in the case of soil erosion, financial incentives and arguments failed to institutionalize conservation because policy makers overlooked innovative, controversial ideas that challenged the paradigm of perpetual capitalization and higher yields and that promoted stewardship and land ethics. A federal or regional campaign emphasizing farmer responsibility and deemphasizing economic motivations for conservation had difficulty gathering momentum because stewardship had never been a priority for either farmers or farm leaders. By the 1950s the suggestion that farmers should address ethical or ecological concerns seemed antiquated, as farmers' ties to older agrarian traditions faded with each generation, and it would take years for the agricultural establishment to change course.

Occasional signs of progress surfaced, however, and augured some hope for the future. Through the 1940s and 1950s Palouse conservation districts, often in conjunction with local chambers of commerce, sponsored yearly "soil rallies" and "conservation days" to broaden the appeal of soil conservation and to make it a community event. The towns of Colfax, Pullman, Palouse, Moscow, Genesee, and Uniontown all staged popular gatherings that included field demonstrations and lectures from area specialists. Sponsors tried to make their events fun, informative, and family-oriented to engender a greater respect for the land and a fuller appreciation for better farming practices. At one rally in Moscow in 1954, seventy-five local Future Farmers of America and 4–H members teamed up to move nearly fifteen tons of soil by hand from the bottom of a slope back to the top of a hill. An estimated crowd of four hundred watched as this one field, which had lost over ninety tons of soil per acre to erosion, was partially restored. The work repaired a mere fraction of one farm and could hardly be replicated on a large scale—nor could it be guaranteed that the soil would not erode away the following spring. But the effort clearly showed the tenacity of a few committed citizens in the fight against erosion and in the promotion of a conservation ethic.[57]

Conservationists occasionally used religious appeals to publicize the need for stewardship. The National Association of Soil Conservation Districts, an umbrella organization that oversaw local work, began promoting Soil Stewardship Sunday in 1946. The association called on religious leaders in farming communities to devote one sermon per year to soil conservation issues and to remind parishioners of their Christian duty to protect God's green (and brown) earth. Similar in tone to Walter Lowdermilk's Eleventh Commandment idea of 1939, Soil Stewardship Sunday implored farmers to acknowledge their unique responsibilities as caretakers of the land and warned them of the repercussions of neglect and abuse. At least one local conservation district concurred that godliness and stewardship went hand in hand. A North Palouse district official said that the good farmer downplayed the financial aspects of conservation and instead was "motivated by considerations of a different and more lasting nature—his responsibility before God, the well-being and regard of his family, [and] the improvement of the community in which he lives." Though there was "no denying the dollar values of conservation farming," religion, family, and community esprit de corps permeated the discussion on land ethics.[58]

For most of the farming establishment in the Northwest, however, chemical use indicated proper land use. In a milieu that revered technology, farmers saw herbicides and commercial fertilizers as a modern, progressive means of maintaining the long-term health of their land. Herbicides allowed farmers to eliminate weeds with one or two simple spraying applications, thus reducing the use of harrows and cultivators to break up young weeds. And because less tilling meant less erosion, herbicides became an important part of an overall conservation farming plan. The use of fertilizers, especially the powerful anhydrous ammonia, also signified responsible land use. By returning nitrogen to heavily eroded areas, farmers artificially restored fertility and reduced the need for summer fallow, the leading cause of Palouse erosion. But fertilizers also ensured that steep hills would be tilled every year and likely not planted to perennial grasses. The pressure to produce on these vulnerable areas would continue. Moreover, the indiscriminate use of untested chemicals put the farmer and his land at risk. Soil specialists were careful to insist that chemicals were no substitute for other conservation practices such as contour plowing and stubble mulching, but according to Ed Perdue, associate editor of the Washington Farmer, "whenever and however the needed better practices are adopted, continued and increasing use of commercial fertilizers will be among them."[59]

With all the activity and attention that conservation farming generated, it is not surprising that the erosion situation showed occasional signs of improvement. By the end of the 1950s certain locales could boast that through the collective efforts of a majority of farmers, fewer gullies and rivulets formed and more soil stayed in place. Reports filtered in from farms in the vicinity of Uniontown, Palouse, and Endicott, indicating substantial progress in conservation. The SCS and local newspapers praised the efforts of farmers in these areas and urged their neighbors to follow suit. Although such successes could have been the result of low rainfall, the encouraging news suggested that some farms were on the mend. It is also possible that all the hard work and advice of scientists, journalists, and civic leaders had finally been internalized and that a number of farmers had decided to employ soil-saving concepts. In addition, some farmers may have thought about the ecological effects of soil loss and taken to heart the notions of land ethics and stewardship.[60]

C. Max Harper, a farmer in St. John, Washington, was one such convert. He said in 1953 that instead of being a financial burden, "conservation work has paid its way. It hasn't cost me a penny. . . . My land is more valuable by quite a lot than it would have been." Harper was also a realist; when asked if his conservation plan had stopped erosion entirely, he replied, "No, but it has been greatly checked." And he added a note of sentimentality uncommon in the Palouse, saddened by the erosion that still left its marks on his land: "When the mud is running and ditches form I feel like I used to when I lost a horse." Ira Long, who farmed in the shadow of Kamiak Butte, also believed in the restorative powers of conservation farming. Through stubble-mulching old wheat stalks, he claimed to have reversed years of erosion, making clay hilltops fertile again. And after Ted Meinders instituted a comprehensive farm plan on his farm south of Pullman, he found "practically no ditches." He agreed with Long in the ability of crop remnants to build tilth, stating that it is "very important to leave all crop residue on the soil in order to build the soil back to produce more than it has before."[61] The line between financial gain and personal responsibility, at times artificially drawn, could occasionally be breached. Progressive farmers struggled to reconcile the two sides, keeping one foot firmly on the side of immediate maximum gain and the other attempting to gain a toehold in the relatively new realm of conservation.

In contrast to these hopeful signs of improvement, most reports indicated that much work had yet to be done. Newspaper articles from the 1950s and early 1960s were filled with stories of the destructive effects of normal winter and spring rains and the occasional devastation caused by harder downpours. The *Pullman Herald* called the 1952–1953 erosion season the worst on record and noted that some farmers had to reseed winter wheat plots on steep slopes. The *Washington Farmer* called the erosion situation "worrisome" in 1957 and warned that while conservation had become more popular, it was still "not enough to insure wheat production at present yields 25, 50, or more years to come." Reporters from the Tekoa and Colfax areas in 1960 and 1961 observed heavy soil losses, as spring runoff stripped land of not only soil, but of seed and fertilizer as well. The overall impression gleaned from the local press depicted a gloomy picture; erosion may have ebbed in places, but most of the Palouse saw only incremental progress.[62]

Census and scs data corroborated these impressions. Two key indices of conservation farming—summer fallow and contour plowing—both showed disappointing results. The number of acres in summer fallow actually jumped 25 percent from 1944 to 1959, in defiance of the aggressive campaign to end this pernicious tradition. Contour plowing, a relatively simple and inexpensive soil-saving procedure, was conducted on only 24 percent of fields in Whitman and Latah counties in 1964.[63] Widespread erosion continued because of the inconclusive links between erosion and crop performance, ineffective federal programs, the impotence of soil conservation districts, and weak or nonexistent stewardship values. The annual scs survey of Palouse farms confirmed the trend: from 1939 to 1949 average soil losses totaled 9.75 tons per acre and in the 1950s that sum fell to 8 tons per acre—well above what conservationists considered acceptable. The 1950s was also a slightly drier decade than the 1940s, which may account for the reduced soil losses. Testimony from first-hand accounts and empirical evidence suggested that after a long-running, uneven series of land-use propaganda and legislation, erosion was still a major problem.[64]

By the 1960s it was clear that a new approach was needed. Leaving chemical safety and soil conservation up to the individual farmer was not sufficient. Faced with the pressures of fixed costs and unsure about the economic hazards of chemical misuse or erosion, farmers were reluctant conservationists, unlikely to instigate corrective measures on their own. The federal government and conservation districts, as representatives of the farming community, honored the wishes of their constituents by avoiding radical land-use regulations. And the scientific community, the supposed vanguard of agricultural innovation, merely repeated the admonitions and advice of the 1930s. Few people promoted the fresh ideas coming from land ethicists or organic farmers, while the farming establishment seemed inextricably bound to an ethos of maximized production. When problems arose, most farmers sought stopgap solutions and failed to consider the long-term ecological importance of healthier land. In most regards, the farming establishment was economically driven, and so long as the status quo allowed Palouse farming to stay profitable, the chances of comprehensive reform were remote.

7   LESSONS NEGLECTED AND REJECTED

THE UNORTHODOX and gifted American poet, e e cummings, commented on the state of the industrialized world in his 1944 poem, "Pity This Busy Monster, Manunkind":

> pity this busy monster, manunkind,
> not. Progress is a comfortable disease:
> your victim (death and life safely beyond)
>
> plays with the bigness of his littleness
> —electrons deify one razorblade
> into a mountainrange; lenses extend
>
> unwish through curving wherewhen till unwish
> returns on its unself
>   A world of made
> is not a world of born—pity poor flesh
>
> and trees, poor stars and stones, but never this
> fine specimen of hypermagical
>
> ultraomnipotence. We doctors know
>
> a hopeless case if—listen: there's a hell
> of a good universe next door; let's go

The poet felt uneasy about the whirlwind pace of technological and social change that had enveloped much of the world. He sympathized with God's creations—flesh, trees, stars, and stones—that had been exploited by "this fine specimen of hypermagical ultraomnipotence," that is, humans. Brimming with confidence and arrogance, humanity's overarching faith in progress leads so often to ruin that some ecosystems can become unlivable. At the end, the poet and other "doctors" who comprehend the magnitude of the destruction seek asylum in a neighboring universe. This world had lost its way, leading cummings to sarcastically suggest starting over someplace else.

Two decades after cummings penned those words, more Americans became aware of the unpleasant or dangerous implications of intensive agriculture. Most were not as cynical as cummings and supported steps to make the planet a cleaner, more hospitable place. Because of a desire to restore the beauty and ecological health of the nation and because of environmental tragedies such as the Cuyahoga River fire and the Santa Barbara oil spill, both occurring in 1969, farmers faced new pressures in the 1960s and 1970s to modify activities that harmed the environment. In response to the pressures, federal agencies began writing stricter laws governing farm chemicals and surface-water quality. The cultural zeitgeist of maximizing agricultural production, dominant since the days of Euro-American settlement, now had to contend with a nascent environmental movement. The sudden tilt in favor of preserving resources and away from ceaseless exploitation should have augured well for the Palouse, a region that had seen its share of abuse. Implementing America's environmental laws also should have made people like cummings feel better about their world.

As events unfolded, cummings's pessimism seemed apt. Farmers and farm interest groups at the local and national level spent countless hours and dollars refuting claims that agriculture despoiled the land. From the early 1960s through the early 1980s they habitually denied the existence of ecological problems, blamed urbanites and industry for ruining the environment, and resisted government attempts to regulate farm practices. The defensive, rearguard tactics of the agricultural establishment compromised any hopes that farm environments could be improved. By the mid-1980s, erosion in the Palouse hills was as bad as ever and streams were still choked with sediment and chemicals. After years of neglect and a wave of federal laws, Palouse agriculturalists remained determined to maintain the status quo. The intransigence of these "busy monsters" guaranteed exacerbated environmental problems and invited more aggressive legislative remedies in the future.

The 1960s and 1970s saw Palouse farmers more fully express the concept of the agrarian liberal. Subsidized farming, in the form of USDA research, federal price supports, and the construction and maintenance of a marketing and transportation infrastructure, grew tremendously in this period, especially notable after the construction of the dams on the lower Snake River, making grain shipping to the coast all the more appealing. Payments for soil conservation merely capped off what had become a huge network of federal government assistance. Thus, farmers were the polar opposites of conservative, as they received government monies both in cash form and by less direct means. Rather, they were the quintessential liberals, demanding federal help to subsidize what were in many cases multimillion-dollar grain enterprises. Yet at the same time, partly in an effort to deflect criticism from environmentalists, Palouse farmers used the rhetoric of the American agrarian—claiming that they were the noble, responsible food supplier of the world—to win public support for continued aid and to rationalize intensive agriculture. For the most part the tactic paid off, as farmers easily fended off most land-use regulations and kept the federal money flowing, further demonstrating the essential political, ideological, and economic paradoxes in the modern history of the American West.

The publication of Rachel Carson's best seller *Silent Spring* in 1962 marked a turning point in agricultural and environmental history.[1] Carson informed millions of readers that commercially grown food contained substantial amounts of chemicals that harmed birds, fish, people, and beneficial insects. Despite what her critics said, Carson did not wish to outlaw all farm chemicals, but she supported banning some and argued for more rigorous government regulation of all chemical agents. Although others had voiced similar concerns, the reason for Carson's immediate and lasting impact had to do with her eloquence as a writer and with an aggressive promotional campaign from an established publisher, Houghton Mifflin. *Silent Spring* could be found on bookshelves all over the United States in the early 1960s, making it an instant success both commercially and as a catalyst for environmental and social change.

Catcalls descended on Carson even before her book appeared on store shelves and intensified after its release. Most of the angry words came from farmers, university scientists, and chemical manufacturers, while slightly milder criticism came from the USDA.[2] In the Palouse, reaction was flippant and terse. George W. Fischer, dean of Washington State University's College of Agriculture, accused Carson of igniting an unfounded "cancer scare" and declared that "aspirin alone is said to cause almost twice as many deaths per year in the United States as ALL the pesticides do directly." Richard Maxwell, a Washington State University researcher, credited DDT with eradicating tropical diseases from the US and predicted widespread crop failures if it were banned. Entomologist E. W. Anthon argued that "if it were not for insecticides we could very well rival India and China in poverty and misery." The hyperbole of these men belied their stated purpose of exposing Carson as an emotional and unreliable scientific authority; it is ironic that their histrionics made them appear more biased than Carson.[3]

The scientific community's counterattack could not change political inertia. A better-informed public demanded tighter regulations. Congress revised the Federal Insecticide, Fungicide, and Rodenticide Act (FIFRA) in 1964 and 1972, making the registration process for new and existing chemicals more stringent. Several states issued DDT bans in the late 1960s and the federal government began limiting its use to certain crops until it imposed a national moratorium in 1973.[4] In Washington and Idaho the number of restrictions on chemicals jumped sharply after 1962 and continued to climb through the 1970s. Although neither state outlawed DDT before 1973, its use in Washington dropped quickly after 1970, when several processing plants in the Columbia Basin refused to handle crops exposed to the pesticide. Regional farming interests touted all the positive aspects of chemical use— feeding the hungry world, fighting disease, and inexpensive food—yet could not convince consumers (i.e., voters) to continue supporting a weak regulatory system. The political landscape was changing in the 1960s, and it forced farmers to adapt.[5]

Nitrates in surface and groundwater also drew more attention in the 1960s. Because nitrogen fertilizers such as anhydrous ammonia washed into streams after heavy rainfalls, they stimulated plant growth and caused streams to become algae-choked and oxygen-depleted. Speculation rose that nitrates leached through the soil and tainted municipal drinking-water supplies. Although less toxic than most pesticides, the presence of nitrates in the soil and water worried rural communities and put farmers in a defensive mode.[6]

Farming interests accepted polluted water and shifted blame for its occurrence away from agriculture. The Columbia Plateau Resources Council, a consortium of Northwest soil experts, downplayed the significance of polluted watersheds. The council stated in a 1967 report that farm communities "can tolerate lower [water quality] standards than demanded by other segments of business and society" and added that remedies would be costly to implement and maintain. William Schmidtman, chairman of the Washington State Soil and Water Conservation Committee, exonerated farmers when he told a Spokane audience that "scarcely a single lake, river, or stream has escaped the pollution onslaught" caused by residential and industrial development.[7] In a speech to the US Chamber of Commerce the following year, agriculture secretary Orville Freeman acknowledged the "algal blooms" in ponds and streams that excessive nitrogen caused, but insisted that farm chemicals were only a "minor contributor" to water pollution. At a Washington State University fertilizer and pesticide conference in 1970, one scientist claimed that fertilizers contributed only a "drop in the bucket" to nitrate levels in Palouse waters.[8] Journalists wrote that farmers could not afford fertilizers in quantities that would cause stream eutrophication and that only small amounts of nitrates could leach through dryland soils to the water table.[9] Although the agricultural establishment worked to reassure an increasingly edgy public that farming did not cause serious environmental harm, studies in the 1970s and 1980s would prove them wrong.

The definition of water pollution expanded in the 1960s to include sediment. Long considered only a nuisance or a sign of decreased soil fertility, sediment accumulation in streams and behind dams became an important regional and national issue. John Wilson, a USDA geologist working in the Spokane SCS office, wrote in 1967 that "sediment pollution is one of the most serious problems of water quality" confronting the Northwest. In addition to the economic losses associated with sedimentation, "the aesthetic value of . . . clean water" warranted action. USDA secretary Freeman voiced similar concerns in 1968, stating that "sediment is a terrible example of a resource out of place. It hurts the land where it comes from and hurts the water where it goes." However, like the nitrogen debate, Freeman excused farmers from any wrongdoing, disingenuously railing against rural housing developments that produced "*from 2 to 200 times* the amount of sediment as nearby farmland."[10]

The dual menace of nitrates and sediment amplified the need to control Palouse erosion. Solutions remained elusive, as governments and local experts continued to rely on shopworn and ineffective policies. The failed Soil Bank program expired in 1965, but the USDA revived it under a different name later that year. Under the "new" plan, farmers received cash payments for strip cropping, stubble mulching, and for planting grasses and legumes. They were also partially compensated for the cost of planting trees, installing drainage systems, and building ponds and small dams. Participation in the program was limited and any impact on erosion or pollution was probably minimal. After a slight surge in interest in 1965 and 1966, Washington and

Idaho farmers devoted few acres to the program. By the 1970 planting season, the program had enlisted roughly 90,000 acres in both states for vegetative cover, another 90,000 acres for stubble mulching, and only 781 acres for new tree plantings—a low rate of participation considering the increased attention to water quality and soil erosion.[11]

Soil conservation districts continued their efforts against erosion. Unable to raise tax revenues or to create local land-use ordinances, Washington and Idaho districts were helpless to make demands on farmers. They could only offer advice when asked for help and there was no way to ensure that prescriptive measures would be instituted on a long-term basis.[12] According to soil scientist Leonard C. Johnson, few farmers were inclined to solicit district services. He wrote in 1973 that interest in erosion "stems mostly from public concern and disgust with pollution of streams and reservoirs by soil sediments, not from landowners' concern for the soil they are losing." Johnson predicted that unless soil conservation districts were granted a broader mandate, farmers could look forward to "the appearance to some rather unusual words in legislation dealing with soil erosion: words such as *mandatory, authority,* and *compel.*"[13] Federal and state legislation in fact *was* in the offing, but it did not involve empowering conservation districts, which were increasingly superfluous by the 1970s.

Progressive agricultural states considered strict land-use regulations a necessity. After citizens in Iowa became aware of the costs associated with river and stream sedimentation, the state legislature passed a law in 1971 granting conservation districts broad powers to reduce erosion. The law allowed districts to set maximum erosion levels according to soil type and required landowners to adopt conservation practices. In southwestern Wisconsin, the Vernon County conservation district won approval of an ordinance in 1976 requiring farmers to either strip-crop their land or submit to an overall conservation plan. In each case a majority of farmers put aside property-rights qualms and allowed a quasi-governmental body to make decisions in the public's interest. By the early 1980s twenty-eight states had given conservation districts the power to regulate land use, and fifteen states allocated revenues directly to individual districts. The steps taken in these states, many of which had relatively minor erosion problems compared to the Palouse, stood in sharp contrast to the laissez-faire situation in Washington and Idaho—two states that sorely needed improvement.[14]

Soil conservation correctives in the Palouse were neither mandatory nor inexpensive. After SCS or soil conservation district field workers visited a farm, they usually drew up several conservation alternatives for the farmer to consider. The options ranged from radical—converting all acres to grasses, legumes, and trees—to conservative—installing drainage pipes, planting grasses only on the steepest slopes, and keeping most of the land in grains. In every proposal experts advised farmers to eliminate or curtail summer fallow, to stop stubble burning, and to till-under all crop remnants. Most of those suggestions entailed some expenditure and several, especially tree planting and drainage work, were costly to install and maintain. The cost per acre for implementing these plans could be as low as $4 or $5 per acre, but more ambitious proposals ran close to $20 an acre. If a farmer owned 1,500 or 2,000 acres (an increasingly common occurrence in the 1960s and 1970s) the cost of a conservation plan could prove prohibitive, even with government cost-sharing incentives. The price tag for soil conservation was considerable, especially when extended over the entire region.[15] A study conducted by conservation districts in the Palouse and northeastern Oregon in 1971 found that a comprehensive soil conservation plan for the area's 10 million acres would cost from $250 to $500 million. And after the initial outlay, the government would be compelled to spend millions more annually on maintenance and for increased subsidies for acres taken out of production. The longer farmers waited, however, the more soil they lost, and the more expensive erosion control would become.[16]

In response to the ongoing problem, a host of regional soil associations formed in the 1960s. The Columbia Plateau Resources Council, first convened in 1965, proposed to use private donations to fund conservation projects that it hoped would inspire participation in all programs. But the council was short-lived and by decade's end it fell victim to tepid public support and dwindling revenues. Conservation district officials from Washington, Idaho, and Oregon organized the Pacific Northwest Conservation Program in 1968 to offer advice to the incoming Nixon administration. Its main goal— a revival of long-term conservation contracts—was never popular during the Soil Bank years and new agriculture secretary Clifford Hardin quickly rejected the idea. Another collection of Northwest conservation district officials banded together in 1970 to lobby once again for long-term land contracts, including increased cost-sharing for restoration work. Washington representative Tom Foley introduced legislation for the plan in 1972, but could not convince Congress to support it, and yet another erosion program was stillborn. The most surprising aspect of these proposals was their blatant repetitiveness; the creation of new conservation organizations did not translate into bold initiatives that might have made a difference.[17]

Market forces and government subsidy programs were partly responsible for the persistence of soil erosion problems and the unpopularity of conservation. The Green Revolution associated with agricultural chemicals, first experienced in Western countries in the 1940s and 1950s, began to affect the developing world in the 1960s. Despite periodic bouts with famine, the result was a better fed and growing world population; in the 1960s, worldwide population increased 22 percent, in large measure because of an expanding agricultural sector. Because most developing countries still relied on food imports, the appearance of growing markets encouraged farmers to maximize productivity and made acreage reduction look illogical. Karl Hobson, a Washington State University agricultural economist, wrote in 1966 that wheat production had increased, "but not as fast as it needs," implying that unless more acres went into wheat and unless yields increased, hunger and famine would follow. Other economists reasoned that maximized production was a necessary foreign policy tool, enabling the US to use its agricultural prowess to feed the poor and fend off communism in developing nations.[18] Soil conservationists, on the other hand, argued that if Americans wished to feed the world in the long term, they should accept less than full production in the short term. The two sides agreed on the final goal but differed on how to get there.

Government subsidy programs that encouraged summer fallow and intensive wheat production stymied conservation. From the mid-1950s, the USDA set production targets to regulate supplies and prices. To receive payments, farmers reduced their acreage and were partly reimbursed for the idle land according to its average yield over previous years. Farmers typically put idled land into summer fallow, the scourge of soil conservationists and a leading cause of erosion. They fallowed land to hold soil moisture in order to benefit the following year's crop—a tradition that had proven effective and which had endured despite the admonishments of countless conservationists. Farmers could have planted allotted acres to grass, but fallowed land gave them more flexibility because it could be returned to grains quickly; grasses required three to four years before reaching full maturity, thus committing the farmer for a longer period. Many farmers also tilled previously retired acres, including land planted to trees, to leave it fallow to satisfy subsidy requirements. As a result of these policies and beliefs, more than 380,000 acres were fallowed in 1969. Farmers disregarded years of scientific advice and continued market strategies that would secure federal dollars.[19]

If people wanted less erosion and cleaner water, they would need to look beyond the agricultural establishment. Forty years of research, planning, and federal programs had attained only modest improvement. Tabulating an exact dollar amount spent on conservation would be impossible, but it certainly ran into the hundreds of millions. The Washington state legislature finally seized the opportunity to promote better land use in 1971. Growing support for a cleaner environment, coupled with persistent pollution, prodded lawmakers in Olympia to pass the Washington State Environmental Policy Act (SEPA). If fully implemented, this law had the potential to impose strict conservation measures on the state's industries and cities.

Among SEPA's key precepts was a recognition that "each person has a fundamental and inalienable right to a healthful environment and that each person has a responsibility to contribute to the preservation and enhancement of the environment." To achieve this end, the law required the state government and businesses to submit to a review process before engaging in new projects that might harm the environment. If state regulators believed that damage might occur, they could demand a more thorough environmental impact statement and ultimately require modifications to a proposed action. Bowing to political pressures, the legislature exempted many activities from this review, including those relating to farming. But the state also added a key provision that allowed municipalities and counties to establish Environmentally Sensitive Areas (ESAs)—places with vulnerable soil and water resources or with unique natural features—that could be subject to state review, even if activities were on the "exempt" list. In other words, SEPA and its ESA proviso opened the way for assertive communities to pressure farmers into adopting conservation.[20]

Saddled with the responsibility of addressing a key part of SEPA, Whitman County chose a nonconfrontational course. While eight other Washington counties designated ESAs, Whitman County listed none. In its comprehensive plan for 1978, a document used to guide economic development, the county claimed that erosion, water quality, and wildlife habitat were high priorities, but added, "no agricultural activities will be discouraged." Commissioners supported places dubbed "natural conservation areas" without clearly defining them or their specific location. The county seemed to be in no mood to challenge farmers through aggressive planning, resulting in an anemic, vague, and wholly forgettable policy statement.[21]

Idaho showed even less interest in preserving resources. Its legislature never passed a SEPA-like bill, indicative of the state's reactionary attitude toward government regulation. Some Idaho counties developed comprehensive plans in the 1970s in an attempt to control excessive sprawl and to promote wise resource use. The Latah County plan, written in 1979, was equally as hollow as Whitman County's. The authors acknowledged the importance of soil, calling it the source of its "heritage and livelihood," yet avoided any mention of farming practices. Instead, Latah County commissioners asked for more detailed soil data before considering land-use policies—a curious request, considering all the soil and erosion surveys that had existed for years.[22]

Before SEPA proved ineffective, the federal government again stepped to the fore. On the heels of the first Earth Day celebrations and at the dawn of the modern environmental movement, Congress passed the Federal Water Pollution Control Act (FWPCA) in 1972. The law recognized the foul condition of many waterways and took unprecedented steps "to restore and maintain the chemical, physical, and biological integrity of the nation's waters." Its provisions included the elimination of pollutants in navigable waters by 1985, making waters fishable, swimmable, and drinkable by 1983, and the construction of wastewater treatment plants to process water from industries and municipalities. Congress turned over the enforcement of the Pollution Control Act to a new agency—the Environmental Protection Agency (EPA)—to avoid conflict of interest problems that plagued the Departments of Interior and Agriculture. The EPA in turn handed over the regulatory reins to states to assuage congressional conservatives who loathed federal resource planning.[23]

The Pollution Control Act's preamble was ambitious, but for the Palouse the fine print contained the most provocative material. Section 208 of the act recognized for the first time the role of nonpoint pollutants in surface waters. Nonpoint pollution is that which comes from diffuse sources, not from a single factory, smokestack, or drain pipe, and is a primary concern in Western states where runoff from neighborhoods, farms, ranches, logging operations, and mines account for most of the region's water pollution. This provision was the first of its kind in US environmental law, a landmark decision in which Congress tried to get control over a complex array of environmental threats. Section 208 required states to institute the latest, most efficient means at their disposal to control nonpoint pollution. These best management practices were intended to be the strongest medicine to date in the struggle to save America's dying waters.[24]

After years of fretting over the possibility of heavy-handed regulations, Palouse farmers now faced the reality of the Pollution Control Act and Section 208. With the lofty goal of making all waters at least fishable and swimmable, farmers braced for the worst. As the process unfolded, however, their fears must have subsided. Work on developing new policies began soon after the Pollution Control Act became law when Washington state's Department of Ecology (DOE) summoned Washington State University, conservation districts, and concerned farmers to solicit their opinions. This amalgam of technical and lay constituents formed the Dryland Technical Advisory Committee, which would create a list of best management practices to satisfy Section 208 requirements. The makeup of the committee did not bode well for Palouse conservation; its members had an undistinguished record in reducing erosion in the past and gave no indication that their tune had changed in the 1970s.[25]

The committee exposed its sensibilities in its 1976 draft plan of action. The committee issued three goals to accompany proposed regulations and best management practices: (1) economic feasibility; (2) social acceptability; and (3) water quality improvement. The committee's priorities were alarming. The Pollution Control Act and Section 208 contained language that stressed cost efficiency, but it was not to be the primary concern of local regulators. Nor did the law express interest in its local popularity; Congress was well aware that reducing pollution would mean offending some interest groups. The technical committeee's demotion of water quality goals reflected the conservative views of its members who engaged in the Section 208 process to protect their narrow interests and to subvert a congressional directive.[26]

The committee staged dozens of public meetings in the mid-1970s. When the Washington State University Cooperative Extension Service and conservation districts publicized these events, anxious farmers came out in droves, eager to dilute any ambitious ideas. Perceived threats to their economic health and property rights energized them to resist change. Environmental advocates were scarce and a virtual nonfactor in developing the committee's policy. The environmental movement, still in its incipient stages, was no match for well-organized farmers and their university allies.[27]

One critical voice left to fend for himself was Morley Hagen, a local conservationist from the National Audubon Society. His opening remarks at one of these hearings spelled out the obvious: "I don't think I have very many friendly faces here." Hagen was about to indict farmers for abusing their land and seemingly everyone in the room knew it. He accused them of selfishly wasting soil at the expense of future generations, claiming "you are only robbing us all—not only yourselves—but everyone else." Hagen, like Verle Kaiser had years before, anguished over the thick brown soup that washed over Palouse falls, especially in late winter and spring. He said, "It looks exactly like someone was pouring rich, heavy chocolate over the cliff."

Like most westerners, Hagen would have preferred a local solution to this local and regional problem—it could have been the "ideal method." "But," he added, "regulations are the result of failure to do a good job." Whether his actions were foolish or productive, Hagen bravely stood up to farming orthodoxy in the Palouse, a place where dissent was rarely rewarded.[28]

The overwhelming bulk of public opinion on the Section 208 matter came down firmly against federal, state, or local control over land use. Wheat grower Chris Rangbold insisted that any regulation or law used to implement Section 208 "not be in conflict with constitutional and traditional property rights." In a transparent attempt to simultaneously prevent erosion and avert federal action, Clyde Wilsey of the Palouse Soil Conservation District supported the idea of "more and better farm chemicals for weed and pest control with reasonable regulations." This was an idea that dated back to at least the 1950s, when chemical agents were a more central feature of the soil conservationist's message. By the late 1970s, however, a more astute and sensitive culture was less willing to trade erosion for chemicals. Robert Stuhlmiller clearly took exception to Morley Hagen's remarks, and defended himself against the charge of land abuse: "I am a farmer, and an environmentalist, not maybe by Morley Hagen's interpretation, but I think by Webster's I am." Stuhlmiller, too, was strongly against implementing the Section 208 regulations. Wheat farmer Maynard Cutler might have been the most defensive of the dozens of participants. He questioned whether or not Palouse waters were even polluted in the first place. "Are our rivers and streams not fishable and swimmable?" he asked. "And if so, which ones?" Anyone at those meetings, most farmers included, probably could have pointed to the small creeks that ran through their own land to answer Cutler. But his questions accurately reveal the level of farmer frustration with what they perceived as the heavy hand of government, lording over them and making them jump through bureaucratic hoops to solve problems that they did not consider urgent.[29]

Before the technical committee and the state DOE issued new policies, based in part on these public hearings, several scientific studies pointed to problems with Palouse waters. A Washington State University Agricultural Experiment Station bulletin in 1973 examined surface water quality in the South Fork of the Palouse River and two tributaries and found high levels of nitrogen and phosphorous, both from farm and municipal sources. It also discovered that water temperatures were alarmingly high, with normal summer temperatures of 20 to 26 degrees Celsius and occasional readings of 29 degrees. A University of Idaho study two years later downplayed agriculture's impact on nitrogen levels but showed high sediment and phosphorous levels attributable to farm runoff, adding scientific backing to years of lay observation.[30]

A 1974 joint report of the Washington and Idaho universities warned of increasing nitrate levels in Northwest streams. While a broader debate raged over whether the pollution had originated from artificial fertilizers, naturally occurring nitrates, or from cattle, all agreed it was transported to streams via erosion. The report found that the Palouse River and its tributaries contained elevated levels of fecal coliform, low levels of dissolved oxygen, tremendously high levels of sediment, and had high water temperatures— a drastic change for the state, which had deemed Palouse River waters suitable for drinking, recreation, and wildlife in 1967. Although the political climate had shifted, time worked against a quick fix; several of the authors of the 1974 report expressed grave doubts that watersheds such as the Palouse could be cleaned up by the mid-1980s, even with generous public support.[31]

The Section 208 process also included the USDA. The Washington DOE asked the USDA for a new report on Palouse erosion and climate. The USDA complied in 1978 by submitting the Palouse Cooperative River Basin Study, a thorough 180-page examination of the entire Palouse River basin that further dramatized the need for conservation. USDA researchers began using a new formula in the mid-1970s for establishing erosion rates, and it showed a far worse problem than earlier surveys. They now believed that fourteen tons of soil per acre eroded from farmland per year, up significantly from the eight-to-ten-ton figure from older SCS models. On the area's steepest hills, an average of twenty tons of soil were lost each year. The study concluded that 90 percent of the land had an erosion problem, and that roughly 10 percent had lost all its topsoil and was producing grains only because of massive fertilizer use. New data revealed disturbing information that had serious consequences for the agricultural community.[32]

The USDA basin study traced the relationship between erosion and chemical pollutants and found a direct relationship between erosion and nitrate levels in streams and determined that most pollutants originated from farmlands. The report noted that if erosion rills cut deeply into the ground, nitrogen fertilizers could easily be disturbed. Phosphorous was another concern, even though the state had not yet set tolerance standards. Both anhydrous ammonia and phosphorous caused locally heavy algae growth, making water unfit for drinking and damaging fish habitat. USDA researchers mentioned herbicides but decided against further study because so many were in use with toxicity levels that were "extremely variable." Nevertheless, they believed that "even very low levels of these chemicals in the runoff may be enough for environmental concern."[33]

The USDA study looked at stream channels and waterflow. When water became thick with silt, it moved faster and tended to cut into soft stream-banks—which loosened more sediment. Researchers estimated that 390 of 533 stream miles in the basin had erosion problems, losing an average of fifty-five tons of sediment per mile every year. Moreover, silt and debris eventually settled behind dams on the lower Snake River where it created problems for salmon and steelhead habitat and forced the Army Corps of Engineers to dredge the channel repeatedly. The USDA helped explain that the costs of foregoing soil conservation extended well beyond the Palouse.[34]

Researchers also indicated that erosion affected crop yields. The department's data showed that had erosion been held in check since the 1930s, technological advancements since then "should have produced an average yield of 65–70 bushels per acre instead of the present 50 bushels per acre." The USDA concluded that "because improved technology has produced much greater benefits on non-eroded land than on eroded land, erosion *is* adversely affecting crop yields in the Palouse." After decades of soil losses of fourteen tons per acre per year, the USDA estimated that farmers were now losing approximately 150,000 bushels of potential wheat every season.[35]

The USDA served notice with this study that current practices were neither sustainable nor profitable. Drawing from data on soils, climate, and topography, the department devised working farm regimens that would keep farming profitable and reduce erosion. The good news was that "the problem of soil erosion and water pollution from sediments can be solved. The farmer can do little to change the weather, kind of soil, or steepness of the land he farms, but he can change the way he farms the land." The prescriptions were simple: "reduce acreages of summer fallow, till the soil less, retire the steepest, most erosive areas from cultivation, change cropping systems, divide long slopes with two or more crops and install terraces on long, gentle slopes." If politicians implemented a program of "thorough application of maximum levels of conservation practices," including the permanent retirement of thirty-five thousand acres of highly erodible land, the USDA claimed that erosion could be reduced by 80 percent.[36]

Researchers demanded that "much more conservation should be applied in the basin as County water quality plans are implemented," but they also knew that sweeping changes were controversial and expensive and that "someone will have to pay this cost, either the farmer or the taxpayer or both." In the end the USDA was pessimistic about Section 208 being adequate to clean up the watershed: "Legislative changes may be needed before adequate conservation can be achieved." The department sensed that a weak Section 208 regulation was coming and thus called on the state to devise "improved methods to motivate people to make needed changes in farming practices."[37]

The state DOE's final Section 208 plan, released in September 1979, put almost no constraints on farmers. An exhaustive amount of research and resources produced a weak and gelded document, with the adoption of best management practices being entirely voluntary. After receiving a federal directive to stop erosion and clean up watersheds, Washington's agricultural establishment ensured that regulations would be voluntary and ultimately ineffectual. Palouse farmers subverted the will of Congress in order to protect their own short-term interests while undermining an entire watershed and the ability of future generations to farm the land. Only if a conservation district saw a glaring problem with a particular farm could it appeal to the DOE for authority to take action. As one of the charter members of the agricultural establishment, Palouse districts never made any requests. The DOE fully understood the weaknesses of its regulations, stating, "the lack of an enforcement element could affect achievement of the plan objectives." Instead of setting an aggressive course, the DOE "has taken the position that the voluntary elements of the program will be given every opportunity to work before a decision would be made whether to seek broader regulatory authority."[38]

The final list of best management practices for dryland farming was inadequate and vaguely worded. Rather than invoke stinging condemnations, the DOE mildly reprimanded farmers. The final draft permitted stubble burning "in certain areas" because farmers found plowing thick wheat stalks difficult and costly, and the DOE told farmers to limit moldboard plow use to "certain situations." Fertilizers were to be "kept to the minimum necessary to grow an optimum crop yield," and the new policy allowed summer fallow as an acceptable alternative to grasses or legumes for farms with moderate precipitation. These regulations were essentially recommendations; even if an individual or conservation district indicted a particularly erosive farm, a landowner could nearly always comply with these indeterminate rules.[39]

The DOE seemingly could not decide if implementation of Section 208 would help the environment. On one hand, the department believed that a "reduction in soil erosion and the resultant sediment delivery to the stream systems" would result. The final draft also touted future improvements in river recreation, wildlife habitat, the longevity of hydroelectric dams, and public awareness of fragile rural environments. But the DOE also conceded that "the future environment without the proposed program would not differ significantly from the existing environment. Concerned producers would continue to improve their management with ongoing conservation district activities and research." That last comment casts doubt on the DOE's commitment to conservation and its knowledge of past farmer performance. Later the authors noted that they could not predict if clean water guidelines would be met by 1983. Their equivocation indicated at best ignorance and at worst a willingness to accept a permanently degraded ecosystem.[40]

The *Washington Farmer-Stockman*, the sounding board for Columbia Basin agriculture, voiced support for a weak Section 208 before and after its inception. The newspaper published helpful articles explaining the Byzantine process of implementing the law and kept readers abreast of new developments, with their support contingent on the absence of mandatory land-use provisions. Nevertheless, the *Farmer-Stockman* believed that recent attention on farm environments was "beginning to bear fruit" in the form of voluntary adoption of best management practices. One writer referred to Northwest farmers as "the first environmentalists," explaining that "rural people did not shape the present-day anti-pollution drive because they already live in a pleasant environment."[41]

Verle Kaiser, the longtime SCS soils expert, viewed the events of the 1970s with a growing resignation that the new regulations would do little to improve conditions. Although he supported firm land-use laws, he was incensed with the USDA policy that allowed farmers to classify summer-fallowed land as "set aside" acres for subsidy programs. Kaiser thought that summer fallow alone accounted for two-thirds of all Palouse erosion and pinned blame squarely on the USDA for tacitly encouraging the practice. "THIS IS WRONG!" he told an audience in 1978, as he asked them to join his crusade against erosion. Summer fallow and the federal policies that perpetuated it, he argued, would "destroy more soil than all the efforts of SCS, ACP [Agricultural Conservation Program], and EPA thru the 208 program combined can conserve." Kaiser said he felt a deep sense of sorrow that wiser heads had not prevailed. He felt despondent, too, "for my grandchildren, because *they* are the ones who will pay for our folly."[42]

US census information indicated a lack of progress in conservation following the implementation of Section 208. Summer fallow acres dropped slightly between 1978 and 1982, probably because high commodity prices motivated farmers to take land out of fallow and into wheat production. The double-digit inflation of the late 1970s pushed grain prices higher, boosting wheat production and easing federal wheat subsidies. The amount of summer fallow reduced in this period corresponded almost exactly with an increase in wheat production. When prices fell in the mid-1980s, fallow acres increased quickly and wheat acres dropped. Indeed, Kaiser's angst over USDA subsidy policy was misplaced; fallow acres mirrored the price of wheat, which triggered subsidies and encouraged more fallow. Kaiser neglected to mention that erosion had existed well before government subsidies. On another front, fertilizer use increased, contrary to the DOE's hopes. As erosion worsened over the years and as farmers continued to experiment with quantities, farmers injected upwards of one hundred pounds of anhydrous ammonia per acre into the soil every season. Statistics gave no sign of this trend abating. Nor did new regulations inspire farmers to plant more cover crops; acreages of soil-protecting crops stayed consistently low at about twenty-five thousand acres in the early 1980s—a statistical blip in a region of two million acres.[43]

Government surveys of water quality and erosion showed a similar lack of progress. The state of Idaho conducted studies on the South Fork of the Palouse River and Paradise Creek (a major tributary) in 1981 and found elevated levels of suspended sediments, phosphorous, nitrates, and fecal coliform. Using a new ranking system for assessing water quality—with zero representing the best score and one hundred the worst—the two streams earned the lamentable score of ninety-nine.[44] The following year the National Resources Institute, the federal agency in charge of compiling erosion data, found that an annual average of 7.6 tons per acre eroded from croplands in all of Washington and 9.4 tons per acre in Idaho. At the Idaho branch of the SCS, officials estimated that the Palouse lost 11.3 tons per acre in 1983. Section 208 "regulations" were but a few years old, but these statistics, in addition to census data, revealed no improvement whatsoever.[45]

When Section 208 proved to be a futile means of controlling erosion and pollution, Palouse farmers could have taken some initiative to alter behavior. Instead, farmers resented the notion that they were ruining their own land and cited the magnificent yields as contrary evidence. Most took a dim view of environmentalists, those "wide-eyed dreamers who find coordinating idealism with reality just a bit beyond their capabilities." Farmers argued that they were the *real* environmentalists—people who knew the land intimately and whose consideration for its well-being was "as natural as a rooster's crow."[46]

Plenty of people differed with this interpretation. Wildlife Resources, one of the few environmental advocacy groups in the Palouse in the 1970s, chided farmers for the annual "chocolate colored mixture of soil and water [that] races from hillside to stream to the rivers." The organization asked, "Why aren't farmers responsive to deteriorating soil erosion signs with a willingness to correct conditions that are destroying the mechanism that produces their livelihood?"[47] Chaplin Barnes, editor of the *Journal of Soil and Water Conservation*, proclaimed ten new "land use prescriptions" for farmers in 1980. They included a plea to consider the long-term ramifications of their actions and to put community goals ahead of individual gain. Seven of the ten dealt directly with government land-use regulations, and one of them bluntly read, "You *ought* to accept that the use of land should be subject to public scrutiny and control and to exercise your responsibility, with others, in ensuring that no use is permitted that is damaging to society as a whole."[48] These detractors were hinting at an old problem—the persistent lack of stewardship values. "We don't have a 'soil ethic,'" Verle Kaiser remarked in 1981. "Anybody who owns soil is allowed to do whatever he wants to it. Even if it means destroying it."[49] Kaiser believed that the Palouse was being slowly run out of business because too many farmers believed in a self-centered, individualistic version of the American dream that ignored the future. To these people, any surrender of property rights was tantamount to an encroaching Leviathan state. So long as property rights forces held sway, the only result could be the sacrifice of their most vital resource.

Further study in the early 1980s nullified the economic argument against conservation farming. Farmers had long believed that soil-saving techniques would hurt their bottom line. After the Palouse Cooperative River Basin Study debunked that idea in 1978, other scientists joined the fray. Soil specialists Douglas Young and David Walker published a report in 1982 that showed diminishing returns from technological advances if used on eroding soil. Better seed, chemicals, and machinery might increase yields but not as much as they should. Moreover, Young and Walker warned that if erosion continued at historical levels, technology could not prevent the eventual *decline* in yields.[50] Another group of researchers published more disturbing data in 1984, suggesting that in certain soil types on north-facing slopes, erosion would cause yields to drop 25 percent over the next fifty years.[51]

Farmers ignored this research. In addition to weak stewardship values, a preoccupation with short-term profits and hypocritical attitudes on the role of government impeded the adoption of conservation farming. A University of Idaho questionnaire from 1980 produced telling information. A majority of farmers polled responded that summer fallow helped their net income and about half said that reduced tillage exacerbated weed problems and cut profits. The survey determined that "farmers believe the erosion problem is not a problem of knowing how to control erosion, but rather one of economic feasibility." A majority of farmers believed that they needed more government money to make best management practices more attractive. When asked whether the government should set maximum allowable erosion limits, nine out of ten said "no." Farmers were willing to accept payments for conservation and balked at having their feet held to the fire to ensure compliance.[52] The most rational approach might have been to give farmers increased funding for conservation and hope for better participation. Or the government could have ended payments altogether and told farmers to stop summer fallow and annual cropping on hills and steep slopes. The former would have caused an outcry from taxpayers and the latter would have possibly resulted in violent protests.

A more thorough study of farmer attitudes was published in 1985, one that further exposed the paradoxes of the agrarian liberal. Wheat growers submitted to a battery of questions about their farming practices and views on soil conservation. They were asked to comment on the requirement of implementing conservation practices to receive federal subsidies and crop insurance, on federal cost sharing for soil-conserving farmers, and on conservation rules and fines for noncompliance self-imposed on farmers through their own quasi-governmental agencies, such as soil conservation districts. All requirements and programs were judged poorly and were regarded as unacceptable or inadequately funded. Like those in the University of Idaho study, these farmers were amenable to using government money for conservation, yet firmly opposed mandatory practices. This intellectual inconsistency surprised one farmer, who said, "I just told you I don't think any governmental agency should require or tell farmers what to do. Now I'm telling you that I think government should help pay for soil conservation/erosion control practices. That doesn't seem right, does it?" Another farmer sounded less conflicted when he said, "If they [the federal government] start telling me what I can and cannot do with my land, I'll get out of farming!" Entrenched individualistic values such as these were not unusual. Generations of inertia, both environmental and political, created an atmosphere that was hostile to change—unless someone else was picking up the bill.[53]

A group of rural sociologists from Washington State University, the University of Idaho, and Oregon State University conducted another farmer survey from 1976 to 1985. Although this study examined attitudes over time, it shared the disheartening tone of earlier reports. The study concluded that "attitudes and behaviors of farmers do not reflect large changes in most areas over the past decade. Dramatic changes in the use of erosion control practices are not likely to occur." When farmers were asked if they were doing all they could to stop erosion, more than 80 percent said "yes" in 1976, 1980, and 1985. The percentage favoring land-use regulations hovered between 26 and 31 percent over the same period. And the percentage recognizing stream siltation as a serious problem remained low—18 percent in 1976, 14 percent in 1980, and 29 percent in 1985. The more that scientists studied Palouse farmers, the more these farmers revealed beliefs that were antithetical to improving environmental conditions.[54]

Ideological rigidity did not cause mechanical innovation to slow. First introduced to the Palouse in the mid-1970s, the no-till planting method used a new type of seed drill to plant in and around the past year's remnant crop. It eliminated the need for plowing and harrowing and left wheat stalk residues intact through the winter. No cultivation meant the soil was covered all year, drastically reducing erosion. Proponents of the system said it could protect soil, save money, and would gain the support of environmentalists and traditional farmers alike.

No-till had considerable advantages over conventional tillage. Superior erosion control was the foremost difference; the absence of tilling reduced annual erosion to minuscule amounts. Soil moisture improved, allowing farmers to seed winter wheat earlier and generate more ground cover before the winter-spring erosion season. Fewer tractor hours meant lower fuel and depreciation costs. The USDA added a cost-sharing program in the 1980s to encourage the spread of no-till, paying 75 percent of the cost of seed-drill rentals and extra herbicides. The farm-implement industry embraced no-till, and by the mid-1980s farmers had dozens of seed-drill models from which to choose. The positive aspects of no-till attracted a significant following. About 25 percent of Palouse farmers had experimented with the practice by the mid-1980s, most of whom were innovative farmers who thought they could save money.[55]

That early optimism faded when no-till farming proved troublesome and costly, with weeds being the biggest problem. Without cultivation, grasses such as downy brome and wild oats and broadleaf weeds like prickly lettuce and wild mustard proliferated. Farmers used a barrage of 2,4–D, atrazine, and Roundup with decent but costly results. Moreover, environmentalists recoiled from the Faustian deal of heavier herbicide applications for the sake of erosion control. Decaying matter on the ground caused fungal growth to increase, including a new fungus that had never been seen in the Palouse. The alternatives available to combat these outbreaks—burning crop residues and plowing under old stalks—defeated the purpose of no-till. Bacteria in root systems became a problem for the same reason. Microbes multiplied in the decaying matter and killed young wheat sprouts. The increased costs of reduced tillage negated much of the savings, which put the future of no-till in doubt.[56]

Lower yields sounded the death knell for no-till. After some initially promising studies, farmers discovered that conventional tillage consistently outperformed no-till. When Palouse growers realized that no-till wheat produced less, they quickly abandoned it. Only 7 percent of farmers used no-till on some portion of their land by 1985. The environmental benefits were largely dismissed, both in the early experimental phase and in the 1980s. According to a 1987 study, "Promoters of no-till should not assume that this practice is being tried by farmers mostly because of its conservation implications." The evidence suggested those who tried it did so "more for its economic appeal than because of a conservation ethic."[57]

Nonetheless, experiments with no-till raised public awareness on the fragility of agricultural ecosystems. In spite of farmers' economic motivations, no-till in part shifted the public focus toward environmental issues and agricultural sustainability. No-till and environmental debates taught people to consider the limits of their ability to manipulate nature and to question the wisdom of unfettered growth.[58]

In more practical terms, the attention given to environmental issues in the 1970s also made it easier for researchers to receive money. Congress was willing to fund programs that showed economic as well as ecological promise. The primary beneficiary of this trend was the STEEP (Solutions to Environmental and Economic Problems) program, a broad coalition of scientists and professors from Washington, Idaho, and Oregon devoted to making inland Northwest farming environmentally sustainable and more profitable. The federal government provided $200,000 in 1976 and millions more in years to come for scientists to write a new blueprint for dryland agriculture. Over the next fifteen years, STEEP researchers generated over fifty publications on such topics as conservation farming profitability, alternative crops, insects, weeds, fungi, soil-conserving crop rotations, and seed design. These academics did more than talk to each other; the STEEP program publicized its work to a wider audience with frequent lectures and press releases. How much it affected erosion and water quality remains unknown, but STEEP elevated the level of discourse on farming and promoted sound land-use decisions.[59]

A year before his death in 1982, Verle Kaiser was asked if he had any regrets over his near half-century of public service. He said, "I regret that we did not get the job done in the Palouse. We believed when we started forty-five years ago that we would see the time that we would have the Palouse tied down. And we have not. That is my regret." This simple statement exposed a man who seemed tired and defeated from his many battles. Gone was the driving energy of his early days, depleted like the soil he worked to protect. He had lost and he knew it. At the end of the interview Kaiser expressed thanks for the dozens of people who had helped him in his career, people who knew the troubles that lay ahead.[60]

That was the problem: Kaiser only had to thank *dozens* of people. Through no fault of his own, his message failed to resonate with enough farmers to make a difference. Conservation advocates asked them to look fifty or one hundred years into the future to consider the kind of farm their progeny would inherit, while most farmers thought only one season at a time. Such agricultural myopia, somewhat forgivable in an earlier era, became inexcusable as the evidence mounted against standard farming methods. The terrible irony of this era was that agrarian liberals, bent on maintaining personal sovereignty for themselves and for generations to come, behaved as if there were no tomorrow.

8 A GLIMMER OF HOPE?

A FTER ALL THE WATER—and soil—that has flowed under the proverbial bridge, one way to judge the performance of Palouse conservation is to reexamine the goals laid out earlier in the twentieth century. It is instructive to ponder again the ideas of Hugh Hammond Bennett, progenitor of the Soil Conservation Service and early conservation agitator. In a 1932 radio address, Bennett outlined the basic steps needed to preserve the nation's soils:

> We must stop cultivating unmanageable steep slopes. We must plant these slopes to trees or grass, or not plant on them at all. Beyond this, we must increase our practice of soil and water conserving methods on the erosive slopes that we do plow. . . . Now is a good time to inaugurate better systems of soil management, using our smoother lands for cultivated crops, and giving these lands the best protection possible.[1]

Bennett's recommendations evolved into the USDA's policy template for the next seventy years. Scientists and politicians knew that the task was difficult but remained confident that American agriculture could be reformed.

For more than fifty years the farming community thwarted compulsory conservation measures and Bennett's grand design never fully materialized. Despite ongoing setbacks, soil conservationists were determined to realize those dreams and the 1985 agricultural bill gave cause for optimism. It was a law that required farmers to adopt soil conservation plans in order to be eligible for federal income and price support programs, yet another example of the expansion of the liberal statist model.

But like earlier programs, the 1985 farm bill did not bring fundamental changes to farming regimens nor substantial improvements in erosion control or water quality. The federal government failed to offer adequate funding for land retirement and did nothing to end summer fallow, the most essential components of the Palouse conservation program. More than half of all Palouse farmland would need to be permanently set aside to reduce erosion to sustainable levels, and the USDA was unwilling to retire agricultural lands that were profitable in the short term. Although the USDA's strategy for encouraging participation had improved, it had created only another stopgap measure. The New Deal reformers' objectives would go unrealized in the Palouse into the next century.

Government officials had become increasingly impatient with federal conservation policies by the 1970s. The misuse of funds and a noticeable lack of erosion abatement upset both auditors and Congress. In a 1977 report, the General Accounting Office, the investigative branch of Congress, criticized the SCS for not pursuing farmers who abused their land and for allowing land planted to grasses to revert back to crops. Government auditors also found fault with cost-sharing programs that included drainage systems, fertilizing, and other activities that farmers would have financed on their own.[2] Kansas senator Bob Dole introduced legislation the same year requiring proof that conservation programs would result in less erosion, and he offered new initiatives to improve soil health. The bill passed both houses of Congress but it also restricted cost-sharing activities; Dole and his colleagues were more interested in an efficient, cost-effective bureaucracy than in preventing erosion.[3]

When Ronald Reagan took office in 1981, erosion control faced an uncertain future. Incoming USDA secretary John Block supported heavily capitalized farming interests but also lobbied for soil conservation, a cause célèbre of progressives. Block's plans to continue long-standing soil programs rankled Interior secretary James Watt, a man notorious for fiscal conservatism and scathing denouncements of environmental regulations. Watt and other Reaganites argued that soil conservation measures were costly and unnecessary. When confronted with powerful farmer interest groups who wanted conservation and price and income support programs maintained, however, opposition quickly melted away. In his first term Reagan was content to keep federal dollars flowing to this key constituency, even if USDA soil policies were ineffective.

Reagan administration officials were the inheritors of an overheated agricultural economy. Richard Nixon's diplomatic recognition of China in 1972 and a gradual thawing of Cold War tensions with the Soviet Union opened two huge markets to American farmers. For the balance of the 1970s, commodity prices, land values, and production rose sharply, and farmers quickly saw a revival of the heady days of 1910–1920—the golden age of American agriculture. Eastern Washington wheat prices rose from $1.41 per bushel in 1971 to nearly $5 in 1973 and hovered near $4 in 1981. The average value of a Palouse farm (land and buildings) more than tripled during the 1970s and the average Whitman County farm expanded to more than a thousand acres by 1978. Lending institutions and implement dealers fared well because farmers eagerly went into debt to purchase more land and new equipment. The boom extended into the early 1980s, giving farmers the mistaken impression that the rally would continue.[4]

Like other economic surges in the American West, the 1970s boom crashed hard in the mid-1980s. After Great Plains farmers began cultivating marginal lands and when other industrial nations (e.g., Canada and Australia) began boosting agricultural production, export markets shrunk and prices fell. Moreover, because many farmers had incurred recent debt, conditions were ripe for the worst farm crisis since the Depression. Government purchases of surplus crops and support payments increased in 1983 and 1984, but it was not enough to forestall thousands of farm bankruptcies across the nation. According to a Moscow loan officer, foreclosures were less frequent in the Palouse than in other regions, but nearly all farmers suffered from low prices and narrow profit margins. The cycle of boom and bust had visited the Palouse once again.[5]

Wheat farmers needed help and Congress obliged. The Farm Security Act of 1985 (FSA) relieved immediate financial pressures by promoting strategies that marketed surpluses more aggressively while maintaining price floors and generous subsidies. Economic necessity and political expediency forced the White House to accept this affront to free-market philosophy, and President Reagan grudgingly signed the bill into law. Imbedded within the law was a new USDA erosion control plan, the Conservation Reserve Program (CRP), which the department believed would reduce erosion and government stockpiles of staple goods and provide cash payments to farmers. The plan reflected previous efforts: farmers could retire erodible land for ten years and would receive money (not to exceed $50,000 annually) based on past yields. The USDA insisted that idled land be seeded to grass or planted to trees, with the government paying half of the expenses. Nothing about the program was innovative. On the other hand, the means of enlisting CRP participants was radically different. Under the Farm Security Act, all farmers with highly erodible land (i.e., most of the Palouse) were required to submit a conservation plan that, in most cases, called for the removal of acres from production, which could be enrolled in the CRP. Farmers who failed to obtain a conservation plan by 1990 and implement it by 1995 would be ineligible for any government subsidy payments. The USDA and Congress cleverly manipulated the 1985 farm bill to make the carrot more enticing and the stick far more threatening. According to Peter Myers, assistant secretary of agriculture, "The government is not telling you [farmers] what to do, but it is saying that if you abuse your land, you aren't eligible for federal payments."[6]

The Farm Security Act of 1985 succeeded in keeping farmers afloat and in increasing exports, and the late 1980s witnessed a moderate recovery in the agricultural sector with slightly higher prices. The prolonged bailout came at a considerable price, and when federal budget deficits became politically untenable at the end of Reagan's second term, Congress drafted a new farm bill. The new legislation presented an opportunity to expand the scope of the CRP, which was popular with farmers and environmentalists alike. The Food, Agriculture, Conservation, and Trade Act of 1990 (FACTA) kept subsidy levels intact and amended the CRP. FACTA allowed farmers to put land in the CRP for water quality and wildlife habitat purposes; marginal pasturelands also could be used to stabilize riparian zones. According to the USDA, what began as a modest soil conservation tool became a sweeping environmental improvement plan and an expression of growing concern for the ecological health of America's hinterland.[7]

Farm leaders were aware that they needed to improve their image on environmental issues. Chris Laney, president of the Washington Association of Wheat Growers, acknowledged in 1990 that in recent years, "substantial damage has occurred. Not only to our sustaining resource, the soil, but to our credibility as its stewards. The consumer public [sic] wants and needs to be reassured that we care about the land." Dan Blankenship, vice president of the association, voiced similar sentiments, writing that "soil is the only medium in which we can produce our crops. . . . It would be suicidal to do anything but preserve the integrity and health of that medium." Because of this relationship, "farmers are environmentalists by necessity." The CRP was an important step in fixing both public relations and environmental problems, and the program enjoyed broad support in the Northwest and else-where. SCS chief Paul Johnson asked farmers to take a proactive stance. "It is essential agriculture gets on the offensive on environmental issues," he said in a 1994 interview, because farmers needed to show "how good we can be" rather than settle for "how good we have to be."[8]

Rank-and-file farmers greeted the CRP with ambivalence. Many delayed drafting conservation plans because they believed the USDA would never cut subsidies to uncooperative farmers. Others created conservation plans then ignored them for the same reason. Some farmers avoided the CRP alto-gether, because they could earn more by planting on all their land. As a result, a scant 2 percent of highly erodible land in Whitman County had been enrolled by early 1988.[9] According to Read Smith, a wheat grower from St. John, Washington, once farmers realized that the new protocol would endure, compliance increased. Smith believed that only a few had not signed on by 1993, but added that "producers tend to strive for the very minimum standards to barely get by."[10] Other farmers agreed that their neighbors cared little about the soil. One said in 1990 that "I still hear lots of farmers say, 'I don't care what happens to it after I die. I'm going to get what I can out of it.'" Another quipped that, "The closest most farmers get to their soil is on the seat of their tractor or driving by in their pickups. . . . As long as they are getting their yield they don't think about what they are doing." This widely shared lack of stewardship at the close of the twentieth century indi-cated that little had changed in the effort to curb erosion. It seemed likely that the CRP would fail as a strategy to reduce erosion.[11]

The acreage set aside under the CRP was disappointing. Farmers enrolled 3.9 percent of their cropland in 1992 and 6.4 percent in 1997 and received an average of $11,000 per farm in 1997—well below the $50,000 per annum ceiling. The data suggests that the CRP did not provide a sufficient subsidy to influence behavior; growing wheat was still more profitable in the short term. Farmers were certainly not opposed to government assistance per se. Whitman County ranked third in the nation in 1992 and fourth in 1997 in total government farm assistance.[12] Farmers were eager to accept govern-ment dollars but were opposed to regulations or programs that might injure the bottom line. Farmers on the Palouse adhered to the maxim that Don-ald Worster ascribed to Great Plains farmers: "do not interfere with us when we are making money, but rescue us when we are going bankrupt."[13]

Participation should have been high because the USDA tied subsidies to conservation, but inadequate enforcement of department rules led to some gaping loopholes. When pressured by farm interest groups, the department lowered minimum standards for erosion, thus farmers were required to show only slight improvements to stay on the federal dole. Darrell Kaufman, inspector general of the USDA (the department's in-house auditor), reported that SCS officials often allowed farmers to reschedule inspections. He also noted that SCS agents conducted field tests when farmers were most likely to be in compliance, that some officials failed to report growers in violation, while still others refused to report violators to higher authorities. The root of the problem, according to Kaufman, was that the same SCS personnel providing technical assistance were sometimes also responsible for measuring compliance. Although the opportunity to circumvent the law was obvious, the USDA monitoring process did not change.[14]

The auditor's findings expressed farmers' desire to evade regulation as well as their implicit denial that there was an erosion problem. A joint Washington State University–USDA survey released in 1988 found that in one Palouse watershed farmers believed that only 4,300 acres were highly erodible; in contrast, the USDA designated close to 18,000 acres. Some operators were not sure if they had a problem. When asked if he had an erosion problem, one farmer remarked, "that's tough to answer when you don't know what five tons [of soil] looks like." More than three-quarters of the respondents had no conservation plans in place, and most farmers felt their practices controlled erosion better than their SCS-sanctioned neighbors. The survey concluded that the "inaccurate perception of the erosion problem can only mean that soil erosion control in the Palouse is hit-or-miss at best."[15]

This haphazard policy was nevertheless capable of producing modest results. The USDA and US Geological Survey reported that by the mid-1990s erosion had been reduced 10 percent compared to the late 1970s. Even more promising was the steep drop in stream sediment loads. The Palouse River and its major tributaries carried roughly half as much sediment from 1993 through 1996 as the streams had from 1962 through 1971. Part of the reason for the sharp difference stemmed from an inordinately wet year in 1963, which affected the average for the decade. But even when that year is omitted from the equation, the improvement was notable.[16]

The USDA cheered such statistics and attributed the change to the CRP, which it called "the federal government's single largest environmental improvement program—and one of its most effective." Nationwide, farmers had enrolled more than thirty-six million acres by 1996, nearly reaching the program's target. The department estimated that the CRP had increased net farm income by as much as $6.3 billion, and that upwards of $1.7 billion worth of soil had been saved. The plan saved 28 billion tons of soil per year in Washington and Idaho, or about 15 tons per acre on the farms enrolled.[17]

Eager to tout its environmental accomplishments, the department also publicized its forestry and wildlife programs. In nearly all its CRP-related publications in the 1990s, the USDA reminded people that good farming led to healthier, more diverse ecosystems. On CRP grasslands nationwide, the majority of the land in the program, the department claimed that it had doubled the areas held in the National Wildlife Refuge System. The program was supposedly responsible for planting three million acres in trees by 2001, which annually removed 3.7 million tons of carbon from the atmosphere and reduced agricultural chemical use on retired land. Duck populations grew in the northern Great Plains, pheasant numbers soared in Montana, and various big-game species thrived on CRP areas in many Western states. In an era when environmental ethics became an important political issue, the USDA was keen to accentuate the positive. But the department also provided no raw data as proof; its claims could have been nothing more than self-aggrandizing propaganda.[18]

As a result of CRP incentives, farming practices improved. Key indicators of conservation farming—stubble mulching, strip cropping, and tree planting—showed massive acreage gains from 1979 to 1994. No-till acreage also increased, as did the number of terraced acres. Since all these practices could be used to satisfy new government standards, it is logical to give credit to the 1985 farm bill; conservation was infrequent before that year and commonplace a decade later. The national attention generated by environmental issues could have affected farmer behavior, but it seems likely that farmers listened to their accountants' advice first.[19]

After the Republican congressional landslide of 1994, an intense spate of fiscal conservatism swept through the halls of Congress that threatened many conservation programs. Because CRP supporters spanned the political spectrum, however, the program was spared the budgetary ax. The 1996 Agriculture Improvement and Reform Act, dubbed the "Freedom to Farm Act," extended the life of the CRP and added to the list of eligible conservation practices. It allowed farmers to enroll acres at any time of the year—an important provision for those making last-minute decisions based on weather or markets. But the Republicans' ideological contempt for government regulation removed the regulatory teeth from the 1985 Farm Security Act. The 1996 measure relieved farmers from the requirement of implementing a conservation plan in order to continue receiving subsidies. The one powerful and effective law mandating stewardship had been partially eviscerated. Despite the setback, the fact that the CRP survived attested to its broad appeal and the political strength of liberal farmers and their pet programs. If the CRP could withstand this draconian period, it seemed destined to become a permanent part of American agriculture. When the CRP again came up for renewal in 2002, Congress increased the total cap on acres and made water quality, wildlife habitat, and soil erosion equally important priorities.[20]

There was little doubt that some combination of government action and a shift in values had alleviated certain environmental problems. But what constituted "sufficient" or "substantial" change in erosion or water quality? In other words, what was the overall environmental assessment of the Palouse? Two reports in the 1990s offered clues. A Washington State University study released in 1994 determined that the Paradise Creek watershed in eastern Whitman County failed to meet minimum water quality standards in Washington and Idaho. Researchers placed a good deal of blame not on erosion, but on a wastewater treatment plant in Moscow that raised fecal coliform and phosphorous levels above acceptable limits and depleted oxygen levels below minimum standards. And despite recent drops in erosion, excess sedimentation and the removal of riparian vegetation made it impossible for cold-water fish species to survive. The study deemed this Palouse River tributary unfit for drinking, salmonid spawning, or as "primary contact recreation." The creek was cleaner than in past years but still horribly polluted.[21]

Instead of buying costly new equipment to comply with water quality standards, the city of Moscow in 2001 considered diverting all Paradise Creek water below the plant during summer months. The city already had been sending much of the water to the municipal golf course and had been discussing plans to use it in city parks. The downstream city of Pullman had been distressed about the diversion proposal because less flow in the creek would lower the amount of pollutants Pullman itself could legally discharge. Pullmanites also worried about the aesthetics of having a dry creek running through town for months at a time. Pullman city supervisor John Sherman said in 2001 that "we prefer having a low-flow to no flow at all. The creek doesn't have to be the purest in the world to be enjoyable."[22]

A second report, this one conducted by the USGS and other government and nonprofit agencies, gave a mixed review of the region's water quality. By the late 1990s data suggested that groundwater and surface water contamination from nitrates and farm chemicals was far worse in western portions of the Columbia Basin than in the Palouse. Slower groundwater recharge rates and more judicious use of anhydrous ammonia left people in the Palouse in a better condition than those in the Tri-Cities, Moses Lake, and Othello areas.[23] Nevertheless, Palouse soil and waters were in the top twenty-fifth percentile nationally for nitrates in water, and several sites showed high levels of PCBs, which had been used in electrical transformers. Whitman County ranked thirty-eighth in the nation in 1997 in farm chemicals purchased and sixteenth in commercial fertilizers purchased.[24] Overall pesticide contamination has been minimal, yet DDT and several other chemicals remain a problem. DDT, a persistent pesticide banned in 1972, stays trapped in soil until erosion or some outside force exposes it to a wider environment. Three locations on the Palouse River showed excessive levels of the pesticides DDT, lindane, and diazinon, and the herbicide triallate in 1998. Such residues indicate how the agricultural decisions of generations past will continue to affect the region well into the twenty-first century.[25]

Another popular chemical, the herbicide 2,4–D, has come under renewed scrutiny. The American Medical Association found in 1986 that Kansas farmers with prolonged exposure to the chemical contracted non-Hodgkin's lymphoma at alarmingly high rates. Ten years later a University of Minnesota study linked 2,4–D to birth defects. The Environmental Protection Agency began a new study in 1997 to determine its toxicity. Although its report has not yet been filed, at least one EPA statistician believes the herbicide responsible for nine kinds of cancer. After nearly half a century of use, the jury is still out on the safety of one of the chemical mainstays of Palouse agriculture.[26]

In recent years genetically modified (GM) crops, also known as genetically modified organisms (GMOs), have become a contentious issue nationally and in the Palouse. Unlike traditional plant breeding where specimens of the same plant species are crossed to produce hybrids, GM plants are created by incorporating genes from totally different organisms. In theory, GM crops can be engineered to resist disease and pests, to survive extreme heat and cold, and to require less fertilizer. But potential complications abound, making genetic modification perhaps the most heated topic in world agriculture today.

When GMOs came on the scene, proponents proclaimed them a potential godsend for farmers and environmentalists alike. They considered this microscopic frontier the "gene revolution," an opportunity to increase productivity and end hunger once and for all. In addition to fending off diseases and pests, GM crops could plausibly reduce erosion and improve water quality. By using GM grains that fight weeds and need less fertilizer, Palouse farmers could plow less frequently, thereby disturbing the soil less and keeping more of it in place. If wheat could be made to require less water, summer fallow might become less prevalent and this tradition could finally be discarded. Advocates claimed that the decreased inputs and boost in productivity would surely improve farm profitability and stabilize the regional economy. Genetically modified plants promised to lower the need for government subsidies and taxpayers everywhere could rejoice. If the calculus proved correct, everyone seemed to benefit.[27]

Despite the confident predictions, waves of protest descended upon the supporters of GM crops. Environmentalists from all over the world worried that GMOs were unsafe; they chafed at the notion of "Frankenfood"—plants constructed from the genes of different organisms. They demanded longer and more rigorous testing procedures, arguing that regulations on biotechnology were less thorough than tests on farm chemicals. Moreover, insect, weed, and fungi resistance remained a problem. Scientists could engineer plants to require less chemical treatment, but eventually pests and diseases would adapt, necessitating still more genetic modification. Above all, opposition galvanized around the idea that manipulating DNA to "invent" new plants was intuitively wrong. The bizarre molecular combinations smacked of science fiction, and genetic modification proved particularly upsetting to people not enamored of technology in the first place.[28]

The debate over GM crops intensified when farm economics and equity entered the discussion. Critics believed the new technology caused food production to become more commercialized and that it would increase Third World dependency and thwart developing countries' agricultural self-sufficiency. These nations would endure more poverty and become less stable politically. Because engineered seed is private property, it can be patented and used as a political and economic weapon. Insect and weed tolerance would require the constant innovation of newer varieties, thereby making Western farmers and developing countries perpetually reliant on biotech giants such as Monsanto and Novartis. Genetically modified crops would also encourage the cultivation of submarginal land in the US and elsewhere if they increased yields as promised. Biotechnology thus has become yet another cog in the treadmill theory of industrial agriculture: it favors those with capital and prolongs unsustainable practices.[29]

Washington State University scientists were at the leading edge of the biotech revolution and were quick to counter their detractors. R. James Cook, a plant pathologist, believed GM crops to be fundamentally the same as plants produced by conventional breeding: "There's no scientific reason to discriminate between genes based on where they come from or how they get into the plant. The safety of a new plant should be assessed by looking at the plant, not how it was created."[30] Cook remarked that European nations and some corporations have been reluctant to embrace GMOs because of economic self-interest. New technology creates competitive advantages that some nations and businesses cannot exploit, making them defensive. "There are winners and losers with any change," Cook explained, "and the real resistance to biotechnology is actually a natural resistance to change."[31] Europeans, like Americans, are capitalists motivated by economic self-interest. James Carrington, a Washington State University biochemist, added that there have been no documented cases of illness caused by GM food and that organic foods often pose serious health concerns, such as high levels of fungal toxins. Washington State University geneticist Paul Lurquin acknowledged concerns over GM plants cross-pollinating with unmodified plants but insisted that no examples had ever been shown. Because most GM seeds are no more than ten to fifteen years old, however, the long-term possibility of such an event is unknown. He noted ominously, "As long as nothing goes wrong, it's hard to predict how often these things might happen."[32]

Carrington called biotechnology "a wonderful, relatively non-toxic way to control pests" in grain fields. Along with other industry and university researchers, he praised GM seed as a less intrusive and costly way to battle insects. But Carrington also warned that overuse of bug-tolerant seed could backfire: "indiscriminate use ... can lead to the development of resistant bugs that would make [a] relatively benign pesticide less useful." His proposed solution involved a heavy dose of government oversight to prevent overuse and to maintain effectiveness.[33] This approach has proven only moderately effective in controlling improper chemical use in the US and Europe and has been compromised by industry and farming lobbyists who pressure lawmakers and bureaucrats to create weak regulations. Moreover, in the developing world, where government oversight is often negligible or nonexistent, the opportunities and temptations to use GM seed indiscriminately are considerable.

The controversy surrounding GMOs is the latest installment in a long line of food safety issues confronting industrial agriculture. Questions about the safety of synthetic herbicides and pesticides surfaced, albeit quietly, in the 1940s and became a charged political issue in following decades. While debates on farm chemicals intensified, industrial giants and the farming establishment continually professed their products to be scrupulously tested and fit for human consumption. Often they were right, but when they were wrong, the consequences were severe. Clearly the objectivity of the chemical industry in such matters should be doubted, since its economic viability depended on continued production. Scientists also stood to profit from industry-funded research, and they too often generated reports to satisfy their clients. As the evidence against certain chemicals grew in the 1960s and 1970s, those in charge of assuring the safety of the nation's food supply came under increasing criticism.[34]

The public should be wary about GM food for the same reasons. Although GMOs may not all precipitate the apocalypse, we should not blindly accept the assurances given by the biotech industry or those on its payroll. According to many in the industry, genetic modification has not undergone an exhaustive battery of tests. Because unforeseen consequences always follow new technologies, erring on the side of caution would have helped the farm chemical industry in the 1950s and it would be a prudent approach for biotech corporations today. But as long as market forces dictate government policy, GM crops will proliferate quickly. Biotech supporters have also been successful in casting themselves as victims of an obsessive, neo-Luddite environmental movement. Donald Duvick, an agronomist at Iowa State University, condemned the "blanket denunciation" of biotech scientists, which "comes close to the concept of 'ethnic cleansing.'"[35] Hyperbole aside, environmentalists' admonitions are no match for the scientific, financial, and public relations power of the biotech empire.

Although GM plants have not conclusively been shown to cause environmental harm, seed specialists have been working on wheat varieties that may be ecologically beneficial. Using traditional breeding methods, researchers at Washington State University have been developing perennial wheat strains since 1991. Perennial wheat continues to grow after harvest and for several years and could reduce cultivation and erosion by a considerable amount. Although early test plots showed poor second-year growth, scientists will continue pursuing better strains that may one day be marketable. In many ways technology caused the erosion problem; it also might help reverse it.[36]

Federal price supports became another political battleground during the Clinton and Bush presidencies. As a major component of the Freedom to Farm Act of 1996, Congress lifted all restrictions on what farmers planted and ordered all subsidies phased out over the following seven years. If implemented, this would have constituted the most significant piece of farm legislation since the New Deal or perhaps the Homestead Act. As it turned out, Congress's bark was worse than its bite.[37]

Faced with continued high farm output, low prices, and thousands of potential foreclosures, the Clinton administration and Congress restored price supports to avoid a repeat of the crisis in the early 1980s. Farmers were granted $5.9 billion in subsidies in 1998 and another $8.7 billion the following year. President George W. Bush and a new Congress crafted a farm bill in 2002 that restored the perennial price support system, a retreat from free-market economics and an open acknowledgment of the failed attempt to let market forces determine farm income. But the perpetual support network drew protest because many wealthy farmers received federal aid and were in no danger of foreclosure. Subsidies were paid out according to acres and output, not income. As a result, corporate farms, representing 10 percent of American farmers, received nearly two-thirds of all subsidy dollars. Family and corporate farms were not the only ones lining up at the federal trough: Fortune 500 companies, universities, and even state prisons all collected, simply because they grew commercial crops.[38]

Whitman County has long prospered from federal subsidies. Several southeastern Washington corporate farms took in staggering sums in 1999 and 2000. The Broughton Land Company received nearly $600,000 in 1999 and a whopping $1.2 million in 2000—tops in the state. General manager Dan McKinley called the aid "an absolute necessity." Wheatlife Company ranked second in the state, pulling in $1.08 million in 2000, and Klaveano Brothers ranked third, netting $918,000 from the USDA. Because of federal support, Keith Klaveano remarked, "We're making a living, making payments on land and machinery and that's about it. We're not having a fancy living by any means. There is nothing extra."[39]

Not all were convinced of such farmers' dire straits. Washington State University economist Paul Barkley observed that even after the Freedom to Farm Act, subsidies "never seem to end. . . . Even when we end it, it doesn't end." He commented that those who own their land had "big smiles" after the bailouts of 1998–2001. Barkley added that farmers "are doing what you and I would do if we won the lottery."[40] Palouse farmers countered that while some received extraordinary sums, the end result was the cheapest, most reliable food supply in the world. Duane Grant, president of the Idaho Grain Producers, summarized the farmers' viewpoint: "I think Joe American taxpayers are getting an incredible return on their investment."[41]

The 1980s and 1990s presented farmers with a better approach to erosion control than had policies of previous decades. Policy makers finally understood that if they wanted better results they had to make soil conservation more attractive from a financial standpoint. The USDA poured millions of dollars into programs that were feasible and appealing to farmers, and the Palouse saw moderate reductions in erosion. Although the erosion problem continues, the USDA has discovered what works and can now focus on improving the CRP template.

Palouse farmers will likely never become environmentalists (in spite of their claims to the contrary), and they will continue to be economically motivated. For erosion to be reduced to sustainable levels, the USDA needs to add even more money to the CRP program, but at least a logical (if expensive) framework is in place. In the near absence of stewardship values in the Palouse and because strict land-use regulations seem a political impossibility, this may be the best we can do in the short term. It is a strange twist that in order to fix the long-term erosion problem, policy makers and environmentalists must craft proposals that deal with farmers' immediate needs. To survive into the next century, it seems that agrarian liberals will need to reinvent themselves once more.

EPILOGUE

THE PALOUSE has alternately been called "the best poor man's land," "the garden spot of the Northwest," a "desert of wheat" (by novelist Zane Grey), and a "paradise." These phrases were most common in the late nineteenth and early twentieth centuries when agriculturalists discovered how well this dry land met their needs, transforming one of the last remaining tracts of arable land in the United States into an endless expanse of wheat. The belief that this was an agricultural paradise seemed justified. As the years went by, the Palouse became synonymous with wheat, transforming European and American agrarians, raised on older notions of self-sufficiency, into a blend of agrarian and nineteenth-century classical liberal. Later in the twentieth century, Palouse agrarian liberals convinced a majority in Congress and the nation that federal assistance in the form of research, price supports, soil conservation support, and lax regulations was in their best interest. Along the way some farmers became wealthy, others made modest livings, and a few succumbed to bad luck or bad business decisions. None experienced a weather-related crop failure.

That all this occurred just north of the lower Snake River is remarkable. The few Euro-Americans who visited the Palouse before 1860 were unimpressed with its agricultural potential. But once settlers learned of its fertility, a steady stream of people and matériel filled the earth like never before. A manipulation of the landscape ensued that made the Palouse a very different place at the dawn of the twenty-first century. These changes are the central concern of this book.

White settlement put an unprecedented human imprint on the land. While precontact Indian population estimates range from a few hundred to 2,300, Whitman and Latah counties totaled 42,000 residents in 1910, and the regional hub of Spokane eclipsed the 100,000 plateau the same year.[1] The profuse bunchgrasses were the first environmental casualty after cattle, plows, and exotic weeds had their way with native vegetation. Native mammals and bird species also declined when people and crops eliminated habitat. The land rush at the end of the nineteenth century initiated a series of ecological changes inspired by a desire to convert an overlooked hinterland into reliable farmland.

Commercial agriculture also initiated a less noticeable ecological condition, soil erosion, which had far-reaching implications. First recognized as a serious problem in the 1920s, erosion resulted from a steady dose of plowing and summer fallow. Cultivation exposed the highly erodible soil in this rolling plain, leaving it susceptible to rain and melting snow. Erosion altered the topography of the Palouse by reducing the height of its distinctive hills and making them more rounded. It also deposited sediment in streams, which increased turbidity and water temperatures, spelling the end for cold-water fish species such as trout.

In short, Palouse farming irrevocably altered the landscape. No amount of reclamation could ever replace the millions of tons of soil lost over the years, nor could the bunchgrasses and animals that once dominated the area ever return to their former state. The land has been thoroughly commodified and physically transformed; most of the native vegetation has been removed in favor of crops that are planted, harvested, and replanted indefinitely. Modern farming has literally caused the earth to move.

But was the Palouse experience appreciably different than commercial farming in other locales? Was this environmental story common or unique? Parts of the narrative relate closely with the broader story of American agriculture. Farmers broke sod and repeatedly tilled vast stretches of land in the Southeast, Midwest, Far West, and the Palouse in the nineteenth century with little regard for the environmental consequences. Farmers abandoned subsistence farming as soon as transportation links, markets, and credit sources became available. They went on an endless buying spree for bigger and more efficient machinery and to acquire more land. And they utilized the latest advances in farm science, subjecting the land to a multitude of new products of uncertain toxicity after the Second World War.

Moreover, farmers in the Palouse and the nation resisted land-use regulations and fiercely defended a perceived right to government assistance. To a large extent Palouse farming resembled national trends of exploitation and growth, institutionalizing industrial agriculture. According to historian James Sherow, three recurring features characterized industrial farmers: "they reduced labor costs through greater use of machinery; next they applied petrochemicals to control insects and encourage plant growth; and finally they increased landholdings to maximize economies of scale." When producers made this transition, farming became "an industrial enterprise to be managed in the same manner as a factory."[2] By this criterion, the Palouse was of a piece with modern American agriculture. In fact, I claim that Palouse farmers exceeded most of these national trends in intensity; hence, I have devised the notion of the "agrarian liberal" to more accurately characterize the development of the dominant parallel and paradoxical land-use practices, ideologies, and farmer-government relationships. The Palouse was much like the rest of the United States, except more so. It follows that the term "agrarian liberal" could also be applied across space and time to describe late nineteenth- and twentieth-century American agriculture in general.

Contrasts between the Palouse and other agricultural areas can be traced to the distinctiveness of the land. The countless Palouse hills and valleys, the fertile loess soil, and steady weather patterns are particularly conducive for growing small grains. Other areas of the nation grew wheat, but not as effectively and reliably as the Palouse. The same environmental factors that created favorable farming conditions also threatened to undermine long-term sustainability. The height and slope of the hills, the fine light soils, and heavy precipitation during months with little or no vegetation set the stage for damaging erosion. The Palouse landscape is productive, yet fragile, and it was compromised when settlers removed its top layer of soil and organic matter. It still produces great quantities of wheat, aided to a large extent by chemical fertilizers, but Palouse erosion is among the worst in the nation. It has already reduced productivity and has the potential to cripple the regional economy.

The political and social reactions to erosion in the Palouse also differed from other parts of the country. In the twentieth century in Delaware, Pennsylvania, Colorado, and especially Wisconsin, places where water erosion also created problems, state and local action ameliorated further losses. Strict land-use regulations and provisions that allowed residents to report improper tillage practices distinguished these areas from the Palouse, where property rights have been jealously guarded. Farmers all over the nation often cite freedom and independence, remnants of their pioneer heritage, as reasons why they enjoy their job and why they wish to continue. But in the Palouse this mentality has been taken to the extreme and is a remnant of an older agrarian past. Government intrusion was and is viewed as a threat to the very fabric of farming, an affront to operators' motives. This mentality is partly responsible for the severe erosion problems in the Palouse, conditions that are worse than in any of the aforementioned states.[3] Historian Steven Stoll wrote in 2002 that in the nineteenth century, American farmers "could not and would not be held accountable for their abuse of the land," because of similar attitudes.[4] Palouse agriculture continues to operate under that principle in the twenty-first century but with far more power, machinery, and—ironically—government assistance. In the Palouse, elements of Jeffersonian agrarianism and modern agriculture coexist, in spite of the apparent inconsistency.

The nation's better known wheat belt—the Dakotas, Montana, Nebraska, and Kansas—contends with wind erosion, not water erosion. In the Great Plains states, the problem has tended to be more sporadic; periodic droughts brought soil loss and dust storms, the most severe occurring in the 1930s. Likewise, conservation has been well received in the Plains during these dry spells, only to be ignored when rains return.[5] A more immediate crisis facing the Great Plains today, one that like the Palouse relates to a finite resource, involves groundwater. The Ogallala aquifer, a massive underground water source, has nourished crops there for over half a century. To tap the resource farmers constantly run pumps to bring the water to the surface, a practice that has depleted the aquifer much faster than it can be replenished. Estimates vary, but there is a good chance that 75 percent of the water will be gone by 2020. Yet farmers have resisted turning off their pumps because individual conservation efforts would cause immediate financial hardship and would likely not extend the life of the aquifer more than a few years.[6]

The Palouse suffers from a similar predicament. A limited resource, soil, is being gradually depleted, albeit at a slower rate than groundwater in the Plains. When erosion was at its peak in the 1920s and 1930s, interest in conservation grew when farmers learned for the first time about the tenuous nature of their land. Although soil loss slowed, it continued at a pace that worried scientists and the USDA, because much of the land could not withstand the rigors of intensive agriculture. Farmers resisted permanently taking acres out of production for the same reason Plains farmers keep their spigots open—because it brought short-term financial returns. The land

and water may be in decline, but until the resources are gone they will likely be put to work.

So how long before the Palouse sees a decline serious enough to cause political and social change? A definitive answer is not possible, owing to the technological inputs that farmers and society have thus far been willing to apply to degraded landscapes such as the Palouse; it is entirely possible that we could see wheat in this region for several more generations. Or not. Technological fixes offer only partial solutions to the Palouse erosion and water-pollution problem; as Piers Blaikie notes, "sharpening the tools of policy-making and increasing the 'expertness' of government personnel should no longer be the central problem."[7] Technofixes, to Colin Duncan, offer false hope for a better tomorrow, complicating matters and making permanent solutions more difficult. Duncan suggests that when agricultural societies are confronted with environmental problems, the fork in the agricultural road is clear: "we should imitate nature rather than simplify our activity to spite it."[8]

Depending on who makes land-use decisions in the future, the Palouse could wind up being a very different place. As Steven Stoll reminds us, agriculture has simply not been around that long, when one contrasts it with either the time humans have existed or, especially, with the time life has existed on Earth. And the intensive form of farming that is common today has been around for hardly any time at all, on a geological scale. He writes, "industrial agriculture has been a nanosecond. No one has any reason to believe that it will survive in its present form."[9] Soil scientists Daniel Richter and Daniel Markewitz sound the same notes, claiming, "We cannot take for granted that soil will produce ample and increasing yields of high quality food, fiber, and water over many generations' time." When cast against the backdrop of what one historian calls "big history," or the passage of deep time, agriculture on the Palouse looks rather transient.[10]

And that might not be all bad. If grain farming in the Palouse fails, then what would happen next? It would not make for the imminent collapse of the planet, nor would it cause the automatic ruin of the people who live and work in the region. Asia will not suddenly go without noodles and crackers (the primary uses of Palouse wheat), as other nations would quickly make up for any potential shortfall. If fact, there would be a significant upside, such as the fact that water quality would probably improve, simply because plows would not be running up and down the loess hills every year. In a less tangible sense, the end of Palouse wheat might get residents to think more holistically, consider more carefully the long-term impacts of their actions, and appreciate ecological diversity. And the demise of wheat growing need not result in the end of all forms of agriculture. One possible outcome of an eroded Palouse would be the return of cattle ranching. Grazing animals present their own set of environmental challenges, to be sure, but we need to keep in mind that there are many possible outcomes to the current agricultural situation, and one of them involves the reappearance of large-hoofed creatures. Perhaps some combination of grazing and cropping could work.[11] In all likelihood any new enterprise would not be as profitable as wheat farming has been for the past century, but here too would be another opportunity for growth. There is no special dictum from above that states the Palouse *must* produce annual crops; if this book has shown anything, it is that the Palouse farmer *can* change—provided that either the short-term returns look good or that the immediate consequences of inaction prove costly. Americans have asked all sorts of workers to change with the times or suffer—from factory workers to computer software designers. The Palouse farmer's difficulties might be avoidable, but even if they are not, the region and the nation and the world will press on, perhaps in some diminished form.

It is also not necessary to think about the future in terms of failure or environmental collapse. What might help us realize a better future is a recasting of our notions of "progress" or "success," considering the possibility that the will to exempt landscapes from intensive use might be the truest indicator of wealth and prestige.[12] I admit that it is all too easy to sniff contemptuously at such a notion, dismissing it as yet another unrealistic academic fantasy. Since the Industrial Revolution our consumer-driven wants have been translated into a perceived set of "needs," and anyone who challenges bedrock assumptions about the modern commercial value system quickly gets labeled the town misanthrope. Yet I believe that it will "pay off" to keep some of the Palouse from annual cropping—in ways that are difficult to quantify. Farmers and nonfarmers alike might enjoy—or "profit"—from the feeling that they had limited their physical impact on a part of their world for the sake of future generations. The returns would be nebulous—less erosion and fewer clay points on hills, cleaner water, and more native vegetation—yet people can derive a sense of achievement from these goals that cannot be banked or spent, but instead would be felt and experienced. Indeed, the payoff would be real.

There are people who can envision a future along these lines. Grassroots efforts to confront industrial agriculture have been modest, but they may be the region's best hope for providing farmers with a sense of stewardship. The Palouse-Clearwater Environmental Institute (PCEI), a nonprofit environmental group founded in 1986, sponsors a variety of projects designed to improve the aesthetics and ecology of the Palouse. In its early years the group highlighted dangers from the nearby Hanford nuclear reactor and from farm pesticides, while more recent PCEI efforts included streambank stabilization, wetlands restoration, riparian tree planting and maintenance, and "re-meandering" part of the channelized Paradise Creek. Other concerned groups include the Palouse Land Trust and the Palouse Prairie Foundation, both of which use volunteers to preserve fragments of native vegetation and to acquire conservation easements. Years of erosion and weed infestations make restoration efforts difficult, but the recent interest in semi-arid bunchgrass ecosystems is noteworthy. These environmental groups cannot quantify results in terms of water quality data, but they have popularized the notion of preserving this unique corner of the Northwest.[13]

There are a few small organic producers operating in the Idaho Palouse and there are none who grow grains commercially. Because organic producers in the Palouse are truck farmers operating in a sea of commercial giants, a significant shift away from industrial agriculture appears unlikely. Farmers with arsenals of machinery and mountains of debt would find it financially impossible to risk the possible drop in productivity that organic farming often entails. Creditors would likely throw a fit. Although farmers seek to reduce chemical use and are often aware of its environmental consequences, they cling to industrial agriculture out of fiscal necessity.

There is no wholesale recognition that the Palouse ecosystem today functions as part of nature. The landscape is so transformed that it now appears to run exclusively as a human regimen. Except for rainfall, farmers and scientists have expertly manipulated nature to serve the needs of production. On a national scale, farmer-activist Wendell Berry, renowned for his exposés of California and Great Plains agriculture, argues that a "mentality of exploitation" permeates our culture and encourages ceaseless technological innovation and the constant alteration of resources. Because few people feel a sense of loss, the exploitation of the land appears "natural." Under the prevailing agricultural regime in the US, the notion of sustainability has no place.[14] The American farming establishment has good reason to feel immune from natural forces because it produces bumper crops year after year. This has been made apparent in Whitman County, which led the nation in wheat and barley production in 1997, and to the uncritical eye the future of regional agriculture looks secure.[15] Palouse agriculture in many ways operates according to the national agricultural agenda that preaches short-term gains and deemphasizes landowner responsibilities, creating a kind of dissonance with nature.

Countering the trend are the likes of Wes Jackson, the founder of the Land Institute, who argues that "agriculture depends on nature and is contained in nature."[16] Farmers and their associates should be aware that nature imposes limits on human activity. For years they have mortgaged their future, aided by technology and government support. Predicting when the Palouse will no longer support grain farming is far more difficult than asserting that a problem exists. Certainly agricultural science has made the land incredibly productive and valuable and many farmers believe, quite rationally, that technology will continue to preserve their livelihood. But it also might fail. It is entirely possible that the Palouse has already seen its best days and that declining yields, more expensive inputs, and declining profits are in store for the future. Agricultural improvements might mean little if soil erosion persists and more underlying clay comes to the surface. At some point input costs may prove unbearable, forcing farmers to consider some other crop, ranching, or the outright abandonment of their land. Whatever the outcome, the decisions of the past two centuries will have had a direct bearing on the look, feel, and utility of the land.

1 INTRODUCTION: A PLACE CALLED THE PALOUSE

1. Elliott West, *The Way to the West: Essays on the Central Plains* (Albuquerque: University of New Mexico Press, 1995), 4.

2. The concept of place is crucial to understanding the environmental history of a discrete area. It is best described by the geographer Yi-Fu Tuan, who wrote that space plus culture equals place. In other words, it is the combination and intermingling of the natural world and human society. That union results in a knowable, accessible place that can be studied and analyzed, in this case, the Palouse.

For discussions on place as an organizing principle for environmental and Pacific Northwest history, see William G. Robbins, *The Great Northwest: The Search for Regional Identity* (Corvallis: Oregon State University Press, 2001); Dan Flores, "Place: An Argument for Bioregional History," and William Lang, "From Where We Are Standing: The Sense of Place and Environmental History," in *Northwest Lands, Northwest Peoples: Readings in Environmental History*, ed. Dale D. Goble and Paul W. Hirt (Seattle: University of Washington Press, 1999); the prologue of William G. Robbins's *Landscapes of Promise: The Oregon Story, 1800–1940* (Seattle: University of Washington Press, 1997); and Richard White and John M. Findlay, eds., *Power and Place in the North American West* (Seattle: University of Washington Press, 1999).

3. Other environmental historians have shown interest in agricultural places that contain their own kind of beauty. Mark Fiege, in *Irrigated Eden: The Making of an Agricultural Landscape in the American West* (Seattle: University of Washington Press,

1999), writes that he has a kind of morbid attraction to commercialized, partially despoiled agricultural places: "I have spent a great deal of my life living in or studying unappealing places in the American West" (10). I am not willing to ascribe a similar sentiment to the Palouse. The Palouse is flawed, to be sure, and has plenty of historical fodder to study, but it certainly has its redeeming aesthetic qualities.

4. According to agricultural economist Willard W. Cochrane, extensive agriculture exists when there is "an increase in the total output of goods and services in which output per capita is constant. In this case output increases as the result of an increase in the use of inputs where all inputs continue to be employed in the same ways under the same institutional arrangements." On the other hand, intensive agriculture means "an increase in the total output of goods and services in which output per capita increases. In this case output increases from some combination of an increase in the use of inputs and an increase in the productivity of individual units of inputs as the result of their being employed in new ways under new institutional arrangements." See *The Development of American Agriculture: A Historical Analysis*, 2nd ed. (Minneapolis: University of Minnesota Press, 1993), 5.

5. *Palouse Cooperative River Basin Study* (USDA, Soil Conservation Service, Forest Service, Economics, Statistics, and Cooperatives Service, 1978), xi; Larry J. Puckett, "Nonpoint and Point Sources of Nitrogen in Major Watersheds of the United States," USGS, Water-Resources Investigations Report 94–4001, 1994.

6. *Our Changing Nature: Natural Resource Trends in Washington State* (Washington State Department of Natural Resources, 1998).

7. Gove Hambridge, "Soils and Men—A Summary," in *Soils and Men: Yearbook of Agriculture 1938* (Washington, DC: GPO, 1938), 15.

8. Piers Blaikie, *The Political Economy of Soil Erosion in Developing Countries* (New York: Longman, 1985), 2, 32, 50, 89.

9. Blaikie, 2, 90.

10. William Kittredge, *Owning It All* (St. Paul, MN: Graywolf Press, 1987), 11.

11. Blaikie, 35.

12. Kittredge, 6.

13. My definition of agriculture is purposely broad so as to include Native American land use that was geared toward food production.

14. I have borrowed the term "hybrid landscape" from Mark Fiege, who uses it as the key organizing principle in *Irrigated Eden*.

15. Frieda Knobloch, in *The Culture of Wilderness: Agriculture as Colonization in the American West* (Chapel Hill: University of North Carolina Press, 1996), makes this point abundantly clear. She is concerned most not with the planting of crops in the same space year after year, but with about what happens to people *after* those crops have been planted: "Agriculture . . . has never simply been about raising food

crops or the sciences that make this more productive and efficient. Agriculture is an intensively social enterprise, shaped by inescapably social desires and expectations, even if it is described in simplistic material or natural terms: working the land, improving a breed" (2–3).

16. Steven Stoll, *Larding the Lean Earth: Soil and Society in Nineteenth-Century America* (New York: Hill and Wang, 2002), 8.

17. Stoll, 14.

18. Brian Donahue, *The Great Meadow: Farmers and the Land in Colonial Concord* (New Haven: Yale University Press, 2004), 23, 230.

19. Geoff Cunfer, *On the Great Plains: Agriculture and Environment* (College Station: Texas A&M University Press, 2005), 5–15, 163.

20. Karl Marx, *The Eighteenth Brumaire of Louis Napoleon* (New York: International Publishers, 1998), 124, and *The Communist Manifesto* (New York: Penguin Putnam, 1998), 55. Anyone even slightly familiar with Marx's work knows that if a segment of society appeared unwilling or unable to aid in the toppling of laissez-faire capitalism, they would likely incur his wrath.

21. Richard Hofstadter, *The Age of Reform: From Bryan to FDR* (New York: Alfred A. Knopf, 1955), 46.

22. William Cronon, "The Trouble with Wilderness, or, Getting Back to the Wrong Nature," in *Uncommon Ground: Rethinking the Human Place in Nature*, ed. William Cronon (New York: W. W. Norton, 1995), 85.

23. I am referring here again to the works of Donahue, Stoll, and Cunfer.

24. Cronon, 88.

25. Donald Worster, "Opening Plenary Session: Remarks by Donald Worster," presented at the annual meeting of the American Society for Environmental History, Chapel Hill, North Carolina, March, 2001.

2   THE PRECONTACT PALOUSE

1. Of course, the lack of responses could also have been because Jeff's coworkers were well aware of his academic background; the question may have smacked of scholarly snobbery. Jeff assures me that none was intended.

2. Dan Flores, "Place: An Argument for Bioregional History," in *Northwest Lands, Northwest Peoples: Readings in Environmental History*, ed. Dale D. Goble and Paul W. Hirt (Seattle: University of Washington Press, 1999), 40.

3. In terms of geology and hydrology, the Columbia Basin consists of all the waters drained by the Columbia River—from its headwaters in British Columbia to the north, south to the Blue Mountains, and from the Continental Divide in the

east to the Cascade Range in the west. The basin is roughly 260,000 square miles in size—larger than the state of Texas. See "Columbia River and Tributaries Review Study: Project Data and Operating Limits," US Army Corps of Engineers, North Pacific Division, CRT 69, 1989.

4. Elizabeth L. Orr and William N. Orr, *Geology of the Pacific Northwest* (New York: McGraw-Hill, 1996), 288–291. Steptoe Butte takes its name from nineteenth-century US Army colonel Edward J. Steptoe, who fought, and lost, a battle against several inland tribes in 1858 near Rosalia, Washington. The butte is several miles from the main battle site. Geologists now refer to an older formation or outcrop that protrudes through a younger formation as a "steptoe."

5. Orr and Orr, 291–292.

6. Orr and Orr, 297.

7. Victor Baker et al., "Quaternary Geology of the Columbia Plateau," in *The Geology of North America*, vol. K-2 (Boulder, CO: Geological Society of America, 1991), 215–249.

8. Paul L. Weis and William L. Newman, *The Channeled Scablands of Eastern Washington* (US Department of Interior, Eastern Washington University, 1989). For perspective, ancient Lake Missoula was about half the size of Lake Michigan—its surface area was an estimated three hundred square miles and it reached depths of two thousand feet.

9. John A. Alwin, *Between the Mountains: A Portrait of Eastern Washington* (Bozeman, MT: Northwest Panorama Publishing, 1984), 28–30; Weis and Newman, 12–14. Again for perspective, the Columbia River, at The Dalles, Oregon, runs at an average of 195,000 cubic feet per second. The enormity of the size and violence of this flood simply cannot be related in words that have any real meaning. We are left to use our imaginations to illustrate what must have been the single most otherworldly event the region has ever experienced.

10. Hill Williams, *The Restless Northwest: A Geological Story* (Pullman: Washington State University Press, 2002), 121–122. Determining how many massive floods occurred depends in part on one's definition of "massive." See Alan Busacca, "Long Quaternary Record in Eastern Washington, U.S.A., Interpreted from Multiple Buried Paleosols in Loess," *Geoderma* 45 (1989): 107.

11. John Eliot Allen and Marjorie Burns, *Cataclysms of the Columbia* (Portland, OR: Timber Press, 1986), 87–88; Weis and Newman, 20–21.

12. Baker et al., "Quaternary Geology," 216–217, 224–228; Eric von McDonald, "Correlation and Interpretation of the Stratigraphy of the Palouse Loess of Eastern Washington" (PhD diss., Washington State University, 1987), 189–195; C. A. Richardson, "Late Pleistocene Loess Deposition on the Columbia Plateau," in *Dust Aerosols, Loess Soils, and Global Change: An Interdisciplinary Conference and Field Tour on Dust*

in *Ancient Environments and Contemporary Environmental Management*, ed. Alan J. Busacca (Washington State University, College of Agriculture and Home Economics, Miscellaneous Publications No. MISC 0190, 1998), 175–178.

13. Roald Fryxell and Earl F. Cook, *A Field Guide to the Loess Deposits and Channeled Scablands of the Palouse Area, Eastern Washington* (Pullman: Laboratory of Anthropology, Washington State University, 1964), 30.

14. Don J. Easterbrook and David H. Rahm, *Landforms of Washington: The Geological Environment* (Bellingham: Western Washington University, 1970), 148.

15. Scott M. Lambert, Rodney D. Sayler, and Linda H. Hardesty, "The Palouse Prairie—Does It Still Exist or Is It Extinct?" (n.p., 1997), 1–2.

16. Jerry F. Franklin and C. T. Dyrness, *Natural Vegetation of Oregon and Washington* (Corvallis: Oregon State University Press, 1988), 214–216; Alvin Aller et al., "Plant Communities and Soils of North Slopes in the Palouse Region of Eastern Washington and Northern Idaho," *Northwest Science* 55, no. 4 (1981): 256; Lambert, Sayler, and Hardesty, 2; Harold St. John, *Flora of Southeastern Washington and of Adjacent Idaho* (Escondido, CA: Outdoor Pictures, 1963); Rexford F. Daubenmire, "An Ecological Study of the Vegetation of Southeastern Washington and Adjacent Idaho," *Ecological Monographs* 12 (1942): 75 (Daubenmire also states that 10 percent of this total consisted of nonnative species—imports from Europe, mostly); E. W. Tisdale, "Ecologic Changes in the Palouse," *Northwest Science* 35, no. 4 (1961): 135.

17. J. E. Weaver, *A Study of the Vegetation of Southeastern Washington and Adjacent Idaho* (Lincoln: University of Nebraska, 1917); Anne E. Black et al., "Biodiversity and Land-Use History of the Palouse Bioregion: Pre-European to Present," USGS, Land Use History of North America, August 15, 2000, http://biology.usgs.gov/luhna/chap10.html (accessed 12 October 2000).

18. *Soil Survey of Whitman County, Washington* (USDA, Soil Conservation Service, 1980), 177–182; Daubenmire, "Ecological Study," 59; Helmut K. Beuchner, *Some Biotic Changes in the State of Washington, Particularly During the Century 1853–1953*, Research Studies of the State College of Washington (Pullman: State College of Washington, 1953), 13, 56–59.

19. O. Eugene Maughan et al., "A Comparison of Fish Species Above and Below Palouse Falls, Palouse River, Washington-Idaho," *Northwest Science* 54, no. 1 (1980): 5–8; Daubenmire, "Ecological Study," 59.

20. Lambert, Sayler, and Hardesty, 3.

21. Buechner, 163–164. See also William D. Layman, *Native River: The Columbia Remembered, Priest Rapids to the International Boundary* (Pullman: Washington State University Press, 2002), 42.

22. George Hatley, lecture at the Palouse Audubon Society, Moscow, Idaho, 21 February 2001; Beuchner, 176.

23. Black et al. write that the date is *at least* 12,000 BP. Others claim it to be in the 10,000–11,000 BP range. See Gerald Gross, "Cave Life on the Palouse," *Natural History* 76, no. 1 (February 1967): 42; Christian J. Miss and Bruce D. Cochran, *Archaeological Evaluations of the Riparia (45WT1) and Ash Cave (45WW61) Sites on the Lower Snake River* (Pullman: Laboratory of Archaeology and History, Washington State University, 1982), 16–17; Mary B. Collins and William Andrefsky Jr., *Archaeological Collections Inventory and Assessment of Marmes Rockshelter (45FR50) and Palus Sites (45FR36A, B, C)* (Pullman: Center for Northwest Anthropology, Department of Anthropology, Washington State University, 1995), 44.

24. Clifford E. Trafzer and Richard D. Scheuerman, *Renegade Tribe: The Palouse Indians and the Invasion of the Inland Pacific Northwest* (Pullman: Washington State University Press, 1986), 134.

25. Trafzer and Scheuerman; Click Relander, *Drummers and Dreamers* (Caldwell, ID: Caxton Printers, 1956), *Strangers on the Land* (Yakima, WA: Franklin Press, 1962), and *The Yakimas: Treaty Centennial* (Yakima, WA: Franklin Press, 1955).

26. For example, see Reverend Samuel Parker, *Journal of an Exploring Tour Beyond the Rocky Mountains* (Ithaca, NY: Andrus, Woodruff, and Gauntlett, 1844); David Thompson, *Columbia Journals*, ed. Barbara Belyea (Montreal, PQ: McGill-Queens University Press, 1994); and Ross Cox, *The Columbia River*, ed. Edgar I. Stewart and Jane R. Stewart (Norman: University of Oklahoma Press, 1957).

27. Donald W. Meinig, *The Great Columbia Plain: A Historical Geography, 1805–1910* (Seattle: University of Washington Press, 1968), 26–30.

28. Richard Scheuerman and Clifford Trafzer, "The First People of the Palouse Country," *Bunchgrass Historian* 8, no. 3 (1988): 3; Harry H. Caldwell, "The Palouse in Diverse Disciplines," *Northwest Science* 35, no. 4 (1961): 115.

29. The list of offenders is lengthy. Among them are Garrett D. Kincaid and A. H. Harris, *Palouse . . . in the Making* (n.p., 1934), 1; Alwin, 47.

30. Roderick Sprague, "Palouse," in *Handbook of North American Indians*, vol. 12, ed. Deward E. Walker (Washington, DC: Smithsonian Institution, 1998), 352.

31. Sprague, 352–353; Scheuerman and Trafzer, "First People of the Palouse Country," 4.

32. Meinig, *Great Columbia Plain*, 118–124; Sprague, 357–358.

33. Trafzer and Scheuerman, 42. See also Christopher L. Miller, *Prophetic Worlds: Indians and Whites on the Columbia Plateau* (New Brunswick, NJ: Rutgers University Press, 1985); and Robert T. Boyd, *The Coming of the Spirit of Pestilence: Introduced Infectious Diseases and Population Decline Among Northwest Coast Indians, 1774–1884* (Seattle: University of Washington Press, 1999).

34. Robert H. Ruby and John A. Brown, *A Guide to the Indian Tribes of the Pacific Northwest* (Norman: University of Oklahoma Press, 1986), 162.

35. Eugene S. Hunn, "Mobility as a Factor Limiting Resource Use on the Columbia Plateau," in *Northwest Lands, Northwest Peoples*, ed. Goble and Hirt, 158–159; Eugene S. Hunn, *Nch'i-Wana, "The Big River": Mid-Columbia Indians and Their Land* (Seattle: University of Washington Press, 1990), 110–117.

36. Hunn, "Mobility as a Factor Limiting Resource Use," 165; Alan G. Marshall, "Unusual Gardens: The Nez Perce and Wild Horticulture in the Eastern Columbia Plateau," in *Northwest Lands, Northwest Peoples*, ed. Goble and Hirt, 178.

37. Isaac Stevens et al., *Reports of Explorations and Surveys to Ascertain the Most Practicable and Economic Route for a Railroad from the Mississippi River to the Pacific Ocean* (hereafter cited as *Stevens Report*), vol. 12, bk. 1 (Washington, DC: Thomas H. Ford, Printer, 1860), 199.

38. Rexford F. Daubenmire, "Steppe Vegetation of Washington," Washington Agricultural Experiment Station, Technical Bulletin No. 62, 1970, 7–8; Daubenmire, "Ecological Study," 62.

39. Marshall, 179.

40. Paul S. Martin and Christine R. Szuter, "Megafauna of the Columbia Basin, 1800–1840: Lewis and Clark in a Game Sink," in *Northwest Lands, Northwest Peoples*, ed. Goble and Hirt, 197; Daubenmire, "Steppe Vegetation of Washington," 7.

41. Richard Scheuerman and Clifford Trafzer, eds., "A Palouse Indian Speaks: Mary Jim Remembers," *Bunchgrass Historian* 8, no. 3 (1988): 20.

42. Robert Butler, "Bison Hunting in the Desert West Before 1800: The Paleo-Ecological Potential and the Archaeological Reality," *Plains Anthropologist* 23, no. 82 (November 1978): 109.

43. Marshall, 197; Daubenmire, "Steppe Vegetation of Washington," 7.

3 FROM BUNCHGRASS BACKWATER TO AGRICULTURAL EMPIRE

1. Reuben Gold Thwaites, ed., *The Original Journals of the Lewis and Clark Expedition*, vol. 3 (New York: Antiquarian Press, 1959), 112; David Thompson, *Columbia Journals*, ed. Barbara Belyea (Montreal, PQ: McGill-Queens University Press, 1994), 285; Albert W. Thompson, "The Early History of the Palouse River and Its Names," *Pacific Northwest Quarterly* 62, no. 2 (1971): 71–72; Ross Cox, *The Columbia River*, ed. Edgar I. Stewart and Jane R. Stewart (Norman: University of Oklahoma Press, 1957), 89–92.

2. In *The Culture of Wilderness: Agriculture as Colonization in the American West* (Chapel Hill: University of North Carolina Press, 1996), Frieda Knobloch writes that a reworked or, indeed, a despoiled nature is the source of the very existence of cul-

ture: "Culture exists where nature has been permanently altered, even obliterated, where a society measures its worth by its distance from 'nature'—from its birth—all traces of which have been relegated to the past" (75). She states that the most significant step in this process is plowing the soil.

3. T. C. Elliott, ed., "Journal of John Work, June–October 1825," *Washington Historical Quarterly* 5, no. 2 (1914): 89–90.

4. Donald Meinig, *The Great Columbia Plain: A Historical Geography, 1805–1910* (Seattle: University of Washington Press, 1968), 125–151.

5. *Thirteenth Census of the United States* (Washington, DC: GPO, 1913); Meinig, 201–240.

6. Charles A. Geyer, "Notes on the Vegetation and General Character of the Missouri and Oregon Territories, Made During a Botanical Journey in the State of Missouri, Across the South Pass of the Rocky Mountains, to the Pacific, During the years 1843 and 1844," *London Journal of Botany* 5 (1845): 286–287.

7. Lansford W. Hastings, *The Emigrants' Guide to Oregon and California* (Princeton, NJ: Princeton University Press, 1932), vii–xiv, 38–43.

8. Martha Berry Parker, *Washington and Oregon: A Map History of the Oregon Country* (Fairfield, WA: Ye Galleon Press, 1988), 38–41; Derek Hayes, *Historical Atlas of the Pacific Northwest: Maps of Exploration and Discovery* (Seattle: Sasquatch Books, 1999), 137.

9. George A. Northrup, interview by James E. Lindsey, n.d., James Emerson Lindsey Papers, 1934 (hereafter cited as Lindsey Papers), Washington State University, Manuscripts, Archives, and Special Collections (hereafter cited as WSU MASC).

10. *Stevens Report*, vol. 1, 216.

11. *Stevens Report*, vol. 12, bk. 1, 199.

12. For a complete analysis of Stevens's motivations and subsequent councils, see Kent D. Richards, *Isaac Stevens: Young Man in a Hurry* (Provo, UT: Brigham Young University Press, 1979).

13. Clifford E. Trafzer, "The Palouse Indians: Interpreting the Past of a Plateau Tribe," in *Spokane and the Inland Empire: An Interior Pacific Northwest Anthology*, ed. David H. Stratton (Pullman: Washington State University Press, 1991), 64–68.

14. Keith Roy Williams, "The Agricultural History of Latah County and the Palouse: An Overview and Three Case Studies" (master's thesis, Washington State University, 1984), 19–21; George W. Fuller, *A History of the Pacific Northwest* (New York: Alfred A. Knopf, 1931), 36–37.

15. Harold R. Boyd, "Terror in the East Palouse," *Pacific Northwesterner* 2, no. 3 (Summer 1958): 33–38; Whitman County probate records, Whitman County Historical Association, Pullman, Washington.

16. Alan G. Marshall, "Unusual Gardens: The Nez Perce and Wild Horticulture

in the Eastern Columbia Plateau," in *Northwest Lands, Northwest Peoples: Readings in Environmental History*, ed. Dale D. Goble and Paul W. Hirt (Seattle: University of Washington Press, 1999), 178; Rexford F. Daubenmire, "Steppe Vegetation of Washington," Washington Agricultural Experiment Station, Technical Bulletin No. 62, 1970, 51.

17. Arthur Cox, interview by Harry M. Crumbaker, 3 February 1941, in *History of Grazing in the State of Washington* (n.p.), WSU MASC; J. Orin Oliphant, *On the Cattle Ranges of the Oregon Country* (Seattle: University of Washington Press, 1968), 85, 91, 101; Fred R. Yoder, *Stories of Early Pioneers in Whitman County* (n.p., 1938), 70; *An Illustrated History of Whitman County* (W. H. Lever, 1901), 104–105; Keith Roy Williams, "Agricultural History of Latah County and the Palouse," 10–12. For an extended account of all US agricultural land-law issues, see Paul W. Gates, *History of Public Land Law Development* (Washington, DC: GPO, 1968), especially 466–468.

18. Louis Mathis Ringer Papers, WSU MASC; Meinig, 251–254; Wayne D. Rasmussen, "A Century of Farming in the Inland Empire," in *Spokane and the Inland Empire: An Interior Pacific Northwest Anthology*, ed. David H. Stratton (Pullman: Washington State University Press, 1991), 39–40; Alexander Campbell McGregor, *Counting Sheep: From Open Range to Agribusiness on the Columbia Plateau* (Seattle: University of Washington Press, 1982), 12; Keith Roy Williams, "Agricultural History of Latah County and the Palouse," 19–20.

19. J. Orin Oliphant, "Notes on Early Settlement and on Geographic Names of Eastern Washington," *Washington Historical Quarterly* 22, no. 3 (1931): 172–201; Meinig, 245–247.

20. *Illustrated History of Whitman County*, 105.

21. William H. Brabyn, interview by James E. Lindsey, 7 September 1934, Lindsey Papers, WSU MASC; Oliver Hall, interview by James E. Lindsey, 28 September 1934, Lindsey Papers, WSU MASC; "Asa Calvin Short," Lena Parvin Papers, 1962–1965, WSU MASC. It is also entirely possible that, as Frieda Knobloch suggests, settlers moved away from ranching so as to avoid a permanent nomadic, half-civilized society—but I have found no concrete evidence to support such a notion in this case.

22. Richard Scheuerman puts the date at 1877, in the Rock Creek area, but there is no consensus on the matter. See Richard D. Scheuerman, "Patterns of Settlement in the Palouse Country, 1860–1915" (n.p., 1980), Whitman County Historical Society, 15. See also "Will Our Land Produce," *Colfax Gazette*, 8 December 1878, 1; E. V. Smalley, "In the Palouse Country," *Northwest Magazine*, September 1892, 21–22; Mary W. Avery, *History and Government of the State of Washington* (Seattle: University of Washington Press, 1962), 252; Meinig, 249–251; and Keith Roy Williams, "Agricultural History of Latah County and the Palouse," 12, 43fn.

23. David R. and Ann Judson, interview by James E. Lindsey, 17 September 1934,

Lindsey Papers, WSU MASC; John Morris Klemgard, interview by James E. Lindsey, 26 September 1934, Lindsey Papers, WSU MASC; *Colfax Gazette*, 23 March 1878, 1; Northrup, interview by James E. Lindsey, n.d.

24. *Illustrated History of Whitman County*, 172.

25. Peter J. Lewty, *Across the Columbia Plain: Railroad Expansion in the Interior Northwest, 1885–1893* (Pullman: Washington State University Press, 1995), 27–34; Meinig, 269–272.

26. Leo Marx, *The Machine in the Garden: Technology and the Pastoral Ideal in America* (New York: Oxford University Press, 1964), 191–192.

27. *Farm Lands in the Famous Palouse Country of Eastern Washington and Northern Idaho: How to Get There, How to Get a Farm* (Spokane: Shaw and Borden, 1895), 15; *Pullman, Washington: The Commercial and Educational Center of the Palouse Country* (Pullman Chamber of Commerce, 1912).

28. *Thirteenth Census of the United States*. For a promotional account of regional growth and the importance of Spokane, see *Farm Lands in the Famous Palouse Country*.

29. Colin A. M. Duncan, *The Centrality of Agriculture: Between Humankind and the Rest of Nature* (Montreal, PQ: McGill-Queen's University Press, 1996), 102–103; Robert C. Nesbit and Charles M. Gates, "Agriculture in Eastern Washington," *Pacific Northwest Quarterly* 37, no. 4 (October 1946): 280; *Colfax Gazette*, 18 May 1878, 1, and subsequent issues; John Fahey, *The Inland Empire: The Unfolding Years, 1879–1929* (Seattle: University of Washington Press, 1986), 6; Smalley, 21; "Pullman Is Being Well-Advertised," *Pullman Herald*, 2 April 1909, 1.

30. Ben F. Manning, interview by Josephine Watrous, 26 February 1941, in *History of Grazing*, WSU MASC; Scheuerman, 13; Rural Women's History Project Papers, 1975–1980, University of Idaho, Special Collections and Archives; Walter Scott Getchell, interview by James E. Lindsey, 27 September 1934, Lindsey Papers, WSU MASC.

31. *Eleventh Census of the United States* (Washington, DC: GPO, 1893) 5, 192, 233; Charles O. Kellogg, interview by James E. Lindsey, 29 September 1934, Lindsey Papers, WSU MASC; "Palouse Country Agricultural Society," *Colfax Gazette*, 30 March 1878, 1. See also "Land Values Go Up," *Pullman Herald*, 2 April 1909, 1.

32. William G. Robbins, *Landscapes of Promise: The Oregon Story, 1800–1940* (Seattle: University of Washington Press, 1997), 112.

33. David Danbom, *The Resisted Revolution: Urban America and the Industrialization of Agriculture* (Ames: Iowa State University Press, 1979); James F. Shepherd, "The Development of Wheat Production in the Pacific Northwest," *Agricultural History* 49, no. 1 (January 1975): 263–264; Morton Rothstein, "West Coast Farmers and

the Tyranny of Distance: Agriculture on the Fringes of the World Market," *Agricultural History* 49, no. 1 (January 1975): 272–280.

34. Keith Roy Williams, "Hills of Gold: The Story of Wheat Production Technologies in the Palouse Region of Washington and Idaho," (PhD diss., Washington State University, 1991), 45; "Made Good Run with Harvester," *Pullman Herald*, 4 August 1906, 1; Willard W. Cochrane, *The Development of American Agriculture: A Historical Analysis*, 2nd ed. (Minneapolis: University of Minnesota Press, 1993), 189–208; Wayne D. Rasmussen, "The Impact of Technological Change on American Agriculture, 1862–1962," *Journal of Economic History* 22, no. 4 (December 1962): 578–583; *The Palouse Story* (Palouse Town and Country Study Program, 1962).

35. Within a few years, this long-winded name was shortened to Washington State College. It changed again to Washington State University in the 1950s.

36. George A. Frykman, *Creating the People's University: Washington State University, 1890–1990* (Pullman: Washington State University Press, 1990); Enoch Albert Bryan, *Historical Sketches of the State College of Washington* (Spokane: The Alumni and the Associated Students, 1928); Keith Peterson, *This Crested Hill: An Illustrated History of the University of Idaho* (Moscow: University of Idaho Press, 1987); John Scobey, "Farm Dairying," State College of Washington, Agricultural Experiment Station, Bulletin No. 3, February 1892, 47.

37. Knobloch, 75. She puts the word "breaking" in quotes to liken it to the breaking of a draught animal.

38. See chapters on promotion in Spokane and Palouse settlement in Katherine G. Morrissey, *Mental Territories: Mapping the Inland Empire* (Ithaca, NY: Cornell University Press, 1997). See also Nesbit and Gates, 283; and Verle G. Kaiser, "Historical Land Use in the Palouse—A Reappraisal," *Northwest Science* 35, no. 4 (1961): 140.

39. Richard N. Mack, "First Comprehensive Botanical Survey of the Columbia Plateau, Washington: The Sandberg and Leiberg Expedition of 1893," *Northwest Science* 62, no. 3 (May 1988): 118–128; Charles V. Piper and R. Kent Beattie, *The Flora of the Palouse Region* (Pullman: Allen Brothers, 1901); Bertie J. Weddell, "Changing Perspectives in Nineteenth Century Written Descriptions of Palouse and Canyon Grasslands," Idaho Bureau of Land Management, Technical Bulletin No. 01–13, August 2001, 6.

40. George Hatley, lecture at the Palouse Audubon Society, Moscow, Idaho, 21 February 2001; Helmut K. Beuchner, "Some Biotic Changes in the State of Washington, Particularly During the Century 1853–1953," Research Studies of the State College of Washington, Pullman, 1953, 177–179.

41. Klemgard, interview by James E. Lindsey, 26 September 1934; Hatley, lecture

at the Palouse Audubon Society; Richard J. Poelker and Irven O. Buss, "Habitat Improvement—The Way to Higher Wildlife Populations in Southeast Washington," *Northwest Science* 46, no. 1 (January 1972): 25–26; "Hunters Complain; No Game," *Spokane Spokesman-Review*, 5 October 1909; O. A. Fitzgerald, "Good Deeds by Bad Birds," *Washington Farmer*, 5 June 1952, 6.

42. Verle G. Kaiser, "An Informal Report of the Erosion Damage During the 1945–1946 Run-off Season in Whitman County, Washington" (n.p., n.d.), Verle G. Kaiser Papers, 1932–1982 (hereafter cited as Kaiser Papers), WSU MASC, 3; Jeffrey L. Doke and Gibran S. Hashmi, *Paradise Creek Watershed Characterization Study* (Pullman: State of Washington Water Research Center, 1994), 56–57; Dorothy Presby, *Viola Stump Ranch* (n.p., 1999).

43. Judsons, interview by James E. Lindsey, 17 September 1934; Northrup, interview by James E. Lindsey, n.d; Klemgard, interview by James E. Lindsey, 26 September 1934; E. A. Bryan, interview by George N. Douglas, 21 February 1941, in *History of Grazing*, WSU MASC.

44. *Plat Book of Whitman County* (Seattle: Anderson Map Co., 1910); "Trends in Agriculture in Washington, 1900–1930: Types of Farming Series, Part II," State College of Washington, Agricultural Experiment Station, Bulletin No. 300, 1931, table 8.

45. *Illustrated History of Whitman County*, 187; *Farm Lands in the Famous Palouse Country*, 2.

46. Brabyn, interview by James E. Lindsey, 7 September 1934; Fred A. Hodges, interview by James E. Lindsey, 15 September 1934, Lindsey Papers, WSU MASC.

47. Leonard Hegnauer, *86 Golden Years: The Autobiography of Leonard Hegnauer* (n.p., n.d.), Leonard Hegnauer Papers, 1954–1963, WSU MASC.

48. R. C. McCroskey, "Wheat Growing," Washington Agricultural College and School of Science Experiment Station, Bulletin No. 1, 1892, 55; "Experiments in 'Dry Farming' by Local Station Prove Successful," *Pullman Herald*, 23 October 1908, 1. Byron Hunter, a USDA scientist, concurred. See "Dry Farming in the Columbia River Basin," *Colton News-Letter*, 21 October 1910, 1.

49. Ben H. Pubols and Carl P. Heisig, "Historical and Geographic Aspects of Wheat Yields in Washington," State College of Washington, Agricultural Experiment Station, Bulletin No. 355, 1937, 8.

50. Nicholas E. J. Gentry, interview by James E. Lindsey, 22 September 1934, Lindsey Papers, WSU MASC; Walter Glaspey, interview by James E. Lindsey, 22 September 1934, Lindsey Papers, WSU MASC; Kellogg, interview by James E. Lindsey, 29 September 1934; John Eikum, interview by Sam Schrager, 8 December 1975, *Transcribed Oral History Indexes*, University of Idaho, Special Collections and Archives.

51. Brabyn, interview by James E. Lindsey, 7 September 1934.

52. Kaiser, "Historical Land Use in the Palouse," 140.

53. R. W. Thatcher, "The Nitrogen and Humus Problem in Dry Farming," State College of Washington, Agricultural Experiment Station, Bulletin No. 105, June 1912, 4–16.

54. William Cronon, *Nature's Metropolis: Chicago and the Great West* (New York: W. W. Norton, 1991), 50.

4 THE IMPLICATIONS OF PROSPERITY

1. "Uncle John on the War," *Washington Farmer*, 1 November 1914, 1.

2. *FAO Commodity Series: Wheat* (Washington, DC: Food and Agriculture Organization of the United Nations, 1947), 7.

3. "Annual Average Wheat Prices, 1910–1989," Rosalia Producers Warehouse, n.d.

4. "Wheat Prices Soar; Farmers Jubilant," *Pullman Herald*, 31 July 1914, 1; "Dollar Wheat," *Pullman Herald*, 31 July 1914, 4; "Grain Quotations Again on Upgrade," *Pullman Herald*, 5 February 1915, 1.

5. *Fourteenth Census of the United States, 1920: Agriculture*, vol. 6, pt. 3 (Washington, DC: GPO, 1922), 144; "Trends in Agriculture in Washington, 1900–1930: Types of Farming Series, Part II," State College of Washington, Agricultural Experiment Station, Bulletin No. 300, 1931, table 8; "World Faces a Shortage in Wheat," *Washington Farmer*, 26 October 1916, 1.

6. *Washington Farmer*, 15 August 1914, 4; *Washington Farmer*, 15 February 1915, 4. These "marketing methods" probably refer to discriminatory rail freight rates.

7. Greg Hall, *Harvest Wobblies: The Industrial Workers of the World and Agricultural Laborers in the American West, 1905–1930* (Corvallis: Oregon State University Press, 2001), 1–2, 71–72, 226–229; John Fahey, *The Inland Empire: Unfolding Years, 1879–1929* (Seattle: University of Washington Press, 1986), 64–65.

8. "Use All the Land," *Washington Farmer*, 4 January 1917, 6; "Calamity or Blessing?" *Washington Farmer*, 4 January 1917, 4; "We Must Save Wheat," *Colfax Gazette*, 12 April 1918, 5.

9. *Proceedings of the 32nd Annual Session of the Washington State Grange* (Aberdeen: Washington State Grange, 1920).

10. "Fortyfold Wheat at Eighty Cents," *Pullman Herald*, 28 August 1914, 1; "Holding Wheat," *Pullman Herald*, 4 September 1914, 1 (source of quotes this paragraph); "Heavy Yields Are Reported Daily," *Pullman Herald*, 25 August 1915, 1; "Farmers Sell in Wheat Flurry," *Colfax Gazette*, 10 December 1915, 3; "County Warehouses Bulge with Grain," *Colton News-Letter*, 7 January 1916, 8; "Northwest Wheat Rais-

ers and the Grain Trust," *Colton News-Letter*, 3 March 1916, 8–9; "Learn More of Farm Markets," *Colfax Gazette*, 4 January 1918, 5.

11. "Farmers Get War Orders," *Colfax Gazette*, 14 April 1916, 5; *Washington Farmer*, 1 September 1914, 4.

12. "Must Combat Ruinous Slump in Wheat Prices," *Washington Farmer*, 2 December 1920, 1; "Annual Average Wheat Prices, 1910–1989."

13. *Comparative Statements of Condition* (Pullman State Bank and First National Bank of Pullman, 1917–1939).

14. E. F. Landerholm, "The Economic Relation of Tractors to Farm Organization in the Grain Farming Areas of Eastern Washington," State College of Washington, Agricultural Experiment Station, Bulletin No. 310, 1935, 9; "Buys Truck for Wheat Hauling," *Colfax Gazette*, 1 September 1916, 1; "Modern Farming Methods in the Palouse Country," *Colfax Gazette*, 11 March 1917, 2.

15. Landerholm, 9; J. G. Klemgard and G. F. Cadisch, "Cost of Wheat Production by Power Methods of Farming, 1919–1929," State College of Washington, Agricultural Experiment Station, Bulletin No. 255, 1931, 10; "General Report: Statistics by Subject," in *U.S. Census of Agriculture, 1954* (Washington, DC: GPO, 1956), 222–223.

16. F. J. Sievers, "What the War Did for the Palouse Country," *Washington Farmer*, 21 September 1922, 1; J. E. Nessly, "Wheat Will Always Be King in Palouse Country," *Washington Farmer*, 27 December 1923, 3.

17. "Trends in Agriculture in Washington, 1900–1930," tables 2, 4, 5.

18. "Statistics for Counties," in *Sixteenth Census of the United States, 1940: Agriculture*, vol. 1 (Washington, DC: GPO, 1942), Washington: 539.

19. This dynamic is described in a national context in Willard W. Cochrane, *The Development of American Agriculture: A Historical Analysis*, 2nd ed. (Minneapolis: University of Minnesota Press, 1993).

20. J. E. Nessly, "Cost of Producing Wheat in Palouse Country," *Washington Farmer*, 22 September 1921, 1.

21. Deborah Fitzgerald, *Every Farm a Factory: The Industrial Ideal in American Agriculture* (New Haven, CT: Yale University Press, 2003).

22. George Severence, "Grain Production of the Inland Empire," *Washington Farmer*, 27 April, 1916, 1, and "Era of Soil Mining," *Washington Farmer*, 22 February 1923, 6; Leonard Hegnauer, *86 Golden Years: The Autobiography of Leonard Hegnauer* (n.d., n.p.), Leonard Hegnauer Papers, 1954–1963, WSU MASC.

23. Steven Stoll, *Larding the Lean Earth: Soil and Society in Nineteenth-Century America* (New York: Hill and Wang, 2002), 211.

24. J. H. Agee, George W. Graves, and C. B. Mickelwaite, *Soil Survey of Latah County* (Washington, DC: GPO, 1917), 17.

25. Joseph C. Baird, interview by James E. Lindsey, 19 September 1934, Lindsey Papers, WSU MASC; Walter Glaspey, interview by James E. Lindsey, 22 September 1934, Lindsey Papers, WSU MASC.

26. George N. Angell, "The Hills Shall Be Brought Low," *Washington Farmer*, 19 May 1921, 1.

27. "What Spillman Is Doing," *The Ranch*, 1 April 1904; Byron Hunter, "Farm Practice in the Columbia Basin Uplands," USDA Farmers' Bulletin No. 294, 1907, 11; James F. Shepherd, "Soil Conservation in the Pacific Northwest Wheat Producing Areas: Conservation in a Hilly Terrain," *Agricultural History* 59, no. 4 (1985): 232; Alexander C. McGregor, *Counting Sheep: From Open Range to Agribusiness on the Columbia Plateau* (Seattle: University of Washington Press, 1982), 172; Angell, 1.

28. Latah County Soil Conservation District, *10th Anniversary: Program and Work Plan* (Moscow, ID: Latah County Historical Society, 1950).

29. Sievers, 1; George Severence, "Summer Fallow System Is Inferior to Rotation of Crops," *Washington Farmer*, 30 October 1919, 1; "The System Is Changing," *Washington Farmer*, 10 May 1923, 4; "Soil Washing a Menace," *Washington Farmer*, 10 April 1924, 4.

30. John M. Klemgard, interview by James E. Lindsey, 26 September 1934, Lindsey Papers, WSU MASC; George Johnson, interview by James E. Lindsey, 21 September 1934, Lindsey Papers, WSU MASC; Augusta R. Peer, interview by James E. Lindsey, 20 September 1934, Lindsey Papers, WSU MASC.

31. C. E. Ramser, "Prevention of the Erosion of Farm Lands by Terracing," USDA Bulletin No. 512, 1917, 1–3; F. M. Harvey, "The Famous Palouse Country: Granary of the Northwest," *Pullman Herald*, 6 August 1915, 1–6; Keith Roy Williams, "Hills of Gold: A History of Wheat Production Technologies in the Palouse Region of Washington and Idaho" (PhD diss., Washington State University, 1991), 50–54.

32. William J. Spillman, "Staggering Losses from Soil Robbery," *Washington Farmer*, 9 October 1924, 4; "Make the Everlasting Hills Permanent," *Washington Farmer*, 24 March 1927, 7.

33. "Twenty-eighth Annual Report," State College of Washington, Agricultural Experiment Station, Bulletin No. 153, 1919, 28.

34. "Twenty-eighth Annual Report," 28–29.

35. Frederick J. Sievers and Henry H. Holtz, "The Silt Loam Soils of Eastern Washington and Their Management," State College of Washington, Agricultural Experiment Station, Bulletin No. 166, 1922, 21, 33, 43.

36. Sievers and Holtz, "Silt Loam Soils," 31–33, 45.

37. Sievers and Holtz, "Silt Loam Soils," 32–33, 45. Later Washington State College studies in the 1930s and 1940s confirmed their findings.

38. Sievers and Holtz, "Silt Loam Soils," 46–54.

39. Sievers and Holtz, "Silt Loam Soils," 15–21.

40. Frederick J. Sievers and Henry F. Holtz, "The Fertility of Washington Soils," State College of Washington, Agricultural Experiment Station, Bulletin No. 189, 1924, 7–15.

41. Frederick J. Sievers and Henry F. Holtz, "The Maintenance of Crop Production on Semi-Arid Soil," State College of Washington, Agricultural Experiment Station, Popular Bulletin No. 138, 1927, 8–9, 14–15.

42. Sievers and Holtz, "Maintenance of Crop Production," 14–21.

43. M. A. McCall and H. M. Wasner, "The Principles of Summer-Fallow Tillage," State College of Washington, Agricultural Experiment Station, Bulletin No. 183, 1924, 6–7; Ray E. Neidig and Robert S. Snyder, "The Relation of the Yield and Protein Content of Wheat to the Nitrogen Content of the Soil Under Ten Years of Different Systems of Cropping," University of Idaho, Agricultural Research Station, Research Bulletin No. 5, 1926, 22, 31.

44. "Eastern Washington Farmers Complain of Lack of Moisture," *Spokane Spokesman-Review*, 3 November 1929, 14.

45. Fred W. Clemens, "One-Crop Farming Is on the Skids," *Washington Farmer*, 15 March 1923, 3.

46. E. M. Rowalt, "Soil and Water Conservation in the Pacific Northwest," USDA Farmers' Bulletin No. 1773, 1937; Harvey, 2–3; L. T. Babcock, "One Quarter Is Enough for This Family," *Washington Farmer*, 3 May 1923, 3; Ralph Erskine, "A Change Is Coming Over the Palouse," *Washington Farmer*, 17 May 1923, 4; "Can Grow Crop Every Year," *Washington Farmer*, 23 August 1923, 2.

47. "WANTED: Better Slogan than 'Diversified Farming,'" *Washington Farmer*, 5 April 1923, 6; "What Type of Farming Is the Best? Say It with a Slogan," *Washington Farmer*, 3 May 1923, 6.

48. "Time to Start in Livestock," *Colfax Gazette*, 24 December 1915, 4; E. A. Bryan, "Former President Tells of Possibilities in Service," *Colton News-Letter*, 31 March 1916, 3; E. A. Bryan, "Agricultural Outlook No. 1: Difficulties in Establishing Diversified Farming," *Washington Farmer*, 17 January 1924, 13; Ray White, "Is Tractor Farmer in Whitman," *Washington Farmer*, 30 June 1927.

49. William A. Rockie, "Yesterday, Today, and Tomorrow," *Washington Farmer*, 3 November 1932, 6; "Statistics for Counties," 539; "Trends in Agriculture in Washington, 1900–1930," table 8.

50. Carl P. Heisig, "A Graphic Presentation of Changes in Agriculture in Washington from 1930 to 1935," State College of Washington, Agricultural Experiment Station, Bulletin No. 341, 1936, 19.

51. "Forty-first Annual Report," State College of Washington, Agricultural Experiment Station, Bulletin No. 260, 1931, 71–75.

52. Ben H. Pubols and Carl P. Heisig, "Historical and Geographic Aspects of Wheat Yields in Washington," State College of Washington, Agricultural Experiment Station, Bulletin No. 355, 1937, 9; Fred R. Yoder and A. A. Smick, "Migration of Farm Population and Flow of Farm Wealth," State College of Washington, Agricultural Experiment Station, Bulletin No. 315, 1935, 10.

53. "Growing and Handling Wheat," *Washington Farmer*, 21 December 1916, 6.

5 LESSONS LEARNED AND UNLEARNED

1. William A. Rockie, "A Message to All Members of the Northwest Scientific Association," *Northwest Science* 9, no. 3 (1935): 3–4.

2. "Wheat Prices Take Sudden Drop," *Oakesdale Tribune*, 25 October 1929, 1; "Thinks Wheat Is on Bottom," *Spokane Spokesman-Review*, 30 October 1929, 6; "Holds to His 50,000 Bushels," *Spokane Spokesman-Review*, 1 November 1929, 10; "Wheat Higher but Unsettled," *Spokane Spokesman-Review*, 2 November 1929, 11; "Annual Average Wheat Prices, 1910–1989," Rosalia Producers Warehouse, n.d..

3. "What's Behind This Crash in Wheat?" *Washington Farmer*, 27 February 1930, 3; "Grain Price Low," *Oakesdale Tribune*, 1 August 1930, 1; "Grain Market Is Depressed," *Oakesdale Tribune*, 13 November 1931; "Wheat Climbs to New Highs," *Oakesdale Tribune*, 29 July 1932, 1; "Annual Average Wheat Prices, 1910–1989."

4. "Wheat 50¢ at Tribune Office," *Oakesdale Tribune*, 18 September 1931, 1; Fred R. Yoder and A. A. Smick, "Migration of Farm Population and Flow of Farm Wealth," State College of Washington, Agricultural Experiment Station, Bulletin No. 315, 1935, 5, 16; "Timely Economic Information for Washington Farmers," State College of Washington, Extension Service, No. 1, 1931, 4–6.

5. "Wilmer to Talk Marketing Plan," *Oakesdale Tribune*, 12 November 1929, 1; "Colfax Farmers Will Organize," *Spokane Spokesman-Review*, 25 November 1929, 8; "Fifteen Local Co-ops Organized in This Region," *Sprague Advocate*, 26 December 1929, 2.

6. Washington State Grange Papers, 1889–1953, WSU MASC.

7. "No Need to Get Excited," *Sprague Advocate*, 14 November 1929, 2; "What Is the Future of Wheat Farming?" *Washington Farmer*, 3 April 1930, 3.

8. David E. Hamilton, *From New Day to New Deal: American Farm Policy from Hoover to Roosevelt, 1929–1933* (Chapel Hill: University of North Carolina Press, 1991); Gladys L. Baker et al., *Century of Service: The First 100 Years of the United States Department of Agriculture* (Washington, DC: Centennial Committee, USDA, 1963), 136–137; Bushrod W. Allin, "The U.S. Department of Agriculture as an Instrument of Public Policy: In Retrospect and Prospect," *Journal of Farm Economics* 42 (1960): 1094–1103.

9. George F. Dunning, "The War Is Over," *Washington Farmer*, 14 August 1930, 3. See also "Begs Wheat Men to Join Co-ops," *Spokane Spokesman-Review*, 12 December 1929, 6; "Federal Grain Man Talks to Farmers," *Sprague Advocate*, 13 February 1930, 1; "Legge Makes Frank Answer," *Oakesdale Tribune*, 7 March 1930, 1; "Legge Outlines Year of Work," *Oakesdale Tribune*, 4 July 1930, 1.

10. Paul de Hevesy, *World Wheat Planning and Economic Planning in General* (New York: Oxford University Press, 1940), 664, 706; Alden E. Orr, Carl P. Heisig, and J. C. Knott, "Trends and Desirable Adjustments in Washington Agriculture," State College of Washington, Agricultural Experiment Station, Bulletin No. 335, 1936, 9; "Report for States with Statistics for Counties and a Summary for the U.S.," in *U.S. Census of Agriculture, 1935* (Washington, DC: GPO, 1936), 836–837.

11. "Timely Economic Information for Washington Farmers," State College of Washington, Extension Service, No. 5, 1932, 7. See also "State Intends No Increase in Wheat," *Washington Farmer*, 11 September 1930, 5.

12. "Annual Average Wheat Prices, 1910–1989."

13. Wayve Comstock, interview by Corky Bush, Rural Women's History Project Papers, 1975–1980, University of Idaho, Special Collections and Archives; Vincent L. Higgins Diaries, 1892–1936, WSU MASC; John Jacob Bauer Papers, WSU MASC.

14. *Comparative Statements of Condition* (Pullman State Bank and First National Bank of Pullman, 1917–1939).

15. "Wheat Holiday Gets Approval," *Oakesdale Tribune*, 2 September 1932, 1.

16. Perspectives on Roosevelt and the New Deal abound. Standard works include Arthur Schlesinger Jr.'s *The Age of Roosevelt* trilogy (New York: Houghton Mifflin, 1966); William Leuchtenberg, *Franklin D. Roosevelt and the New Deal, 1932–1940* (New York: Harper and Row, 1963); and Howard Zinn, *New Deal Thought* (New York: Bobbs-Merrill, 1966).

17. For an analysis of the New Deal's legacy west of the Mississippi, see Richard Lowitt, *The New Deal and the West* (Bloomington: Indiana University Press, 1984); and Leonard J. Arrington, "Western Agriculture and the New Deal," *Agricultural History* 44, no. 4 (1970): 337–353.

18. "Timely Economic Information for Washington Farmers," State College of Washington, Extension Service, No. 19, 1933, 1–3; "Farmers Willing to Sign Contracts," *Garfield Enterprise*, 11 August 1933, 1; "Wheat Money Tops $100,000,000," *Garfield Enterprise*, 10 November 1933, 1; "Estimate Sign-up at About 94%," *Oakesdale Tribune*, 27 October 1933, 1; "Solve Wheat Problem from On High," *Washington Farmer*, 1 November 1934, 4; "Whitman Farmers Get Most AAA Cash," *Pullman Herald*, 11 September 1936, 8. For farm surpluses, see "Overproduction Vanishes," *Washington Farmer*, 6 April 1933, 6; and "Malthus Guessed Wrong," *Washington Farmer*, 22 February 1934, 21.

19. "Discuss Erosion at Farm Meeting," *Garfield Enterprise*, 30 March 1934, 1; "Approve More Soil Practices," *Uniontown Journal*, 23 July 1934, 1; *Sixteenth Census of the United States, 1940: Agriculture*, vol. 1 (Washington, DC: GPO, 1942), Idaho: 112, Washington: 551.

20. "Erosion Is of Two Types," *Washington Farmer*, 30 November 1933, 6; "While We Slept an Enemy Came," *Washington Farmer*, 14 December 1933, 12–13; "Tons of Soil Go into Sea," *Washington Farmer*, 21 December 1933, 6.

21. Baker et al., *Century of Service*, 139; "Soil Nitrogen Disappearing," *Oakesdale Tribune*, 17 January 1930, 1; "Pacific Northwest to Get Erosion Experiment Station," *Latah Citizen*, 31 January 1930, 1; "Discuss Vital Wheat Problems," *Oakesdale Tribune*, 14 February 1930, 1.

22. William A. Rockie and Paul C. McGrew, "Erosive Effects of Heavy Summer Rains in Southeastern Washington," State College of Washington, Agricultural Experiment Station, Bulletin No. 271, 1932, 4–8; "Forty-second Annual Report," State College of Washington, Agricultural Experiment Station, Bulletin No. 275, 1932, 67–75; "Forty-third Annual Report," State College of Washington, Agricultural Experiment Station, Bulletin No. 291, 1934, 59–63; "Forty-fourth Annual Report," State College of Washington, Agricultural Experiment Station, Bulletin No. 305, 1934, 64–67.

23. "Forty-second Annual Report," 74.

24. Rockie and McGrew, 4–8. See also "Cloudburst Hits Colfax Vicinity," *Oakesdale Tribune*, 7 August 1931, 1; and "Township Lost in Cloudburst," *Oakesdale Tribune*, 14 August 1931, 1.

25. The definitive analysis of Bennett's career is D. Harper Simms, *The Soil Conservation Service* (New York: Praeger Publishers, 1970). See also Robert J. Morgan, *Governing Soil Conservation: Thirty Years of the New Decentralization* (Baltimore, MD: Johns Hopkins Press, 1965); and Wellington Brink, *Big Hugh: The Father of Soil Conservation* (New York: Macmillan, 1951).

26. Simms, 10–13; Baker et al., *Century of Service*, 190–194; Morgan, 4–22. See also Edgar B. Nixon, ed., *FDR and Conservation, 1911–1945*, 2 vols. (Hyde Park, NY: General Services Administration, 1957); and Rexford G. Tugwell, *The Brains Trust* (New York: Viking Press, 1968).

27. Kaiser Papers, WSU MASC; Earl Victor Papers, 1933–1939, WSU MASC (source of quote this paragraph); Renee Guillierie and Sharon Norris, *Serving People and the Land: A History of Idaho's Soil Conservation Movement* (Meridian: Idaho Association of Soil Conservation Districts, 1985).

28. "Erosion Control to Be Discussed," *Garfield Enterprise*, 16 March 1934, 1; "Stress Need for Suitable Legumes," *Whitman County Farmer*, 23 March 1934, 1; "Greeters Admonished to Help Save Soil," *Whitman County Farmer*, 16 August 1935, 1; "Soil Erosion Perils Revealed by Survey; Remedies Are Named," and "600,000

Farm Folk Learn More about Soil Conservation," *Whitman County Farmer*, 13 December 1935, 1; "Chamber Erosion Trip Is June 17," *Palouse Republic*, 12 June 1936, 1; "Over 100 Enjoy Erosion Survey," *Palouse Republic*, 19 June 1936, 1.

29. "Wallace Visits Palouse Country," *Garfield Enterprise*, 2 August 1935, 1; "Wallace Visits Washington," *Washington Farmer*, 25 July 1935, 5.

30. Orr, Heisig, and Knott, 9.

31. George F. Johnson, interview by James E. Lindsey, 21 September 1934, Lindsey Papers, WSU MASC; David R. and Ann Judson, interview by James E. Lindsey, 17 September 1934, Lindsey Papers, WSU MASC; Charles O. Kellogg, interview by James E. Lindsey, 29 September 1934, Lindsey Papers, WSU MASC; Christian Naffziger, interview by James E. Lindsey, 13 September 1934, Lindsey Papers, WSU MASC.

32. Simms, 12–13; Morgan, 20–24; James F. Shepherd, "Soil Conservation in the Pacific Northwest Wheat-Producing Areas: Conservation in a Hilly Terrain," *Agricultural History* 59, no. 4 (1985): 235. In other parts of the nation, CCC soil conservation work accelerated after the SES transfer. At its peak, the SCS administered 454 camps across the country.

33. Simms, 18–19.

34. Guillierie and Norris, 3; "Soil Erosion Unit Sought for Here," *Palouse Republic*, 6 November 1936, 1; "Petitions Request Soil Conservation," *Palouse Republic*, 13 November 1936, 1; "North Palouse Conservation District Organization Is Made," *Palouse Republic*, 20 November 1936, 1; "Chamber Backs Soil Program," *Garfield Enterprise*, 16 April 1937, 1.

35. "Wheat Allotment Work Stopped," *Uniontown Journal*, 9 January 1936, 1; "Supreme Court Halts AAA Work," *Garfield Enterprise*, 10 January 1936, 1; "Court Smashes AAA Farm Plan," *Palouse Republic*, 10 January 1936, 1.

36. "Soil Program Highlights," *Whitman County Farmer*, 17 April 1936, 1; "Soil Conservation Act Liberalized," *Washington Farmer*, 30 April 1936, 6; "Payments for Soil Conservation," *Washington Farmer*, 28 May 1936, 4; "110 Sign Up for Erosion Program," *Palouse Republic*, 5 June 1936, 1; "Figure Pay Rates for Saving Soil," *Washington Farmer*, 11 June 1936, 4.

37. "Dad Showed the Boys Up," *Washington Farmer*, 29 October 1936, 2; N. D. Showalter, "The Land on Which We Live," *Washington Farmer*, 12 November 1936, 6 (source of "the true heritage . . . " quote); "What Is Soil Consciousness?" *Washington Farmer*, 15 April 1937, 6 (source of "to husband the land . . . " quote).

38. Oliver Hall, interview by James E. Lindsey, 28 September 1934, Lindsey Papers, WSU MASC; Walter A. Fiscus, interview by James E. Lindsey, 3 October 1934, Lindsey Papers, WSU MASC.

39. Earl Victor, "Some Effects of Cultivation Upon Stream History and Upon

the Topography of the Palouse Region," *Northwest Science* 9, no. 3 (1935): 18–19; Rockie, "Message to All Members," 4; William A. Rockie, "Man's Effects on the Palouse," *Geographical Review* 29, no. 1 (1939): 34–35.

40. Russell Lord, *To Hold This Soil*, USDA Miscellaneous Publication No. 321 (Washington, DC: GPO: 1938), 6, 116.

41. *An Eleventh Commandment* (National Association of Soil Conservation Districts, 1955).

42. These dueling interpretations can easily be seen in the book of Genesis, where humans are told to conquer *and* preserve the earth. Jews and Christians have been perplexed ever since. See also Psalms 8:5–8, 96:11–13, 148:1–13; and Leviticus 25:1–7. For contemporary sources, see David Kinsley, *Ecology and Religion* (Englewood Cliffs, NJ: Prentice-Hall, 1994); Roger S. Gottlieb, ed., *This Sacred Earth: Religion, Nature, Environment* (New York: Routledge, 1996); and H. Paul Santmire, *The Ambiguous Ecological Promise of Christian Theology* (Philadelphia: Fortress Press, 1985).

43. James F. Shepherd, "The Development of Wheat Production in the Pacific Northwest," *Agricultural History* 49, no. 1 (1975): 266–267; "Tractor Keeps Balance on Hill," *Washington Farmer*, 20 August 1936, 6; "Palouse Farmers Are Tractor Minded," *Pullman Herald*, 21 August 1936, 6; "Diesel Plowing Costs Seven Cents an Acre," *Washington Farmer*, 17 September 1936, 10; "Our Farm Forces Require Good Equipment Too," *Washington Farmer*, 26 February 1942, 2–3.

44. "The Machine and Rural Prosperity," *Latah Citizen*, 14 February 1930, 4; "General Report: Statistics by Subject," in *U.S. Census of Agriculture, 1954* (Washington, DC: GPO, 1956), 216–217.

45. Verle G. Kaiser, "Historical Land Use and Erosion in the Palouse—A Reappraisal," *Northwest Science* 35, no. 4 (1961): 142; Shepherd, "Development of Wheat Production," 267.

46. "Trashy Fallow Pins Down Soil," *Washington Farmer*, 22 July 1937, 8; "Check Next Year's Erosion Now," *Washington Farmer*, 13 April 1939, 7; "Farmers and Manufacturers Seek Erosion Control Machinery," *Washington Farmer*, 16 January 1947, 5; "Stubble Puncher Helps Prevent Runoff," *Washington Farmer*, 1 January 1948, 2; "This 'Whatsit' Reduces Erosion," *Washington Farmer*, 16 June 1948, 9; "Straw Spreading Devices Make Fall Plowing a Pleasure," *Washington Farmer*, 20 July 1944, 5; "Picture Tells a Vital Story," *Washington Farmer*, 21 August 1947, 6.

47. Kaiser, "Historical Land Use," 145.

48. "Statistics for Counties," in *Sixteenth Census of the United States, 1940: Agriculture*, vol. 1 (Washington, DC: GPO, 1942), Idaho: 112, Washington: 551.

49. *Sixteenth Census of the United States, 1940: Agriculture*, vol. 1, Idaho: 130, 134, Washington: 569, 573. This list is not comprehensive. Other crops not listed include small amounts of corn, potatoes, and sugar beets.

50. *AAA Conservation Guide* (State of Washington, 1942), table 16.

51. Ben H. Pubols, Alden E. Orr, and Carl P. Heisig, "Farming Systems and Practices and Their Relationship to Soil Conservation and Farm Income in the Wheat Region of Washington," State College of Washington, Agricultural Experiment Station, Bulletin No. 374, 1939, 32–41.

52. E. A. Norton, *Soil Conservation Survey Handbook*, USDA Miscellaneous Publication No. 352 (Washington, DC: GPO, 1939).

53. Oscar A. Camp and Paul C. McGrew, *History of Washington's Soil and Water Conservation Districts* (n.p., 1969), 7; Verle G. Kaiser, "Background of the State Soil Conservation District Act" (n.p., n.d.), Kaiser Papers, WSU MASC, 1–4.

54. *Pacific Northwest Erosion Control*, annual report (Soil Conservation Service, 1934–1935), 8; "Forty-fifth Annual Report," State College of Washington, Agricultural Experiment Station, Bulletin No. 325, 1935, 68; *Agricultural Conservation, 1936: A Report of the Activities of the Agricultural Adjustment Administration* (Washington, DC: USDA, 1936), 32; Paul C. McGrew and G. M. Horner, *Soil and Water Conservation Investigations* (Washington, DC: USDA, Soil Conservation Service, 1937), 43–46; *Soil Conservation in Outline* (Northwest Regional Council, 1940). The USDA did retire land in the Dust Bowl area of the Great Plains, but only a small amount and under heavy farmer protest.

55. *Sixteenth Census of the United States, 1940: Agriculture*, vol. 1, Idaho: 112, Washington: 551. The increase in farm size could have come at the expense of small tracts of Palouse woodland; woodland acres fell steadily in the 1930s.

56. Verle G. Kaiser, "An Informal Report of the Erosion Damage During the 1945–1946 Run-off Season in Whitman County, Washington" (n.p., n.d.), Kaiser Papers, WSU MASC, 5.

57. David E. Stephens, *Conservation Practices on Wheat Lands of the Pacific Northwest* (Washington, DC: USDA/SCS, 1944), 7; "Report for States, with Statistics for Counties and a Summary of the U.S.," in *U.S. Census of Agriculture, 1925* (Washington, DC: GPO, 1927), 157, 391; *Sixteenth Census of the United States, 1940: Agriculture*, vol. 1, Idaho: 130, Washington: 569.

58. "Timely Economic Information for Washington Farmers," State College of Washington, Extension Service, No. 34, 1939, 1; No. 36, 1940, 2; No. 40, 1940, 5–6. See also Bela Gold, *Wartime Economic Planning in Agriculture: A Study in the Allocation of Resources* (New York: Columbia University Press, 1949), 66; and "Defense Demands Production, but Not Over-Production," *Washington Farmer*, 11 September 1941, 5.

59. "Farmers Are Called Upon for All-Out Food Production," *Washington Farmer*, 25 September 1941, 5; "Still Greater Production Is Urged," *Washington Farmer*, 25 January 1942, 5; "Timely Economic Information for Washington Farmers," State

College of Washington, Extension Service, No. 42, 1942, 3, 19; No. 46, 1943, 6–9; "Annual Average Wheat Prices, 1910–1989"; Morgan, 178–181. Parity price is defined as the "fair" price farmers received for their goods as compared to the cost of items they consumed.

60. "High Lights in Agricultural Research in Idaho," University of Idaho, Agricultural Extension Station, Bulletin No. 244, 1941, 3.

61. "The Old Chip Basket," *Washington Farmer*, 3 June 1943, 2.

62. For example, see Glenn K. Rule, "Working Plans for Permanent Farms," USDA Miscellaneous Publication No. 411, 1940; Edward H. Graham, "Legumes for Erosion Control and Wildlife," USDA Miscellaneous Publication No. 412, 1941; *Soil and Water Conservation: An Introduction to the Problem and Its Control* (Spokane, WA: Soil Conservation Service, 1942).

63. "Statistics for Counties," in *U.S. Census of Agriculture, 1945*, vol. 1 (Washington, DC: GPO, 1946–1947), Idaho: 24, 38, 47, Washington: 25, 37, 45.

64. *U.S. Census of Agriculture, 1945*, vol. 1, Idaho: 47, Washington: 45. Barley and livestock production increased over this period, which also explains the drop in fallow and wheat acreage. See also George Severence, "Field Peas on a Palouse Wheat Farm," State College of Washington, Agricultural Experiment Station, Bulletin No. 36, 1911, 1–3; and Otis W. Freeman, "The Pacific Northwest Pea Industry," *Economic Geography* 19, no. 2 (1943): 118–120.

65. McGrew and Horner, 110; Kaiser, "Historical Land Use," 141; Maurice Taylor and Vernon W. Baker, "Economic Aspects of Soil Conservation in the Palouse Wheat-Pea Area," State College of Washington, Agricultural Experiment Station, Bulletin No. 494, 1947, 1–11.

66. "Soil Erosion Is Arch Fifth Columnist," *Washington Farmer*, 3 April 1942, 5; "Neighbors Stage Summer-Fallowing Bee That Was a Real Honey," *Washington Farmer*, 15 July 1943, 3; "This Can Be Stopped—This MUST Be Stopped—This WILL Be Stopped," *Washington Farmer*, 18 January 1945, 3.

67. Latah County Soil Conservation District, *10th Anniversary: Program and Work Plan* (Moscow, ID: Latah County Historical Society, 1950).

68. Kaiser, "Historical Land Use," 145.

6   BETTER FARMING THROUGH CHEMISTRY

1. The counterpoint to this argument can be found in David Danbom, *The Resisted Revolution: Urban America and the Industrialization of Agriculture, 1900–1930* (Ames: Iowa State University Press, 1979).

2. It should be noted that this is not a comprehensive analysis of all farm chem-

icals used in the Palouse. Many important, effective, and potentially hazardous products have been omitted from this discussion simply because they are too numerous. In one agricultural chemicals handbook from 1952, I counted well over one thousand different farm chemical products. It would be impossible to write a meaningful narrative on all of them—or even half of them—and therefore I have decided to focus on the three that made the biggest impact on Palouse farming: 2,4–D, anhydrous ammonia, and DDT.

3. W. B. Ennis Jr., "Use of Herbicides, Growth Regulators, Nematocides, and Fungicides," in *The Nature and Fate of Chemicals Applied to Soils, Plants, and Animals: A Symposium Held April 27, 28, and 29, 1960, at the Plant Industry Station and Agricultural Research Center, Beltsville, Maryland* (Washington, DC: USDA, 1960), 18.

4. The US Army also took notice of this new weed killer. It conducted tests during World War II on the ability of 2,4–D to kill broadleaf plants in the tropical South Pacific. It would later mix this herbicide with another, 2,4,5–T, to produce Agent Orange—used to defoliate large areas of Vietnam during the war in the 1960s and 1970s.

5. D. L. Klingman, "Effects of Spraying Cereals with 2,4–D," *Journal of the American Society of Agronomy* 39 (1947): 445–447; H. B. Tukey, "Historical Changes in Bindweed and Sowthistle Following Applications of 2,4–D in Herbicidal Concentrations," *Botany Gazette* 107 (1945): 62–73; Alvin Overland, "Some Effects of 2,4–D Formulations in Herbicidal Concentrations on Wheat and Barley" (master's thesis, Washington State University, 1950), 3–6; Hugh C. McKay et al., "Control Canada Thistle for Greater Profits," University of Idaho, Agricultural Experiment Station, Bulletin No. 321, 1959, 1–14; John T. Schlebecker, *Whereby We Thrive: A History of American Farming, 1607–1972* (Ames: Iowa State University Press, 1975), 270–271.

6. "2,4–D—Its Future in Weed Control," *Agricultural Chemicals*, May 1946, 20.

7. "Predicts Use of 2,4–D on Vast Scale," *Washington Farmer*, 5 December 1946, 8; Schlebecker, 314.

8. See the USDA annual publication *The Pesticide Situation* for a complete rundown on the production of all agricultural chemicals during this period. See also Ardith L. Many and Donald F. Hadwiger, "Taking 'Cides: The Controversy Over Agricultural Chemicals," in *Farmers, Bureaucrats, and Middlemen: Historical Perspectives on American Agriculture*, ed. Trudy Huskamp Peterson (Washington, DC: Howard University Press, 1980).

9. J. K. R. Gasser, "Some Biological Effects of Ammonia Injected into Soils," in *Anhydrous Ammonia: Proceedings of a Symposium on Aspects of Its Technology and Use as a Fertilizer*, ed. J. K. R. Gasser et al. (Surrey, UK: IPC Science and Technology Press, 1971), 30–31; Hans Jenny, "The Making and Unmaking of a Fertile Soil," in *Meeting the Expectations of the Land: Essays in Sustainable Agriculture and Stew-*

ardship, ed. Wes Jackson, Wendell Berry, and Bruce Coleman (San Francisco: North Point Press, 1984), 44–45.

10. Henry W. Smith, S. C. Vandecaveye, and L. T. Kardos, "Wheat Production and Properties of Palouse Silt Loam as Affected by Organic Residues and Fertilizers," State College of Washington, Agricultural Experiment Station, Bulletin No. 476, 1946, 4; Cecil Hagen, "Ammonia New Nitrogen Fertilizer Source," *Washington Farmer*, 18 August 1949, 6; C. B. Harston, "Fertilizers in Eastern Washington," State College of Washington, Agricultural Experiment Station, Bulletin No. 385, 1954.

11. "Pesticide Production Since 1953," *Farm Chemicals*, October 1963, 57–58; *Reports for the 1964 Census of Agriculture*, vol. 1 (Washington, DC: GPO, 1967), Washington, 315; Idaho, 259; "The Whitman County Farm and Home Reporter," State College of Washington, Extension Service, 11 May 1946, 15 July 1946. Unfortunately, the USDA did not track insecticide use on a county-by-county basis prior to 1964. DDT also helped stop a World War II typhus epidemic in Italy. For more general treatments on DDT and other farm chemicals, see Thomas Dunlap, *DDT: Scientists, Citizens, and Public Policy* (Princeton, NJ: Princeton University Press, 1981); and Edmund Russell, *War and Nature: Fighting Humans and Insects with Chemicals from World War I to "Silent Spring"* (New York: Cambridge University Press, 2001).

12. *Agricultural Chemicals Handbook*, State College of Washington, Agricultural Experiment Station, 1958, 53–60, 79–87; C. B. Harston, "Nutrient Needs of Our State Soils," *Washington Farmer*, 16 August 1956, 10.

13. George W. Fischer and J. P. Meiners, "Comparative Value of Several Fungicides in the Control of Head and Stripe Smuts in Certain Forage Grasses," State College of Washington, Agricultural Experiment Station, Bulletin No. 532, 1952, 1–17. Dozens of different kinds of fungi infect wheat and they fall into three basic categories: rusts, bunts, and smuts. Among the agents used to eliminate fungi were zineb, Ceresan M2X, mercury dusts, and hexachlorobenzene.

14. James F. Shepherd, "The Development of Wheat Varieties in the Pacific Northwest," *Agricultural History* 54, no. 1 (1980): 57–60; Dana D. Dalrymple, "Changes in Wheat Varieties and Yields in the United States, 1919–1984," *Agricultural History* 62, no. 3 (1988): 20–36; O. A. Vogel, S. P. Swenson, and C. S. Holton, "Brevor and Elmar—Two New Winter Wheats for Washington," State College of Washington, Agricultural Experiment Station, Bulletin No. 525, 1951, 1–8; "Whitman County Tops N.W. with 46 Pct. Smut in Wheat," *Pullman Herald*, 22 January 1953, 5; "Wheat Smut Conditions Were Increased During Past Year," *Daily Idahonian*, 10 January 1955, 5; "County Agents' Corner," *Tekoa Sentinel*, 19 August 1960, 2; "County Agents' Corner," *Tekoa Sentinel*, 23 September 1960, 2.

The struggle against fungi continues to this day. Washington State University researchers introduced Zak in 2002, a wheat bred for high yield and fungal resistance. Several years of field testing looked promising, but in its first year on the market farmers in eastern parts of the Palouse reported a devastating stripe rust outbreak. See John Stucke, "New Wheat Disappoints," *Spokane Spokesman-Review*, 3 July 2002, 1, 6.

15. "Counties and State Economic Areas," in *U.S. Census of Agriculture: 1945*, vol. 1 (Washington, DC: GPO, 1956), Washington: 47–87, Idaho: 44–94; "State and County Statistics," in *Reports for the 1964 Census of Agriculture*, vol. 1 (Washington, DC: GPO, 1967), Washington: 282–351, Idaho: 220–304. For an international perspective on the Green Revolution, see Craig R. Humphrey, *Environment, Energy, and Society* (Belmont, CA: Wadsworth Publishing, 1982).

16. Lester W. Hanna, *Hanna's Handbook of Agricultural Chemicals* (Forest Grove, OR: Lester W. Hanna, 1952), ii; John Boyd Orr, *The White Man's Dilemma* (London: George Alwin and Unwin, 1953), 80.

17. *U.S. Census of Agriculture: 1945*, vol. 1, Washington: 25, 32; Idaho: 24, 33; *Reports for the 1964 Census of Agriculture*, vol. 1, Washington: 315; Idaho: 241. See also "'Side-hill Dodger's' Short Leg Levels Tractor," *Washington Farmer*, 1 December 1949, 12; "Farm Machinery Will Get Bigger and Better," *Washington Farmer*, 5 December 1957, 5; "Farm Mechanization Will Proceed Apace," *Washington Farmer*, 3 January 1963, 12.

18. *U.S. Census of Agriculture: 1945*, vol. 1, Washington: 25; *U.S. Census of Agriculture: 1954*, vol. 1, (Washington, DC: GPO, 1956), Washington: 47; *Reports for the 1964 Census of Agriculture*, vol. 1, Washington: 283. Idaho figures are not included in these tallies because many Latah County farms in the foothills of the Clearwater Mountains did not produce grains and were much smaller operations. Still, farms in that county also grew considerably in the postwar era.

19. "Company Says 'Slow' on Own 2,4–D Spray," *Washington Farmer*, 5 July 1945, 2.

20. "Stinginess with 2,4–D Costly," *Washington Farmer*, 16 February 1950, 13.

21. "2,4–D—Its Future in Weed Control," 21.

22. Howard B. Roylance and K. H. Klages, "Winter Wheat Production," University of Idaho, Agricultural Extension Service, Bulletin No. 314, 1959, 16–17.

23. "County Agents' Column," *Tekoa Sentinel*, 26 August 1960, 2.

24. "Fertilizers for Eastern Washington," State College of Washington, Extension Service, Bulletin No. 385, 1950. A mad rush to overuse anhydrous may have been tempered because farmers had been using other forms of nitrogen-based fertilizers for some time; see Roylance and Klages, 11–13; and O. A. Fitzgerald, "Nitrogen Can Backfire," *Washington Farmer*, 15 February 1951, 5.

25. "Sweet Clover Damage Laid to Weed Killers," *Genesee News*, 4 June 1954, 1; "Herbicides in Ground Water?" *Washington Farmer*, 16 September 1954, 5; "Bee Poisoning: A Hazard of Applying Agricultural Chemicals," State College of Washing-

ton, Agricultural Experiment Stations, Stations Circular No. 356, 1959, 1–3; "Contamination of Milk to Be Institute Topic," *Pullman Herald*, 4 February 1960, 1; Suzanne Myklebust, "Crop Dusting in the Palouse," *Latah Legacy* 13–14 (Winter 1984–Spring 1985): 1–23.

The problem of drifting chemicals also plagued farmers in neighboring Oregon. See William G. Robbins, "The Wonder World of Pesticides," in *Landscapes of Conflict: The Oregon Story, 1940–2000* (Seattle: University of Washington Press, 2004).

26. "Farm News of the North Palouse SCS District," *Palouse Republic*, 22 February 1952, 4; "Short Course on Fertilizers Set at WSU," *Pullman Herald*, 11 February 1960, 6; "A Seminar on Nitrogen," *Organic Farmer* 1, no. 11 (1950): 22–24.

27. "County Agents' Column," *Tekoa Sentinel*, 15 January 1960, 2.

28. Walter Weber, "A Safety Side in Every Pesticide," *Agricultural Chemicals* (May 1971), 18; Gordon L. Berg, "Nature, Mr. Alnutt, Is What We Are Put in This World to Rise Above," *Farm Chemicals* (April 1968), 132.

29. *Where the Buffalo Roamed* (Phillips Petroleum, 1956).

30. Christopher J. Bosso, *Pesticides and Politics: The Life Cycle of a Public Issue* (Pittsburgh: University of Pittsburgh Press, 1987), 30; James Whorton, *Before Silent Spring: Pesticides and Public Health in Pre-DDT America* (Princeton, NJ: Princeton University Press, 1974), 253; William H. Eyster, "What About DDT?" *Organic Farmer* 1, no. 2 (1949): 19–22. The literature on DDT is voluminous. See also Thomas R. Dunlap, "Farmers, Scientists, and Insects," *Agricultural History* 54 (1980): 93–107; Angus A. MacIntyre, "Why Pesticides Received Extensive Use in America: A Political Economy of Agricultural Pest Management to 1970," *Natural Resources Journal* 27 (Summer 1987): 533–578; and John H. Perkins, *Insects, Experts, and the Insecticide Crisis: The Quest for New Pest Management Strategies* (New York: Plenum Press, 1982).

31. R. L. Webster, "New Insecticides: Their Use, Limitations, and Hazards to Human Health," State College of Washington, Agricultural Experiment Station, Circular No. 64, 1951.

32. For example, see "The Pesticide Problem," *Agricultural Chemicals*, March 1958, 33; L. C. Terriere, "What to Do About Insect Resistance?" *Washington Farmer*, 6 March 1958, 16; Dr. H. S. Telford, "Watch Out for Residue Tolerances," *Washington Farmer*, 5 February 1959, 10; and "Chemicals—Farming's Lifeblood," *Washington Farmer*, 16 February 1961, 7.

33. Terriere, 16.

34. Land-grant universities spent (and continue to spend) a tremendous amount of time and chemical industry money on the research and development of new chemicals. Jim Hightower explores this and related issues in *Hard Tomatoes, Hard Times: A Report of the Agribusiness Accountability Project on the Failure of America's Land Grant*

Colleges (Cambridge, MA: Schenkman, 1973). See also Frank Graham Jr., *Since Silent Spring* (Boston: Houghton Mifflin, 1970), 166; C. M. Packard, "Cereals and Forage Insects," in *The Yearbook of Agriculture, 1954* (Washington, DC: GPO, 1954), 581–594; Cecil Hagen, "Weed Men Have Bear by Tail in Chemicals," *Washington Farmer*, 19 February 1948, 12; "New Soil Herbicides," *Washington Farmer*, 15 March 1956, 29; and "New Form of 2,4-D Now on Market," *Washington Farmer*, 7 May 1958, 13.

35. Mary Devine Worobec, *Toxic Substances Controls Primer*, 2nd ed. (Washington, DC: Bureau of National Affairs, 1986), 41–43; Edward C. Gray, "A Short History of Pesticide Registration," in *Regulation of Agrochemicals: A Driving Force in Their Evolution*, ed. Gino J. Marco, Robert M. Hollingworth, and Jack R. Plummer (Washington, DC: American Chemical Society, 1991), 45–49; Whorton, 243–244.

36. Gustave K. Kohn, "Agrochemicals and the Regulatory Process Before 1970," in *Regulation of Agrochemicals*, ed. Gino J. Marco, Robert M. Hollingworth, and Jack R. Plummer, 4–5; Worobec, 41.

37. *Agricultural Chemicals Handbook*, 1–12; *Washington Pest Control Handbook* (Washington State University, Washington State Department of Agriculture, 1971), 91–103; "Weed Law Up-Dating Discussed," *Washington Farmer*, 17 December 1959, 9; Myklebust, 1–23.

Fraudulent or inaccurate labeling of farm chemicals occurred often. For a complete rundown on the offending parties, see "Annual Report of Commercial Fertilizers, Agricultural Minerals, and Lime," State College of Washington, Washington State Department of Agriculture, Bulletin No. 4, 1954–1955; "Annual Report of Commercial Feeds, Fertilizers, and Economic Poisons," Washington State Department of Agriculture, Agriculture and Marketing Division, 1956–1957; and "Annual Report: Commercial Feeds, Fertilizers, and Economic Poisons," Washington State Department of Agriculture, 1958–1959.

38. "Chemical Future Uncertain," *Washington Farmer*, 2 February 1961, 22. See also "The Editor Comments," *Agricultural Chemicals,* May, 1950, 29; "Stringent Controls Coming for Herbicides?" *Washington Farmer*, 3 September 1959, 4; "County Agents' Column," *Tekoa Sentinel*, 8 July 1960, 2.

39. For an annual breakdown on US and foreign chemical production, sales, stocks, and prices, see the USDA bulletin, *The Pesticide Situation*, for the years 1953 through 1965.

40. Verle G. Kaiser, "Historical Land Use and Erosion in the Palouse—A Reappraisal," *Northwest Science* 35, no. 4 (1961): 145. For more on the continuation of the erosion problem, see "Farm Program News," *Uniontown Journal*, 16 January 1947, 3; "Erosion Damages Fallowed Fields," *Colfax Commoner-Gazette*, 23 January 1947, 1; "Our Soil Is Going, Going, and Some of It Is Gone Forever!" *Washington Farmer*, 15 May 1947, 6; "Pacific Northwest Croplands Took Bad Beating Last Spring," *Wash-*

ington Farmer, 18 November 1948, 5; and "Much Erosion as Rainfall Nears 5–Inch Mark," *Uniontown Journal*, 22 January 1953, 1.

41. "Floods in Palouse Country Spotlight Erosion," *Washington Farmer*, 18 March 1948, 5.

42. Verle G. Kaiser, "An Informal Report of the Erosion Damage During the 1945–1946 Run-off Season in Whitman County, Washington" (n.p., n.d.), Kaiser Papers, WSU MASC.

43. Colin A. M. Duncan, *The Centrality of Agriculture: Between Humankind and the Rest of Nature* (Montreal, PQ: McGill-Queen's University Press, 1996), 122; Piers Blaikie, *The Political Economy of Soil Erosion in Developing Countries* (New York: Longman, 1985), 35; Daniel D. Richter Jr. and Daniel Markewitz, *Understanding Soil Change: Soil Sustainability over Millennia, Centuries, and Decades* (New York: Cambridge University Press, 2001), 17. See also Steven Stoll, *Larding the Lean Earth: Soil and Society in Nineteenth Century America* (New York: Hill and Wang, 2002), 5.

44. The new land ethic, the rise of organic farming, and their impact on future land use and the environmental movement is explored in detail in Randal Beeman, "Friends of the Land and the Rise of Environmentalism, 1940–1954," *Journal of Agricultural and Environmental Ethics* 8, no. 1 (1995); and Randal S. Beeman and James A. Pritchard, *A Green and Permanent Land: Ecology and Agriculture in the Twentieth Century* (Lawrence: University Press of Kansas, 2001).

45. Aldo Leopold, *A Sand County Almanac, and Sketches Here and There* (New York: Oxford University Press, 1949), 46–47.

46. Leopold, 207–209. Leopold wrote many essays that deal with agriculture and ecology. They include "The Conservation Ethic" (1933), "Coon Valley: An Adventure in Cooperative Conservation" (1935), "The Farmer as a Conservationist" (1939), "A Biotic View of Land" (1939), "What Is a Weed?" (1943), "The Outlook for Farm Wildlife" (1945), and "The Ecological Conscience" (1947). They can all be found in Susan L. Flader and J. Baird Callicott, eds., *The River of the Mother of God, and Other Essays by Aldo Leopold* (Madison: University of Wisconsin Press, 1991).

47. Ward Shepard, *Food or Famine: The Challenge of Erosion* (New York: Macmillan, 1945).

48. Karl B. Mickey, *Man and the Soil: A Brief Introduction to the Study of Soil Conservation* (Chicago: International Harvester Co., 1947), 17; Fairfield Osborn, *Our Plundered Planet* (Boston: Little, Brown and Co., 1948), xii.

49. Beeman and Pritchard, 49.

50. Rodale's basic tenets of organic farming can be found in *The Organic Method on the Farm* (Emmaus, PA, 1949), and the monthly magazine *Organic Farmer*, which began circulation in 1949. The Friends of the Land published a quarterly journal simply titled, *The Land*, which ran from 1941 to 1954. An anthology of articles from this

journal can be found in Nancy P. Pittman, ed., *From the Land* (Washington, DC: Island Press, 1988). See also Sir Albert Howard, *The Soil and Health: A Study of Organic Agriculture* (New York: Devin-Adair, 1947); and E. W. Bartlett, *Make Friends with Your Land: A Chemist Looks at Organiculture* (New York: Devin-Adair, 1948).

51. "Conservation Program Ready to Go," *Washington Farmer,* 1 August 1946, 6; "Erosion Control Is Big Objective in 1947 Conservation Program," *Washington Farmer,* 17 October 1946, 5; "Soil Conservation Needs More Support," *Colfax Gazette-Commoner,* 25 April 1947, 1; "Will Pay for Conserving Soil on Diverted Acres," *Uniontown Journal,* 14 October 1947, 1.

52. Harold A. Scales, "Farm Bureau Leans Toward Soil Fertility Bank Plan," *Washington Farmer,* 15 December 1955, 12; "Secretary Benson Likes Soil Bank," *Washington Farmer,* 16 February 1956, 9; Ramon L. Kent, "Insure 'Deposits' in the Soil Bank," *Washington Farmer,* 20 September 1956, 10.

53. For perspective, Whitman County contains about 2 million acres of land. Putting 340,000 acres statewide in the CRP represented a small fraction of the state's agricultural land.

54. *Washington—Our Soil, Our Water: 1960–1964 Annual Report* (USDA, Agricultural Stabilization and Conservation Service, n.d.), 11. For annual statistics on Soil Bank participation, see the USDA publication *Conservation Reserve Program of the Soil Bank: Statistical Summary* for the years 1957 through 1963. For local opinions on the Soil Bank, see "What Should Soil Bank Do for Us?" *Washington Farmer,* 16 February 1956, 21; Harold A. Scales, "Washington State Grange Takes Look at Soil Bank," *Washington Farmer,* 21 June 1956, 5; "Acreage Reserve Signup Underway," *Tekoa Sentinel,* 8 February 1957, 1; and Arthur Cagle, "1960 Conservation Reserve Dollars and Cents," *Washington Farmer,* 17 September 1959, 5.

55. Maurice C. Taylor and Vernon W. Baker, "Economic Aspects of Soil Conservation in the Palouse Wheat-Pea Area," State College of Washington, Agricultural Experiment Station, Bulletin No. 494, 1947, 1–11; "Land Capability Methods for Conserving Washington Soils," State College of Washington, Washington Agricultural Experiment Stations, USDA, Soil Conservation Service, Popular Bulletin No. 200, 1950, 34–35 (source of "continued soil losses . . . " quote); William A. Rockie, "Snowdrift Erosion in the Palouse," *Geographical Review* 61, no. 3 (July 1951): 461–463; Verle G. Kaiser et al., "Soil Losses on Wheat Farms in the Palouse Wheat-Pea Area, 1952–1953: A Progress Report," State College of Washington, Agricultural Experiment Station, Circular No. 255, 1954, 1–11 (source of "the loss of soil by erosion . . ." quote); G. M. Horner, "Effect of Cropping Systems on Runoff, Erosion, and Wheat Yields," *Agronomy Journal* 52, no. 6 (June 1960): 342–344.

56. Latah Soil Conservation District, *10th Anniversary: Program and Work Plan,* (Latah County Historical Society, Moscow, Idaho, 1950); "Conservation Ups Profits

Promptly," *Washington Farmer*, 7 November 1946, 36; "scs Workers Offer Figures As Proof Conservation Pays," *Daily Idahonian*, 21 January 1949, 2; John Armstrong, "Conservation Ups Yields," *Washington Farmer*, 5 May 1955, 13. For other "studies," see R. G. Fowler, "Conservation Farming Can Pay," *Washington Farmer*, 16 August 1951, 20; "Pride and Profit Save Most Soil," *Washington Farmer*, 6 December 1951, 6; "May Double Wheat Yield By Cropping and Fertilizer," *Uniontown Journal*, 10 September 1953, 1; Alfred E. Slinkard, "The Green Leaf," *Tekoa Sentinel*, 24 April 1959, 2; "Conservation Practice Combination," *Washington Farmer*, 18 August 1960, 18; and "County Agents' Column," *Tekoa Sentinel*, 23 December 1960, 2.

57. "Soil Rally Day Plans Complete," *Colfax Gazette-Commoner*, 27 February 1948, 1; "Palouse Farm Scheduled for Face-Lifting Job," *Washington Farmer*, 1 September 1949, 22; "Bursch's Break," *Washington Farmer*, 6 October 1949, 5; "Annual scs Rally Day in Palouse March 15th," *Palouse Republic*, 7 March 1952, 1; "Pullman to Host Soil Rally Day," *Pullman Herald*, 12 March 1953, 1; "Soil Conservation Day at Genesee March 21," *Genesee News*, 13 March 1953, 1; "14th Annual Rally Day in Palouse Next Saturday," *Palouse Republic*, 13 March 1953, 1; "Soil Conservation Rally Day," *Pullman Herald*, 19 March 1953, 8; "'Who Done It First' Wanted for scs Rally Day," *Uniontown Journal*, 21 January 1954, 1; J. M. Rabdau, "Load by Load, They Put It Back!" *Soil Conservation* (November 1954): 88–90.

58. "Soil Stewardship Sunday," National Association of Soil Conservation Districts, 1955, 3–4; "SCD News," *Tekoa Sentinel*, 6 January 1961, 3 (source of quote this paragraph). See also Firman E. Bear, "The Country Beautiful," *Journal of Soil and Water Conservation* 15, no.4 (July 1960): 168.

59. Ed Perdue, "The Right Fertilizers Plus Good Farming Offer Hope," *Washington Farmer*, 1 July 1965, 20–21. See also "Fertilizers Alone Won't Do Job of Building Up Soil," *Daily Idahonian*, 3 January 1949, 4; "Chemicals Replace Cultivators," *Washington Farmer*, 19 March 1959, 12; and Dr. William Furtick, "Chemical Winter Fallow," *Washington Farmer*, 6 October 1960, 4.

60. "Very Little Erosion Reported So Far This Year," *Uniontown Journal*, 31 March 1949, 1; "Israel Cited as Example of 'Final Erosion,'" *Uniontown Journal*, 5 January 1950, 1; "Field Activities Are Increasing," *Palouse Republic*, 18 October 1957, 4; "Farm News of North Palouse S.C. District," *Palouse Republic*, 15 November 1957, 8; "Conservation Picture Improving," *Washington Farmer*, 17 December 1959, 9.

61. Quotes from Harper, Long, and Meinders are from documents in Alfred Wilson Philips Papers, 1952–1954, WSU MASC.

62. "Heavy Erosion Reported as Dry Year Turns Wet," *Pullman Herald*, 22 January 1953, 1; "Erosion Still Plagues Region's Wheatmen," *Washington Farmer*, 5 December 1957, 16; "SCD News," *Tekoa Sentinel*, 2 December 1960, 2; "Erosion 'Bad' in County, Kaiser Finds," *Colfax Gazette*, 16 March 1961, 1. See also W. W. Pawson,

"Here's What Causes Wheatland Erosion," *Washington Farmer*, 19 August 1954, 12; and "Heavy Rainfall Erodes Topsoil," *Pullman Herald*, 11 February 1960, 1.

63. *Reports for the 1964 Census of Agriculture*, vol. 1, Washington: 283, Idaho: 221.

64. Kaiser, "Historical Land Use," 145; Frederick R. Steiner, *The Productive and Erosive Palouse Environment* (Washington State University, Cooperative Extension, USDA, 1987), 42.

7 LESSONS NEGLECTED AND REJECTED

1. Two other important books on the state of modern agriculture and science were published at about the same time, but did not draw nearly the same attention: Murray Bookchin, *Our Synthetic Environment* (New York: Alfred A. Knopf, 1962) and Barry Commoner, *Science and Survival* (New York: Viking Press, 1963).

2. For discussions on the national reaction to *Silent Spring*, see Frank Graham Jr., *Since Silent Spring* (Boston: Houghton Mifflin, 1970); and Christopher J. Bosso, *Pesticides and Politics: The Life Cycle of a Public Issue* (Pittsburgh: University of Pittsburgh Press, 1987). For an analysis of the USDA reaction, see Linda J. Lear, "Bombshell in Beltsville: The USDA and the Challenge of *Silent Spring*," *Agricultural History* 66, no. 2 (Spring 1992): 151–170. For more on Carson's lingering impact on the chemical industry, see Gordon L. Berg, "A Crack in Our Scientific Armor?" *Farm Chemicals*, February 1968, 142; and "Emotion Is a Pollutant, Too," *Agricultural Chemicals*, May 1971, 10.

3. George W. Fischer, "'Silent Spring' Bites the Hand that Feeds Us," *Washington Farmer*, 3 January 1963, 26–28; "Pest Control with Chemicals Not Ideal but Necessary," *Washington Farmer*, 17 January 1963, 5; E. W. Anthon, "Insecticides Important Tools," *Washington Farmer*, 21 January 1965, 11; "Still No Easy Solutions in Sight for Insect Control Problems," *Washington Farmer*, 2 January 1964, 8–9; Dr. M. E. Ensminger, "Good of Agricultural Chemicals Vastly Outweighs the Bad," *Washington Farmer*, 5 August 1965, 19.

4. Edward J. Gray, "A Short History of Pesticide Regulation," in *Regulation of Agrochemicals: A Driving Force in Their Evolution*, ed. Gino J. Marco, Robert M. Hollingworth, and Jack R. Plummer (Washington, DC: American Chemical Society, 1991), 48–50; Bosso, 158–170; Frank Graham, 268; "Birds Are on the Increase," *Farm Chemicals*, June 1968, 112; "What If Pesticide Use Stopped?" *Farmer's Journal* 34, no. 3 (August-September 1970): 29–32.

5. "Pesticide Regulations Announced," *Washington Farmer*, 16 May 1963, 17; "Tolerance Required in Every Food Crop," *Washington Farmer*, 4 January 1968, 17; "Growers Urged to Check with Processors Before Using DDT," *Washington Farmer*,

16 April 1970, 9; *Washington Pest Control Handbook* (Washington State Department of Agriculture, 1971), 96, 102; *Pacific Northwest Pest Control Handbook* (Idaho State Department of Agriculture, Oregon State Department of Agriculture, Washington State Department of Agriculture, 1979), 102, 312.

6. Carl Fanning, "Air and Water Pollution Is Causing Real Concern," *Washington Farmer*, 16 May 1968, 9–10; "Dams and Pollution Choking Columbia," *Los Angeles Times*, 6 June 1971, 26; George E. Smith, "Fertilizer Nutrients as Contaminants in Water Supplies," in *Agriculture and the Quality of Our Environment*, ed. Nyle. C. Brady (Washington, DC: American Association for the Advancement of Science, 1967), 173.

7. *Water Pollution as Related to Agriculture* (Columbia Plateau Resources Council, 1967), 3; Oscar A. Camp and Paul C. McGrew, *History of Washington's Soil and Water Conservation Districts* (n.p., 1969), 34.

8. Remarks by Secretary of Agriculture Orville L. Freeman to the Agriculture and Natural Resources Committee of the US Chamber of Commerce, Washington, DC, 2 February 1968, Kaiser Papers, WSU MASC; Gene Wirth, "Planet 'N,'" in *Sixth and Seventh Annual Eastern Washington Fertilizer and Pesticide Conference, 2 and 3 February 1970, 1 and 2 February 1971* (Washington State University Cooperative Extension Service and College of Agriculture, n.d.), 94.

9. "Nitrates No Threat to Food," *Farm Chemicals*, February 1968, 32–34; "Pollution: Big Problem for Washington Farmers," *Washington Farmer*, 1 January 1970, 7–8; John T. Underwood, "Bum Rap for Farmers on Pollution," *Farmer's Digest* 34, no. 2 (1970): 27–30; "Nitrates in Ground Water?" *Farm Journal*, April 1970, 52B; "Pollution Problem: Seedman's View," *Grange News*, 13 February 1971, 4.

10. John A. Wilson, "Water Pollution by Sediments in the Columbia Plateau Resources Area" (n.p., 1967), Kaiser Papers, WSU MASC; Remarks by Secretary of Agriculture Orville L. Freeman, 10.

11. Statistics on conservation acreage by state can be found in *Agricultural Conservation Program: Practice Accomplishments by States* (Washington, DC: USDA, Agricultural Stabilization and Conservation Service, 1971). For an explanation of cost-sharing amounts and department policy, see *Agricultural Conservation Program: A Conservation Partnership*, USDA, Agricultural Stabilization and Conservation Service, 1965. See also "Wheat Program Details for 1965 Outlined in USDA Statement," *Washington Farmer*, 1 October 1964, 6.

12. Camp and McGrew, 11–13; "Conservation Problems Increase," *Grange News*, 9 November 1968, 4; "SWCDs Aid in Pollution Control," *Grange News*, 28 March 1970, 14.

13. Leonard C. Johnson, "State Legislation to Control Soil Erosion and Sedimentation Through Land Use," in *Ninth Eastern Washington Fertilizer and Pesti-*

cide Conference, Washington State University, January 29 and 30 (Washington State University Cooperative Extension Service and College of Agriculture, 1973), 9–10.

14. Sandra S. Batie, *Soil Erosion: Crisis in America's Croplands?* (Washington, DC: The Conservation Foundation, 1983), 83–108; Frederick R. Steiner, *Soil Conservation in the United States: Policy and Planning* (Baltimore, MD: Johns Hopkins Press, 1990), 34–35.

Geoff Cunfer, in *On the Great Plains: Agriculture and Environment* (College Station: Texas A&M University Press, 2005), writes about similarly impotent conservation districts in the Great Plains. There it was water, not soil, that was the question, and farmers likewise fought against land-use regulations even if it meant they would all run out of groundwater in the near future: "The farmers in the middle of the district did not want their [conservation district] representatives to mandate or restrict irrigation practices. Admirable as is the goal of local, democratic, bioregional management of natural resources, in this instance such a government failed to preserve its common resource over the long term" (200).

15. *Basic Conservation Plans for Sample Farms in Conservation Problem Areas* (Soil Conservation Service, USDA, 1971–1972).

16. Scott Barr, "A Conservation and Environmental Proposal for the Columbia, Snake, Palouse Region," in *Proceedings of the 27th Annual Meeting of the Soil Conservation Society of America*, Portland, Oregon, 6–9 August 1972, 224.

17. Barr, 224; C. B. Harston, "Now, A Step Toward Controlling Erosion," *Washington Farmer-Stockman*, 2 March 1972, 6–7; Fred Wetter, "Neighborhood Watershed Groups Battle Erosion," *Washington Farmer-Stockman*, 16 March 1972, 50; John B. Armstrong, "End in Sight for Erosion in the Palouse Country?" *Washington Farmer-Stockman*, 4 May 1972, 6–8.

18. Karl Hobson, "The Wheat Shortage Is Here," *Farm Journal*, August 1966, 21, 47; *Oxford Economist Calls Population Explosion Good Thing* (Washington State University, Washington State Farm and Home News, 1963), 1–2; Gladwin E. Young, "Water for Peace," *Soil Conservation* 32, no. 10 (May 1967): 220–221; Michael P. Steiner and Gerald Marousek, *Food for Freedom: On the Causes of War and the Conditions for Peace* (Moscow: University of Idaho, 1967).

19. Verle G. Kaiser, oral history interview by Douglas Helms for the Soil Conservation Service, 17 September 1981, WSU MASC, 38–39; *Census of Agriculture, 1969: Area Reports*, vol. 1 (Washington, DC: GPO, 1972), Washington, 307; Idaho, 235.

20. *SEPA Guidelines* (State of Washington, Council of Environmental Policy, 1975). The state law is a near duplicate of the National Environmental Policy Act, passed in 1969.

21. *Comprehensive Planning Program* (Whitman County, Washington, 1978). See also Michael D. Jennings and John P. Reganold, "Policy and Reality of Environ-

mentally Sensitive Areas in Whitman County, Washington, USA," *Environmental Management* 12, no. 3 (1988): 369–370.

22. *Latah County Comprehensive Plan of 1979* (Latah County Planning and Zoning Commission, 1980).

23. John S. Gladwell, "A Preface to the University of Idaho/Washington State University Joint Water Resources Seminar on the Subject of the FWPCA Amendments of 1972—PL 92–500," in *Water Pollution Control Action-Reaction-Inaction*, ed. John S. Gladwell and William H. Funk (Moscow: University of Idaho, Water Resources Research Institute, 1974), 1–10; Harry Harker III, "Developing the 208 Planning Process," in *208 Planning: What's It All About?* ed. Frank L. Cross (Westport, CT: Technomic, 1976), 1–4; C. B. Harston, "Water Quality Management and Nonpoint Sources of Pollution," Washington State University, Cooperative Extension Service, Extension Bulletin No. 672, 1976.

24. Gladwell, 5.

25. *Dryland Agriculture Work Plan* (Olympia: Washington State Department of Ecology, 1976), 4. Frederick Steiner, in *Soil Conservation in the United States*, wrote that the Dryland Technical Advisory Committee was composed of antiregulation farmers and like-minded WSU researchers who "had a tendency to down play the more difficult and controversial aspects of the clean water legislation—regulation and land-use planning" (109).

26. *Dryland Agriculture Work Plan*, 5; Steiner, *Soil Conservation in the United States*, 109–110.

27. Steiner, *Soil Conservation in the United States*, 107–109; *Dryland Agriculture Water Quality Management Plan, Appendix III* (State of Washington Department of Ecology, 1979), 121–123.

28. Felix Entenmann Dry Land Water Quality Project Files, 1976–1981 (hereafter cited as Entenmann Files), WSU MASC.

29. All sources are from Entenmann Files, WSU MASC.

30. Leonard C. Johnson et al., "Surface Water Quality in the Palouse Dryland Grain Region," Washington State University, Washington Agricultural Experiment Station, Bulletin No. 779, 1973, 1–9; Leonard C. Johnson and Myron Molnau, "Hydrograph and Water Quality Relationships for Two Palouse Cropland Watersheds," University of Idaho, Agricultural Experiment Station, Research Bulletin No. 87, 1975, 1–7.

31. Glen H. Fielder, "A Look at P.L. 92–500 by the State of Washington," in *Water Pollution Control Action-Reaction-Inaction*, ed. John S. Gladwell and William H. Funk (Moscow: University of Idaho, Water Resources Research Institute, 1974), 100; "A Regulation Relating to Water Quality Standards for Interstate and Coastal Waters of the State of Washington and a Plan for Implementation and Enforcement of Such Standards," State of Washington, Water Pollution Control Commission (1967), 4–8.

32. *Palouse Cooperative River Basin Study* (USDA, SCS, Forest Service, Economics, Statistics, and Cooperatives Service, 1978), 36–39. For more on the new soil loss formula, see K. G. Renard et al., *Predicting Soil Erosion by Water: A Guide to Conservation Planning with the Revised Universal Soil Loss Equation (RUSLE)* (Washington, DC: GPO, 1997).

33. *Palouse Cooperative River Basin Study*, 53.

34. *Palouse Cooperative River Basin Study*, 45–47.

35. *Palouse Cooperative River Basin Study*, 55.

36. *Palouse Cooperative River Basin Study*, xii.

37. *Palouse Cooperative River Basin Study*, xiii.

38. *Dryland Agriculture Water Quality Management Plan, Final Draft* (State of Washington, Department of Ecology, 1979), 38–39.

39. *Dryland Agriculture Water Quality Management Plan, Final Draft*, 16–17.

40. *Dryland Agriculture Water Quality Management Plan, Final Draft*, 34–35, 39.

41. C. B. Harston, "Water Quality," *Washington Farmer-Stockman*, 15 March 1973, 23–25; "What Lies Ahead for the Palouse?" *Washington Farmer-Stockman*, 17 May 1979, 16–18; "Section 208 May Be Blessing in Disguise," *Washington Farmer-Stockman*, 20 September 1979, 14–15; Norman Herdrich, "Section 208 Is Now Bearing Fruit," *Washington Farmer-Stockman*, 3 September 1980, 6–7; Mike Wohld, "The Concept of Conservation," *Washington Farmer-Stockman*, 15 June 1972, 6–8.

42. Verle Kaiser, "A Critical Look at the Soil Erosion Problem of the Palouse," (n.p., 1978), 17–18, Kaiser Papers, WSU MASC.

43. *1978 Census of Agriculture*, vol. 1 (Washington, DC: GPO, 1980), Washington: 355–359; Idaho: 310–314; *1987 Census of Agriculture*, vol. 1 (Washington, DC: GPO, 1989), Washington: 146–176; Idaho: 144–147.

44. *Water Quality Status Report No. WQ-46: South Fork of the Palouse River/Paradise Creek* (Idaho Department of Health and Welfare, Division of Environment, 1981).

45. "Basic Statistics, 1982 National Resources Inventory," USDA Statistical Bulletin No. 756, 1982; *Idaho's Soil and Water: Condition and Trends* (USDA, Soil Conservation Service, 1983), 11.

46. "Who Is an Environmentalist?" *Washington Farmer-Stockman*, 4 November 1982, 11A.

47. Harvey C. Neese, *The Palouse Wash-out: A 20th Century Tragedy* (Troy, ID: Wildlife Resources, 1973), iii, 20.

48. Chaplin B. Barnes, "A New Land Use Ethic," *Journal of Soil and Water Conservation* (March–April 1980): 61–62.

49. Kaiser, oral history interview by Douglas Helms, 17 September 1981, 18.

50. Douglas Young and David Walker, "Technical Progress in Yields—No Sub-

stitute for Soil Conservation," University of Idaho, College of Agriculture, Current Information Series No. 671, 1982. See also Pierre R. Crosson and Anthony T. Stout, *Productivity Effects of Cropland Erosion in the United States* (Washington, DC: Resources for the Future, 1983).

51. Alan J. Busacca et al., "Dynamic Impacts of Erosion Processes on Productivity of Soils in the Palouse," in *Proceedings of the National Symposium on Erosion and Soil Productivity*, New Orleans, Louisiana, 10–11 December 1984.

52. Steve Berglund and E. L. Michalson, "Economics of the Five-Point Program in Latah County," University of Idaho, Agricultural Experiment Station, Research Bulletin No. 113, 1980.

53. Debra M. Schultz, "Farmers' Perceptions of Soil Erosion and Soil Conservation in the Pleasant Valley Creek Watershed" (master's thesis, Washington State University, 1985).

54. John E. Carlson, Don A. Dillman, and Larry Boersma, "Attitudes and Behavior About Soil Conservation in the Pacific Northwest: 1976–1985," in *STEEP— Conservation Concepts and Accomplishments*, ed. L. F. Elliott (Pullman: Washington State University Publications, 1986), 333–341.

55. Harley Jacquot, "Minimum Tillage as It Applies to West Whitman County— What Are the Trends?" in *Ninth Eastern Washington Fertilizer and Pesticide Conference*, 23–29; Douglas L. Young et al., "Yields and Probability of Conservation Tillage in the Eastern Palouse," Washington State University, Agricultural Research Center, Research Bulletin XB 0941, 1984; Michael D. Jennings et al., "Sustainability of Dryland Farming in the Palouse: An Historical View," *Journal of Soil and Water Conservation* (January–February 1990): 80.

56. Ray Meyer, "Reduced Tillage, Panel Discussion," in *Proceedings of the Eastern Washington Fertilizer and Pesticide Conference* (Pullman: Washington State University Department of Agronomy and Soils, 1978); Hubert W. Kelley, "Conservation Tillage: Hazards Ahead?" *Soil Conservation* 42, no. 6 (January 1977): 9.

57. John E. Carlson, Don A. Dillman, and C. Ellen Lamiman, "The Present and Future Use of No-Till in the Palouse," University of Idaho, Agricultural Experiment Station, Research Bulletin No. 140, 1990; Young et al., 5.

58. Norman Herdrich, "No-Till Farming's Day Is Coming," *Washington Farmer-Stockman*, 4 December 1975, 22–23; Gary Bye, "Zero-Till Farming Is Coming of Age," *Washington Farmer-Stockman*, 1 March 1979, 6–7; "Putting the Plow to Rest," *Inland Farmer*, December 1993, 7.

59. For a comprehensive collection of the most important articles, see L. F. Elliott, ed., *STEEP—Conservation Concepts and Accomplishments* (Pullman: Washington State University Publications, 1987).

60 Kaiser, oral history interview by Douglas Helms, 17 September 1981, 43.

1. Hugh Hammond Bennett, "Some Recent Results of Soil Erosion Research," USDA, Natural Resources Conservation Service, http://www.nhq.nrcs.usda.gov/CCS/history/10_24_32.html (accessed 28 October 1999).

2. US Comptroller General, *To Protect Tomorrow's Food Supply—Soil Conservation Needs Priority Attention* (Washington, DC: GPO, 1977).

3. Sandra S. Batie, *Soil Erosion: Crisis in America's Croplands?* (Washington, DC: The Conservation Foundation, 1983), 96–97.

4. "Annual Average Wheat Prices, 1910–1989," Rosalia Producers Warehouse, n.d.; *Census of Agriculture, 1969*, vol. 1 (Washington, DC: GPO, 1972), Washington: 305, Idaho, 233; *1978 Census of Agriculture*, vol. 1 (Washington, DC: GPO, 1980), Washington: 355; Idaho: 310; *1987 Census of Agriculture*, vol. 1 (Washington, DC: GPO, 1989), Washington: 146; Idaho: 144; Willard Cochrane, *The Development of American Agriculture: A Historical Analysis*, 2nd ed. (Minneapolis: University of Minnesota Press, 1993), 166.

5. "Farming Looks Bleak," *Palouse Sodbuster*, 2 October 1985, 1–2; "Hope for Stronger Prices Is Remote," *Wheat Life*, March 1984, 2–4; Neil E. Hart, *The Farm Debt Crisis of the 1980s* (Ames: Iowa State University Press, 1990); Thomas R. Wessel, "Agricultural Policy Since 1945," in *The Rural West Since World War II*, ed. R. Douglas Hurt (Lawrence: University of Kansas Press, 1998); William P. Browne, *Private Interests, Public Policy, and American Agriculture* (Lawrence: University of Kansas Press, 1988).

6. Mike Wohld, "The Most Significant Conservation Legislation in 50 Years," *Washington Farmer-Stockman*, 6 March 1986, 39A. See also Terence Day, "Farm Conservation Plans Needed by 1990," *Wheat Life*, March 1986, 15; *The Conservation Reserve Program* (USDA, Farm Security Agency, May 1997); "A Brief History of the CRP," *Inland Farmer*, September 1994, 4; William A. Galston, *A Tough Road to Hoe: The 1985 Farm Bill and Beyond* (New York: Hamilton Press, 1985); Bruce L. Gardner, ed., *US Agriculture Policy: The 1985 Farm Legislation* (Washington, DC: American Enterprise Institute for Public Policy Research, 1985); M. C. Hallberg, *Policy for American Agriculture: Choices and Consequences* (Ames: Iowa State University Press, 1992).

7. B. Delworth Gardner, *Plowing Ground in Washington: The Political Economy of US Agriculture* (San Francisco: Pacific Research Institute for Public Policy, 1995), 241–268; Bruce L. Gardner, *American Agriculture in the Twentieth Century: How It Flourished and What It Cost* (Cambridge, MA: Harvard University Press, 2002), 211–217; *The Conservation Reserve Program* (USDA, 1997), 16; James Sherow, "Environmentalism and Agriculture in the American West," in *The Rural West Since World War II*, ed. Hurt.

8. Chris Laney, "'What Was your Grade in World History . . . ?'" *Wheat Life*, February 1990, 2; Dan Blankenship, "Genuine Concern for Long-term Health of the Environment," *Wheat Life*, June 1990, 2; Mike Wohld, "Getting Farmers on the Right Track," *Inland Farmer*, July 1994, 39. See also "Pure Water a Treasure," *Washington Farmer-Stockman*, 4 October 1984, 23A; "Water Contamination," *Washington Farmer-Stockman*, 19 March 1987, 28A; Mike Wohld, "Water Quality a Major Topic," *Inland Farmer*, March 1989, 31.

9. "Many Washington Farmers Will Need Conservation Plans," *Washington Farmer-Stockman*, March 1988, 26–27; "Palouse Wheat Growers Should Consider CRP," *Washington Farmer-Stockman*, March 1988, 57.

10. Jeffrey Zinn, "How Are Soil Erosion Control Programs Working?" *Journal of Soil and Water Conservation* 48 (July–August 1993): 257.

11. Curtis Beus et al., "Prospects for Sustainable Agriculture in the Palouse: Farmer Experiences and Viewpoints," Washington State University, College of Agriculture and Home Economics Research Center, Research Bulletin XB 1016, 1990, 53–55.

12. *Census of Agriculture, 1997: Ranking of States and Counties*, vol. 1, pt. 2 (Washington, DC: GPO, 1999), 22.

13. Donald Worster, *Dust Bowl: The Southern Plains in the 1930s* (New York: Oxford University Press, 1979), 154.

14. Tim Osborn, "The Conservation Reserve Program: Status, Future, and Policy Options," *Journal of Soil and Water Conservation* 48 (July–August 1993): 273; Zinn, 260. See also Peter C. Meyers, "Conservation at the Crossroads," *Journal of Soil and Water Conservation* 43 (January–February 1988): 10–13; and Milton Hertz, "Implementing CRP: Progress and Prospects," *Journal of Soil and Water Conservation* 43 (January–February 1988): 14–16.

15. Douglas A. Osterman and Theresa L. Hicks, "Highly-Erodible Land: Farmer Perceptions versus Actual Measurements," *Journal of Soil and Water Conservation* 43 (March–April 1988). See also Beus et al.

16. James C. Ebbert and Dennis Roe, *Soil Erosion in the Palouse River Basin: Indications of Improvement* (USGS, USDA, 1998); "Inventory Shows Soil Erosion Down," *Inland Farmer*, August 1994, 9.

17. *The Conservation Reserve Program* (USDA, Farm Service Agency, 1997).

18. *The Conservation Reserve Program* (USDA, Farm Service Agency, 1997, 2001); *Contour Buffer Strips* (USDA, Natural Resources Conservation Service, April 1997); *Windbreak/Shelterbelt* (USDA, Natural Resources Conservation Service, January 1998); *Riparian Forest Buffer* (USDA, Natural Resources Conservation Service, January 1998).

19. Ebbert and Roe. See also Mike Wohld, "One Million Acres of 'New' Grassland in Washington," *Washington Farmer-Stockman*, April 1991, 14A.

20. *Conservation Reserve Program*, 2001; *Section-by-Section Summary of Title II of the Farm Security and Rural Investment Act of 2002* (USDA, Natural Resources Conservation Service, 2002). See also Heather Abel, "Farm Bill Helps the Land— Sort Of," *High Country News*, 13 May 1996.

21. Jeffrey L. Doke and Gibran S. Hashmi, *Paradise Creek Watershed Characterization Study* (Pullman: State of Washington Water Research Center, 1994).

22. Ted McDonough, "City Tackles Water Issues," *Moscow-Pullman Daily News*, 8 August 2001, A1.

23. The USGS reported in 1998 that, on average, farmers in Grant County and western parts of Adams and Franklin Counties used 140 pounds of nitrogen fertilizer per acre. By comparison, Palouse farmers used about 55 pounds per acre—a reduction from historical levels that ran as high as 110 pounds per acre. See sources in note 25, below.

24. *Census of Agriculture, 1997: Ranking of States and Counties*, vol. 1, pt. 2, 17, 18.

25. For USGS studies, see Joseph L. Jones and Richard J. Wagner, *Water Quality Assessment of the Central Columbia Plateau in Washington and Idaho—Analysis of Available Nutrient and Pesticide Data for Ground Water, 1942–1992* (Tacoma, WA: USGS, 1995); and Alex K. Williamson et al., *Water Quality in the Central Columbia Plateau: Washington and Idaho, 1992–1995* (Tacoma, WA: USGS, 1998). See also D. N. Erickson and D. Norton, *Washington State Agricultural Chemicals Pilot Study*, Washington State Department of Ecology, 1990; and L. M. Nelson, *Surface Water Resources for the Columbia Plateau—Washington, Oregon, and Idaho* (USGS, 1991).

26. Emily Green, "Weedkiller Cancer Debate Blooms, Has Broad Application," *Spokane Spokesman-Review*, 2 June 2002, A9; J. M. Charles, "Developmental Toxicity Studies in Rats and Rabbits on 2,4–D and its Forms," *Toxicological Sciences* 60 (2001): 121–131; *Pesticides and Epidemiology: Unraveling Disease Patterns* (Purdue University Pesticide Program, July, 1998); J. M. Charles, "Comparative Subchronic Studies on 2,4–D Acid, Amine and Ester in Rats," *Fundamental and Applied Toxicology* 33 (1996): 161–165.

27. The literature on GMOs is considerable, but two articles succinctly lay out the important arguments, pro and con: Martha L. Crouch, "Biotechnology Is Not Compatible with Sustainable Agriculture," *Journal of Agricultural and Environmental Ethics* 8 (1995): 98–111; and Donald N. Duvick, "Biotechnology Is Compatible with Sustainable Agriculture," *Journal of Agricultural and Environmental Ethics* 8 (1995): 112–125. For a multidisciplinary survey, one that includes a thorough scientific explanation of how GMOs are made, their cultural significance, and agribusiness's advertising techniques, see Nick Bingham, "Food Fights: On Power, Contest, and GM," in *Contested Environments*, ed. Nick Bingham, Andrew Blowers, and Chris Belshaw

(Milton Keynes, UK: The Open University, 2003). For unabashed support for GMOs, see Per Pinstrup-Anderson and Ebbe Schiøler, *Seeds of Contention: World Hunger and the Global Controversy over GM Crops* (Baltimore, MD: Johns Hopkins University Press, 2000); and Thomas R. DeGregori, *Bountiful Harvest: Technology, Food Safety, and the Environment* (Washington, DC: Cato Institute, 2002). Genetic modification is another issue in which the environmentalists are the conservatives. See Britt Bailey and Marc Luppé, eds., *Engineering the Farm: Ethical and Social Aspects of Agricultural Biotechnology* (Washington, DC: Island Press, 2002).

28. Hannah Wolfson, "Corn-Belt Farmers Find Modified Crops Tough Sell," *Boston Globe*, 20 February 2003, A1; "US Postpones WTO Move on Modified Foods," *Financial Times*, 6 February 2003; "US Threatens to Act against Europeans over Modified Foods," *New York Times*, 10 January 2002, A1; David Holley, "Biotechnology Debate Takes Center Stage at Food Summit," *Los Angeles Times*, 13 June 2002, A3; David Chandler, "Down on the Farm," *Boston Globe*, 25 August 2001, A1.

29. Crouch, 99–107.

30. Mary Aegerter, "Public, Not Scientists, Determine the Future of GMO Food," *Hilltopics*, August 2001, 12–13. See also R. James Cook, "Biotech Food Great for Farmers, Eaters," *Spokane Spokesman-Review*, 15 June 2002, B4.

31. Mandee Merrill, "Scientists Say Most Americans Support Biotechnology," *Hilltopics*, August 2001, 11–12.

32. Aegerter, 13.

33. Aegerter, 13.

34. The best exposé of the various conflicts of interests in determining food safety is still Jim Hightower, *Hard Times, Hard Tomatoes: A Report of the Agribusiness Accountability Project on the Failure of America's Land Grant Colleges* (Cambridge, MA: Schenkman, 1973).

35. Duvick, 120.

36. Tim Steury, "Full Circle: Perennial Wheat Could Fulfill a Tradition and Transform a Landscape," *Washington State Magazine* (Summer 2004): 33–37; Pamela L Scheinost et al., "Perennial Wheat: The Development of a Sustainable Cropping System for the US, Pacific Northwest," *American Journal of Alternative Agriculture* 16, no. 4 (2001): 147–151; A. S. Moffat, "Agricultural Research: Higher Yielding Perennials Point the Way to New Crops," *Science* 274 (1996): 1469–1470.

37. A detailed account on why government subsidies are so difficult—and expensive—to dismantle can be found in William P. Browne, *The Failure of National Rural Policy: Institutions and Interests* (Washington, DC: Georgetown University Press, 2001).

38. John Kelly, "Mega-farms Harvest Subsidies," *Spokane Spokesman-Review*, 9 September 2001, A1; John Stucke, "Wheat Growers Not Rejoicing Over New Farm

Bill," *Spokane Spokesman-Review*, 2 May 2002, A10; George B. Pyle, "Mega-farming Is Killing the Land," *Spokane Spokesman-Review*, 2 July 2002, A15.

Historian Colin Duncan gives a broader view of this phenomenon, stating, "the 'West' now relies on a chronically overproductive industrialized agriculture that is quite bereft of economic rationale, however politically convenient it may be." See Colin A. M. Duncan, *The Centrality of Agriculture: Between Humankind and the Rest of Nature* (Montreal, PQ: McGill-Queen's University Press, 1996), 114.

39. Mike Lee, "Subsidies Keeping Wheat Farmers from Withering in Price Drought," *Tri-City Herald*, 26 February 2001, A1. See also Brian Peters, "Region Reaps a Bumper Crop of Aid," *Lewiston Morning Tribune*, 11 September 2001, 1A.

40. Lee, A1.

41. Bob Fick, "From the Grass Roots, Subsidies Look Like a Safety Net," *Lewiston Morning Tribune*, 11 September 2001, 1A.

EPILOGUE

1. *Thirteenth Census of the United States* (Washington, DC: GPO, 1913).

2. James Sherow, "Environmentalism and Agriculture in the American West," in *The Rural West Since World War II*, ed. R. Douglas Hurt (Lawrence: University Press of Kansas, 1998), 59.

3. Frederick R. Steiner, *Soil Conservation in the United States: Policy and Planning* (Baltimore, MD: Johns Hopkins University Press, 1990); J. Douglas Helms et al., "National Soil Conservation Policies: A Historical Case Study of the Driftless Area," *Agricultural History* 70 (Spring 1996): 377–394.

4. Steven Stoll, *Larding the Lean Earth: Soil and Society in Nineteenth-Century America* (New York: Hill and Wang, 2002), 8.

5. See the epilogue to Donald Worster's *Dust Bowl: The Southern Plains in the 1930s* (New York: Oxford University Press, 1979).

6. John Opie, *Ogallala: Water for a Dry Land* (Lincoln: University of Nebraska Press, 1993); Geoff Cunfer, *On the Great Plains: Agriculture and Environment* (College Station: Texas A&M University Press, 2005), chapter 7; Dan Flores, *The Natural West: Environmental History in the Great Plains and Rocky Mountains* (Norman: University of Oklahoma Press, 2001), 176; Donald Worster, *Under Western Skies: Nature and History in the American West* (New York: Oxford University Press, 1992), 246.

7. Piers Blaikie, *The Political Economy of Soil Erosion in Developing Countries* (New York: Longman, 1985), 96. Blaikie suggests that bureaucrats' technical reports on erosion might just have to be tossed to the side if we want to truly get at the heart of the issue.

8. Colin A. M. Duncan, *The Centrality of Agriculture: Between Humankind and the Rest of Nature* (Montreal, PQ: McGill-Queen's University Press, 1996), 125.

9. Stoll, 218.

10. Daniel D. Richter Jr. and Daniel Markewitz, *Understanding Soil Change: Soil Sustainability over Millennia, Centuries, and Decades* (Cambridge: Cambridge University Press, 2001), 10; David Christian, *Maps of Time: An Introduction to Big History* (Berkeley: University of California Press, 2005).

11. Geoff Cunfer suggests this very blend of farming and ranching is a possibility on the Great Plains, once they run out of groundwater as expected. See Cunfer, 198.

12. Steven Stoll would like us to consider the advent of conservation in the same way: "conservation did not challenge basic assumptions of material progress; it *recast* progress as timber left standing, as waters running clear, as habitat undiminished." See Stoll, 213.

13. For a complete rundown on PCEI activities, see their quarterly newsletter, *Environmental News*. A statewide nonprofit group, the Washington Environmental Council, also tackles agricultural issues, but operates mostly on the west side of the Cascades.

For a greater understanding of the scientific requirements for the rehabilitation, reclamation, and restoration of bunchgrass steppe and meadow-steppe biomes, see Bertie J. Weddell, "Restoring Palouse and Canyon Grasslands: Putting Back the Missing Pieces," Bureau of Land Management, Technical Bulletin No. 01–15, August 2001.

14. Wendell Berry, *The Unsettling of America: Culture and Agriculture* (New York: Avon Books, 1977), 7.

15. *Census of Agriculture, 1997: Ranking of States and Counties* (Washington, DC: GPO, 1999), 63, 65.

16. Wes Jackson, *New Roots for Agriculture* (Lincoln: University of Nebraska Press, 1980), xi.

SELECTED BIBLIOGRAPHY

AAA *Conservation Guide.* State of Washington, 1942.

Agee, J. H., George W. Graves, and C. B. Mickelwaite. *Soil Survey of Latah County.* Washington, DC: GPO, 1917.

Agricultural Chemicals Handbook. State College of Washington, Agricultural Experiment Station, 1958.

Agricultural Conservation, 1936: A Report of the Activities of the Agricultural Adjustment Administration. Washington, DC: USDA, 1936.

Agricultural Conservation Program: A Conservation Partnership. Washington, DC: USDA, Agricultural Stabilization and Conservation Service, 1965.

Agricultural Conservation Program: Practice Accomplishments by States. Washington, DC: USDA, Agricultural Stabilization and Conservation Service, 1971.

Allen, John Eliot, and Marjorie Burns. *Cataclysms of the Columbia.* Portland, OR: Timber Press, 1986.

Aller, Alvin, et al. "Plant Communities and Soils of North Slopes in the Palouse Region of Eastern Washington and Northern Idaho." *Northwest Science* 55, no. 4 (1981): 248–261.

Allin, Bushrod W. "The U.S. Department of Agriculture as an Instrument of Public Policy: In Retrospect and Prospect." *Journal of Farm Economics* 42 (1960): 1094–1103.

Alwin, John A. *Between the Mountains: A Portrait of Eastern Washington.* Bozeman, MT: Northwest Panorama Publishing, 1984.

"Annual Report of Commercial Fertilizers, Agricultural Minerals, and Lime." State

College of Washington, Washington State Department of Agriculture, Bulletin
No. 4, 1954–1955.

Annual Reports. State College of Washington, Agricultural Experiment Station,
1900–1940.

"Annual Average Wheat Prices, 1910–1989." Rosalia Producers Warehouse, n.d.

Arrington, Leonard J. "Western Agriculture and the New Deal." *Agricultural History* 44, no. 4 (1970): 337–353.

Avery, Mary W. *History and Government of the State of Washington.* Seattle: University of Washington Press, 1962.

Bailey, Britt, and Marc Luppé, eds. *Engineering the Farm: Ethical and Social Aspects of Agricultural Biotechnology.* Washington, DC: Island Press, 2002.

Baker, Gladys, et al. *Century of Service: The First 100 Years of the United States Department of Agriculture.* Washington, DC: Centennial Committee, USDA, 1963.

Barnes, Chaplin B. "A New Land Use Ethic." *Journal of Soil and Water Conservation* (March–April 1980): 61–62.

Barr, Scott. "A Conservation and Environmental Proposal for the Columbia, Snake, Palouse Region." In *Proceedings of the 27th Annual Meeting of the Soil Conservation Society of America*, Portland, Oregon, 6–9 August 1972.

Bartlett, E. W. *Make Friends with Your Land.* New York: Devin-Adair, 1948.

Basic Conservation Plans for Sample Farms in Conservation Problem Areas. Soil Conservation Service, USDA, 1971–1972.

"Basic Statistics, 1982 National Resources Inventory." USDA Statistical Bulletin No. 756, 1982.

Batie, Sandra S. *Soil Erosion: Crisis in America's Croplands?* Washington, DC: The Conservation Foundation, 1983.

Bear, Firman E. "The Country Beautiful." *Journal of Soil and Water Conservation* 15, no. 4 (July 1960): 167–168.

Beeman, Randal. "Friends of the Land and the Rise of Environmentalism, 1940–1954." *Journal of Agricultural and Environmental Ethics* 8, no. 1 (1995).

Beeman, Randal S., and James A. Pritchard. *A Green and Permanent Land: Ecology and Agriculture in the Twentieth Century.* Lawrence: University of Kansas Press, 2001.

"Bee Poisoning: A Hazard of Applying Agricultural Chemicals." State College of Washington, Agricultural Experiment Station, Stations Circular No. 356, 1959.

Bennett, Hugh Hammond. "Some Recent Results of Soil Erosion Research." USDA, Natural Resources Conservation Service, http://www.nhq.nrcs.usda.gov/CCS/history/10_24_32.html (accessed 28 October 1999).

Berg, Gordon L. "A Crack in Our Scientific Armor?" *Farm Chemicals*, February 1968, 142.

Berglund, Steve, and E. L. Michalson. "Economics of the Five-Point Program in Latah County." University of Idaho, Agricultural Experiment Station, Research Bulletin No. 113, 1980.

Berry, Wendell. *The Unsettling of America: Culture and Agriculture*. New York: Avon Books, 1977.

Beuchner, Helmut K. "Some Biotic Changes in the State of Washington, Particularly During the Century 1853–1953." Research Studies of the State College of Washington, Pullman, 1953.

Beus, Curtis, et al. "Prospects for Sustainable Agriculture in the Palouse: Farmer Experiences And Viewpoints." Washington State University, College of Agriculture and Home Economics Research Center, Research Bulletin XB 1016, 1990.

Bingham, Nick, Andrew Blowers, and Chris Belshaw, eds. *Contested Environments*. Milton Keynes, UK: The Open University, 2003.

Blaikie, Piers. *The Political Economy of Soil Erosion in Developing Countries*. New York: Longman, 1985.

Bookchin, Murray. *Our Synthetic Environment*. New York: Alfred A. Knopf, 1962.

Bosso, Christopher J. *Pesticides and Politics: The Life Cycle of a Public Issue*. Pittsburgh: University of Pittsburgh Press, 1987.

Boyd, Harold R. "Terror in the East Palouse." *Pacific Northwesterner* 2, no. 3 (Summer 1958): 33–38.

Brady, Nyle C. *Agriculture and the Quality of Our Environment*. Washington, DC: American Association for the Advancement of Science, 1967.

Brink, Wellington. *Big Hugh: The Father of Soil Conservation*. New York: McMillan, 1951.

Browne, William P. *The Failure of National Rural Policy: Institutions and Interests*. Washington, DC: Georgetown University Press, 2001.

———. *Private Interests, Public Policy, and American Agriculture*. Lawrence: University of Kansas Press, 1988.

Bryan, Enoch Albert. *Historical Sketches of the State College of Washington*. Spokane: The Alumni and the Associated Students, 1928.

Busacca, Alan J., ed. *Dust Aerosols, Loess Soils, and Global Change: An Interdisciplinary Conference and Field Tour on Dust in Ancient Environments and Contemporary Environmental Management*. Washington State University, College of Agriculture and Home Economics, Miscellaneous Publications No. MISC 0190, 1998.

Busacca, Alan J. "Long Quaternary Record in Eastern Washington, U.S.A., Interpreted from Multiple Buried Paleosols in Loess." *Geoderma* 45 (1989): 102–122.

Busacca, Alan J., et al. "Dynamic Impacts of Erosion Processes on Productivity of Soils in the Palouse." In *Proceedings of the National Symposium on Erosion and Soil Productivity*, New Orleans, Louisiana, 10–11 December 1984.

Butler, B. Robert. "Bison Hunting in the Desert West Before 1800: The Paleo-Ecological Potential and the Archaeological Reality." *Plains Anthropologist* 23 no. 82 (November 1978): 106–112.

Caldwell, Harry. "The Palouse in Diverse Disciplines." *Northwest Science* 35, no. 4 (1961): 115–121.

Camp, Oscar A., and Paul C. McGrew. *History of Washington's Soil and Water Conservation Districts*. N.p, 1969.

Carlson, John E., Don A. Dillman, and C. Ellen Lamiman. "The Present and Future Use of No-Till in the Palouse." University of Idaho, Agricultural Experiment Station, Research Bulletin No. 140, 1990.

Charles, J. M. "Comparative Subchronic Studies on 2,4–D Acid, Amine and Ester in Rats." *Fundamental and Applied Toxicology* 33 (1996): 161–165.

———. "Developmental Toxicity Studies in Rats and Rabbits on 2,4–D and its Forms." *Toxicological Sciences* 60 (2001): 121–131.

Chase, Stuart. *Rich Land, Poor Land: A Study of Waste in the Natural Resources of America*. New York: Whittlesey House, 1936.

Cochrane, Willard W. *The Development of American Agriculture: A Historical Analysis*. 2nd ed. Minneapolis: University of Minnesota Press, 1993.

Collins, Mary B., and William Andrefsky Jr. *Archaeological Collections Inventory and Assessment of Marmes Rockshelter (45FR50) and Palus Sites (45FR36A, B, C)*. Pullman: Center for Northwest Anthropology, Department of Anthropology, Washington State University, 1995.

"Columbia River and Tributaries Review Study: Project Data and Operating Limits." US Army Corps of Engineers, North Pacific Division, CRT 69, 1989.

Commoner, Barry. *Science and Survival*. New York: Viking Press, 1963.

Comparative Statements of Condition. Pullman State Bank and First National Bank of Pullman, 1917–1939.

Comprehensive Planning Program. Whitman County, Washington, 1978.

The Conservation Reserve Program. USDA, 1997, 2001.

Conservation Reserve Program of the Soil Bank, Statistical Summary. USDA, 1957–1963.

Contour Buffer Strips. USDA, Natural Resources Conservation Service, April 1997.

Cronon, William. *Nature's Metropolis: Chicago and the Great West*. New York: W. W. Norton, 1991.

Cross, Frank L., ed. *208 Planning: What's It All About?* Westport, CT: Technomic, 1976.

Crosson, Pierre R., and Anthony T. Stout. *Productivity Effects of Cropland Erosion in the United States*. Washington, DC: Resources for the Future, 1983.

Crouch, Martha L. "Biotechnology Is Not Compatible with Sustainable Agriculture." *Journal of Agricultural and Environmental Ethics* 8 (1995): 98–111.

Cunfer, Geoff. *On the Great Plains: Agriculture and Environment.* College Station: Texas A&M University Press, 2005.

Dalrymple, Dana D. "Changes in Wheat Varieties and Yields in the United States, 1919–1984." *Agricultural History* 62, no. 3 (1988): 20–36.

Danbom, David. *The Resisted Revolution: Urban America and the Industrialization of Agriculture.* Ames: Iowa State University Press, 1979.

Daubenmire, Rexford F. "An Ecological Study of the Vegetation of Southeastern Washington and Adjacent Idaho." *Ecological Monographs* 12 (1942): 55–79.

———. "Steppe Vegetation of Washington." Washington Agricultural Experiment Station, Technical Bulletin No. 62, 1970.

DeGregori, Thomas R. *Bountiful Harvest: Technology, Food Safety, and the Environment.* Washington, DC: Cato Institute, 2002.

De Hevesy, Paul. *World Wheat Planning and Economic Planning in General.* New York: Oxford University Press, 1940.

Doke, Jeffrey L., and Gibran S. Hashmi. *Paradise Creek Watershed Characterization Study.* Pullman: State of Washington Water Research Center, 1994.

Donahue, Brian. *The Great Meadow: Farmers and the Land in Colonial Concord.* New Haven: Yale University Press, 2004.

Dryland Agriculture Water Quality Management Plan. State of Washington Department of Ecology, 1979.

Duncan, Colin A. M. *The Centrality of Agriculture: Between Humankind and the Rest of Nature.* Montreal, PQ: McGill-Queen's University Press, 1996.

Dunlap, Thomas R. *DDT: Scientists, Citizens, and Public Policy.* Princeton, NJ: Princeton University Press, 1981.

———. "Farmers, Scientists, and Insects." *Agricultural History* 54 (1980): 93–107.

Duvick, David N. "Biotechnology Is Compatible with Sustainable Agriculture." *Journal of Agricultural and Environmental Ethics* 8 (1995): 112–125.

The Earth Around Us. Ankeny, IA: Soil Conservation Society of America, 1972.

Easterbrook, Don J., and David A. Rahm. *Landforms of Washington: The Geological Environment.* Bellingham: Western Washington University, 1970.

Ebbert, James C., and Dennis Roe. *Soil Erosion in the Palouse River Basin: Indications of Improvement.* USGS, USDA, 1998.

An Eleventh Commandment. National Association of Soil Conservation Districts, 1955.

Elliott, L. F., ed. *STEEP—Conservation Concepts and Accomplishments.* Pullman: Washington State University Publications, 1986.

"Emotion Is a Pollutant, Too." *Agricultural Chemicals*, May 1971, 10.

Erickson, D. N., and D. Norton. *Washington State Agricultural Chemicals Pilot Study.* Washington State Department of Ecology, 1990.

Fahey, John. *The Inland Empire: The Unfolding Years, 1879–1929*. Seattle: University of Washington Press, 1986.

FAO Commodity Series: Wheat. Washington, DC: Food and Agriculture Organization of the United Nations, 1947.

Farm Lands in the Famous Palouse Country of Eastern Washington and Northern Idaho: How to Get There, How to Get a Farm. Spokane, WA: Shaw and Borden, 1895.

Fiege, Mark. *Irrigated Eden: The Making of an Agricultural Landscape in the American West*. Seattle: University of Washington Press, 1999.

Fischer, George W., and J. P. Meiners, "Comparative Value of Several Fungicides in the Control of Head and Stripe Smuts in Certain Forage Grasses." State College of Washington, Agricultural Experiment Station, Bulletin No. 532, 1952.

Fitzgerald, Deborah. *Every Farm a Factory: The Industrial Ideal in American Agriculture*. New Haven, CT: Yale University Press, 2003.

Flader, Susan L., and J. Baird Callicott, eds. *The River of the Mother of God, and Other Essays by Aldo Leopold*. Madison: University of Wisconsin Press, 1991.

Flores, Dan. *The Natural West: Environmental History in the Great Plains and Rocky Mountains*. Norman: University of Oklahoma Press, 2001.

Franklin, Jerry F., and C. T. Dyrness. *Natural Vegetation of Oregon and Washington*. Corvallis: Oregon State University Press, 1988.

Freeman, Otis W. "The Pacific Northwest Pea Industry." *Economic Geography* 19, no. 2 (1943): 118–120.

Frykman, George A. *Creating the People's University: Washington State University, 1890–1990*. Pullman: Washington State University Press, 1990.

Fryxell, Roald, and Earl F. Cook. *A Field Guide to the Loess Deposits and Channeled Scablands of the Palouse Area, Eastern Washington*. Pullman: Laboratory of Anthropology, Washington State University, 1964.

Fuller, George W. *A History of the Pacific Northwest*. New York: Alfred A. Knopf, 1931.

Galston, William A. *A Tough Road to Hoe: The 1985 Farm Bill and Beyond*. New York: Hamilton Press, 1985.

Gardner, B. Delworth. *Plowing Ground in Washington: The Political Economy of US Agriculture*. San Francisco: Pacific Research Institute for Public Policy, 1995.

Gardner, Bruce L. *American Agriculture in the Twentieth Century: How It Flourished and What It Cost*. Cambridge, MA: Harvard University Press, 2002.

———. *US Agriculture Policy: The 1985 Farm Legislation*. Washington, DC: American Enterprise Institute for Public Policy Research, 1985.

Gasser, J. K. R., et al., eds. *Anhydrous Ammonia: Proceedings of a Symposium on Aspects of Its Technology and Use as a Fertilizer*. Surrey, UK: IPC Science and Technology Press, 1971.

Gates, Paul W. *History of Public Land Law Development*. Washington, DC: GPO, 1968.

The Geology of North America. Boulder, CO: Geological Society of America, 1991.

Geyer, Charles A. "Notes on the Vegetation and General Character of the Missouri and Oregon Territories, Made During a Botanical Journey in the State of Missouri, Across the South Pass of the Rocky Mountains, to the Pacific, During the years 1843 and 1844." *London Journal of Botany* 5 (1845): 286–287.

Gladwell, John S., and William H. Funk, eds. *Water Pollution Control: Action-Reaction-Inaction*. Moscow: University of Idaho, Water Resources Research Institute, 1974.

Goble, Dale D., and Paul W. Hirt, eds. *Northwest Lands, Northwest Peoples: Readings in Environmental History*. Seattle: University of Washington Press, 1999.

Gold, Bela. *Wartime Economic Planning in Agriculture: A Study in the Allocation of Resources*. New York: Columbia University Press, 1949.

Gottlieb, Roger S., ed. *This Sacred Earth: Religion, Nature, and Environment*. New York: Routledge, 1996.

Graham, Edward H. "Legumes for Erosion Control and Wildlife." USDA Miscellaneous Publication No. 412, 1941.

Graham, Frank, Jr. *Since Silent Spring*. Boston: Houghton-Mifflin, 1970.

Gross, Gerald H. "Cave Life on the Palouse." *Natural History* 76, no. 1 (February 1967): 38–43.

Guillierie, Renee, and Sharon Norris. *Serving People and the Land: A History of Idaho's Soil Conservation Movement*. Meridian: Idaho Association of Soil Conservation Districts, 1985.

Hallberg, M. C. *Policy for American Agriculture: Choices and Consequences*. Ames: Iowa State University Press, 1992.

Hamilton, David E. *From New Day to New Deal: American Farm Policy from Hoover to Roosevelt, 1929–1933*. Chapel Hill: University of North Carolina Press, 1991.

Hanna, Lester W. *Hanna's Handbook of Agricultural Chemicals*. Forest Grove, OR: Lester W. Hanna, 1952.

Harston, C. B. "Fertilizers in Eastern Washington." State College of Washington, Agricultural Experiment Station, Bulletin No. 385, 1954.

———. "Water Quality Management and Nonpoint Sources of Pollution." Washington State University, Cooperative Extension Service, Bulletin No. 672, 1976.

Hart, Neil E. *The Farm Debt Crisis of the 1980s*. Ames: Iowa State University Press, 1990.

Hastings, Lansford W. *The Emigrants Guide to Oregon and California*. Princeton, NJ: Princeton University Press, 1932.

Hayes, Derek. *Historical Atlas of the Pacific Northwest: Maps of Exploration and Discovery*. Seattle: Sasquatch Books, 1999.

Hegnauer, Leonard. *86 Golden Years: The Autobiography of Leonard Hegnauer*. N.p., n.d. Leonard Hegnauer Papers, 1954–1963, Washington State University, Manuscripts, Archives, and Special Collections.

Heisig, Carl P. "A Graphic Presentation of Changes in Agriculture of Washington from 1930 to 1935." State College of Washington, Agricultural Experiment Station, Bulletin No. 341, 1936.

Helms, J. Douglas, et al. "National Soil Conservation Policies: A Historical Case Study of the Driftless Area." *Agricultural History* 70 (Spring 1996): 377–394.

Hertz, Milton. "Implementing CRP: Progress and Prospects." *Journal of Soil and Water Conservation* 43 (January–February 1988): 14–16.

"High Lights in Agricultural Research in Idaho." University of Idaho, Agricultural Experiment Station, Bulletin No. 244, 1941.

Hightower, Jim. *Hard Tomatoes, Hard Times: A Report of the Agribusiness Accountability Project on the Failure of America's Land Grant Colleges*. Cambridge, MA: Schenkman, 1973.

Hobson, Karl. "The Wheat Shortage Is Here." *Farm Journal*, August 1966, 21, 47.

Horner, G. M. "Effect of Cropping Systems on Runoff, Erosion, and Wheat Yields." *Agronomy Journal* 52, no. 6 (June 1960): 342–344.

Howard, Sir Albert. *The Soil and Health: A Study of Organic Agriculture*. New York: Devin-Adair Co., 1947.

Humphrey, Craig R. *Environment, Energy, and Society*. Belmont, CA: Wadsworth Publishing, 1982.

Hunn, Eugene. *Nch'i-Wana, "The Big River": Mid-Columbia Indians and Their Land*. Seattle: University of Washington Press, 1990.

Hunter, Byron. "Farm Practice in the Columbia Basin Uplands." USDA Farmers' Bulletin No. 294, 1907.

Hurt, R. Douglas, ed. *The Rural West Since World War II*. Lawrence: University of Kansas Press, 1998.

Idaho's Soil and Water: Condition and Trends. USDA, Soil Conservation Service, 1983.

An Illustrated History of Whitman County. W. H. Lever, 1901.

Jackson, Wes. *New Roots for Agriculture*. Lincoln: University of Nebraska Press, 1980.

Jackson, Wes, Wendell Berry, and Bruce Coleman, eds. *Meeting the Expectations of the Land: Essays in Sustainable Agriculture and Stewardship*. San Francisco: North Point Press, 1984.

Jennings, Michael D., et al. "Sustainability of Dryland Cropping in the Palouse: An Historical View." *Journal of Soil and Water Conservation* (January–February 1990): 75–80.

Jennings, Michael D., and John P. Reganold. "Policy and Reality of Environmentally Sensitive Areas in Whitman County, Washington, USA." *Environmental Management* 12, no. 3 (1988): 369–370.

Johnson, Leonard C., et. al. "Surface Water Quality in the Palouse Dryland Grain Region." Washington State University, Agricultural Experiment Station, Bulletin No. 779, 1973.

Johnson, Leonard C., and Myron Molnau. "Hydrograph and Water Quality Relationships for Two Palouse Cropland Watersheds." University of Idaho, Agricultural Experiment Station, Bulletin No. 87, 1975.

Jones, Joseph L., and Richard J. Wagner. *Water Quality Assessment of the Central Columbia Plateau in Washington and Idaho—Analysis of Available Nutrient and Pesticide Data for Ground Water, 1942–1992.* Tacoma, WA: USGS, 1995.

Kaiser, Verle G. "Background of the State Soil Conservation District Act." N.p., n.d. Verle G. Kaiser Papers, 1932–1982, Washington State University, Manuscripts, Archives, and Special Collections.

———. "Historical Land Use and Erosion in the Palouse—A Reappraisal." *Northwest Science* 35, no. 4 (1961): 139–153.

———. "An Informal Report of the Erosion Damage During the 1945–1946 Runoff Season in Whitman County, Washington." N.p., n.d. Verle G. Kaiser Papers, 1932–1982, Washington State University, Manuscripts, Archives, and Special Collections.

———. Oral history interview by Douglas Helms for the Soil Conservation Service, 17 September 1981. Washington State University, Manuscripts, Archives, and Special Collections.

Kaiser, Verle G. et al. "Soil Losses on Wheat Farms in the Palouse Wheat-Pea Area, 1952–1953: A Progress Report." State College of Washington, Agricultural Experiment Station, Circular No. 255, 1954.

Kelley, Hubert W. "Conservation Tillage: Hazards Ahead?" *Soil Conservation* 42, no. 6 (January 1977): 8–17.

Kincaid, Garret D., and A. H. Harris. *Palouse . . . in the Making.* N.p., 1934.

Kinsley, David. *Ecology and Religion.* Englewood Cliffs, NJ: Prentice-Hall, 1994.

Kittredge, William. *Owning It All.* St. Paul, MN: Graywolf Press, 1987.

Klemgard, J. G., and G. F. Cadisch. "Cost of Wheat Production by Power Methods of Farming, 1919–1929." State College of Washington, Agricultural Experiment Station, Bulletin No. 255, 1931.

Klingman, D. L. "Effects of Spraying Cereals with 2,4–D." *Journal of the American Society of Agronomy* 39 (1947): 445–447.

Knobloch, Frieda. *The Culture of Wilderness: Agriculture as Colonization in the American West.* Chapel Hill: University of North Carolina Press, 1996.

Lambert, Scott M., Rodney D. Sayler, and Linda Hardesty. "The Palouse Prairie—Does It Still Exist or Is It Extinct?" N.p., 1997.

"Land Capability Methods for Conserving Washington Soils." State College of Washington, Agricultural Experiment Stations, USDA, Soil Conservation Service, Popular Bulletin No. 200, 1950.

Landerholm, E. F. "The Economic Relation of Tractors to Farm Organization in the Grain Farming Areas of Eastern Washington." State College of Washington, Agricultural Experiment Station, Bulletin No. 310, 1935.

Latah County Comprehensive Plan of 1979. Latah County Planning and Zoning Commission, 1980.

Latah County Soil Conservation District. 10th Anniversary: Program and Work Plan. Moscow, ID: Latah County Historical Society, 1950.

Layman, William D. Native River: The Columbia Remembered, Priest Rapids to the International Boundary. Pullman: Washington State University Press, 2002.

Leopold, Aldo. A Sand County Almanac, and Sketches Here and There. New York: Oxford University Press, 1949.

Leuchtenberg, William. Franklin D. Roosevelt and the New Deal, 1932–1940. New York: Harper and Row, 1963.

Lewty, Peter J. Across the Columbia Plain: Railroad Expansion in the Interior Northwest, 1885–1893. Pullman: Washington State University Press, 1995.

Lord, Russell. To Hold This Soil. USDA Miscellaneous Publication No. 321. Washington, DC: GPO, 1938.

Lowitt, Richard. The New Deal and the West. Bloomington: Indiana University Press, 1984.

MacIntyre, Angus A. "Why Pesticides Received Extensive Use in America: A Political Economy of Agricultural Pest Management to 1970." Natural Resources Journal 27 (Summer 1987): 533–578.

Mack, Richard N. "First Comprehensive Botanical Survey of the Columbia Plateau, Washington: The Sandberg and Leiberg Expedition of 1893." Northwest Science 62, no. 3 (May 1988): 118–128.

Marco, Gino J., Robert M. Hollingworth, and Jack R. Plummer, eds. Regulation of Agrochemicals: A Driving Force in Their Evolution. Washington, DC: American Chemical Society, 1991.

Marx, Leo. The Machine in the Garden: Technology and the Pastoral Ideal in America. New York: Oxford University Press, 1964.

Maughan, O. Eugene, et al. "A Comparison of Fish Species Above and Below Palouse Falls, Palouse River, Washington-Idaho." Northwest Science 54, no. 1 (1980): 5–8.

McCall, M. A., and H. M. Wanser. "The Principle of Summer-Fallow Tillage." State College of Washington, Agricultural Experiment Station, Bulletin No. 183, 1924.

McCroskey, R. C. "Wheat Growing." Washington Agricultural College and School of Science Experiment Station, Bulletin No. 1, 1892.

McDonald, Eric von. "Correlation and Interpretation of the Stratigraphy of the Palouse Loess of Eastern Washington." PhD dissertation, Washington State University, 1987.

McGregor, Alexander Campbell. *Counting Sheep: From Open Range to Agribusiness on the Columbia Plateau.* Seattle: University of Washington Press, 1982.

McGrew, Paul C., and G. M. Horner. *Soil and Water Conservation Investigations.* Washington, DC: USDA, Soil Conservation Service, 1937.

McKay, Hugh C. "Control Canada Thistle for Greater Profits." University of Idaho, Agricultural Experiment Station, Bulletin No. 321, 1959.

Meinig, Donald W. *The Great Columbia Plain: A Historical Geography, 1805–1910.* Seattle: University of Washington Press, 1968.

Meyers, Peter C. "Conservation at the Crossroads." *Journal of Soil and Water Conservation* 43 (January–February 1988): 10–13.

Mickey, Karl B. *Man and the Soil: A Brief Introduction to the Study of Soil Conservation.* Chicago: International Harvester, 1945.

Miss, Christian J., and Bruce D. Cochran. *Archaeological Evaluations of the Riparia (45WT1) and Ash Cave (45WW61) Sites on the Lower Snake River.* Pullman: Laboratory of Anthropology, Washington State University, 1982.

Moffat, A. S. "Agricultural Research: Higher Yielding Perennials Point to the Way to New Crops." *Science* 274 (1996): 1469–1470.

Morgan, Robert J. *Governing Soil Conservation: Thirty Years of the New Decentralization.* Baltimore, MD: Johns Hopkins Press, 1965.

Morrissey, Katherine G. *Mental Territories: Mapping the Inland Empire.* Ithaca: Cornell University Press, 1997.

The Nature and Fate of Chemicals Applied to Soils, Plants, and Animals: A Symposium Held April 27, 28, and 29, 1960, at the Plant Industry Station and Agricultural Research Center, Beltsville, Maryland. Washington, DC: USDA, 1960.

Neese, Harvey C. *The Palouse Wash-out: A 20th Century Tragedy.* Troy, ID: Wildlife Resources, 1973.

Neidig, Ray E., and Robert S. Snyder. "The Relation of the Yield and Protein Content of Wheat to the Nitrogen Content of the Soil Under Ten Years of Different Systems of Cropping." University of Idaho, Agricultural Research Station, Research Bulletin No. 5, 1926.

Nelson, L. M. *Surface Water Resources for the Columbia Plateau: Washington, Oregon, and Idaho.* USGS, 1991.

Nesbit, Robert C., and Charles M. Gates. "Agriculture in Eastern Washington." *Pacific Northwest Quarterly* 37, no. 4 (1946): 279–302.

Ninth Eastern Washington Fertilizer and Pesticide Conference, Washington State University, January 29 and 30. Washington State University Cooperative Extension Service and College of Agriculture, 1973.

Nixon, Edgar B., ed. FDR *and Conservation, 1911–1945.* 2 vols. Hyde Park, NY: GSA, 1957.

Norton, E. A. *Soil Conservation Survey Handbook.* USDA Miscellaneous Publication No. 352. Washington, DC: GPO, 1939.

Oliphant, J. Orin. "Notes on Early Settlements and on Geographic Names of Eastern Washington." *Washington Historical Quarterly* 22, no. 3 (1931): 172–201.

———. *On the Cattle Ranges of the Oregon Country.* Seattle: University of Washington Press, 1968.

Opie, John. *Ogallala: Water for a Dry Land.* Lincoln: University of Nebraska Press, 1993.

Orr, Alden E., Carl P. Heisig, and J. C. Knott, "Trends and Desirable Adjustments in Washington Agriculture." State College of Washington, Agricultural Experiment Station, Bulletin No. 335, 1936.

Orr, Elizabeth L., and William N. Orr. *Geology of the Pacific Northwest.* New York: McGraw-Hill, 1996.

Orr, John Boyd. *The White Man's Dilemma.* London: George Alwin and Unwin, 1953.

Osborn, Fairfield. *Our Plundered Planet.* Boston: Little, Brown and Co., 1948.

Osborn, Tim. "The Conservation Reserve Program: Status, Future, and Policy Options." *Journal of Soil and Water Conservation* 48 (July–August 1993): 273.

Osterman, Douglas A., and Theresa L. Hicks. "Highly-Erodible Land: Farmer Perception versus Actual Measurements." *Journal of Soil and Water Conservation* 43 (January–February 1988): 177–181.

Our Changing Nature: Natural Resource Trends in Washington State. Washington State Department of Natural Resources, 1998.

Overland, Alvin. "Some Effects of 2,4–D Formulations in Herbicidal Concentrations on Wheat and Barley." Master's thesis, Washington State University, 1950.

Oxford Economist Calls Population Explosion a Good Thing. Washington State University, Washington State Farm and Home News, 1963.

Pacific Northwest Erosion Control. Annual report. Soil Conservation Service, 1934–1935.

Pacific Northwest Pest Control Handbook. Idaho State Department of Agriculture, Oregon State Department of Agriculture, Washington State Department of Agriculture, 1979.

Palouse Cooperative River Basin Study. USDA, Soil Conservation Service, Forest Service, Economics, Statistics, and Cooperatives Service, 1978.

The Palouse Story. Palouse Town and Country Study Program, 1962.

Parker, Martha Berry. *Washington and Oregon: A Map History of the Oregon Country*. Fairfield, WA: Ye Galleon Press, 1988.

Parker, Samuel. *Journal of an Exploring Tour Beyond the Rocky Mountains*. Ithaca, NY: Andrus, Woodruff, and Gauntlett, 1844.

Perkins, John H. *Insects, Experts, and the Insecticide Crisis: The Quest for New Pest Management Strategies*. New York: Plenum Press, 1982.

Pesticides and Epidemiology: Unraveling Disease Patterns. Purdue University Pesticide Program, July 1998.

The Pesticide Situation. USDA, 1953–1965.

Peterson, Keith. *This Crested Hill: An Illustrated History of the University of Idaho*. Moscow: University of Idaho Press, 1987.

Peterson, Trudy Huskamp, ed. *Farmers, Bureaucrats, and Middlemen: Historical Perspectives on American Agriculture*. Washington, DC: Howard University Press, 1980.

Pinstrup-Anderson, Per, and Ebbe Schiøler. *Seeds of Contention: World Hunger and the Controversy over GM Crops*. Baltimore, MD: Johns Hopkins University Press, 2000.

Pittman, Nancy P. *From the Land*. Washington, DC: Island Press, 1988.

Plat Book of Whitman County. Seattle: Anderson Map Co., 1910.

Poelker, Richard J., and Irven O. Buss. "Habitat Improvement—The Way to Higher Wildlife Populations in Southeast Washington." *Northwest Science* 46, no. 1 (January 1972): 25–31.

Presby, Dorothy. *Viola Stump Ranch*. N.p., 1999.

Proceedings of the 32nd Annual Session of the Washington State Grange. Aberdeen: Washington State Grange, 1920.

Pubols, Ben H., and Carl P. Heisig. "Historical and Geographic Aspects of Wheat Yields in Washington." State College of Washington, Agricultural Experiment Station, Bulletin No. 355, 1937.

Pubols, Ben H., Carl P. Heisig, and Alden E. Orr. "Farming Systems and Practices and Their Relationship to Soil Conservation and Farm Income in the Wheat Region of Washington." State College of Washington, Agricultural Experiment Station, Bulletin No. 374, 1939.

Pullman, Washington: The Commercial and Educational Center of the Palouse Country. Pullman Chamber of Commerce, 1912.

Ramser, C. E. "Prevention of the Erosion of Farm Lands by Terracing." USDA Bulletin No. 512, 1917.

Rasmussen, Wayne D. "The Impact of Technological Change on American Agriculture, 1862–1962." *Journal of Economic History* 22, no. 4 (December 1962): 578–591.

"A Regulation Relating to Water Quality Standards for Interstate and Coastal Waters of the State of Washington and a Plan for Implementation and Enforcement of Such Standards." State of Washington, Water Pollution Control Commission, 1967.

Relander, Click. *Drummers and Dreamers.* Caldwell, ID: Caxton Printers, 1956.

———. *The Yakimas: Treaty Centennial.* Yakima, WA: Franklin Press, 1955.

Renard, K. G., et al. *Predicting Soil Erosion by Water: A Guide to Conservation Planning with the Revised Universal Soil Loss Equation (RUSLE).* Washington, DC: GPO, 1997.

Richards, Kent. *Isaac Stevens: Young Man in a Hurry.* Provo, UT: Brigham Young University Press, 1979.

Richter, Daniel D., Jr., and Daniel Markewitz. *Understanding Soil Change: Soil Sustainability over Millennia, Centuries, and Decades.* New York: Cambridge University Press, 2001.

Riparian Forest Buffer. USDA, Natural Resources Conservation Service, 1998.

Robbins, William G. *The Great Northwest: The Search for Regional Identity.* Corvallis: Oregon State University Press, 2001.

———. *Landscapes of Conflict: The Oregon Story, 1940–2000.* Seattle: University of Washington Press, 2004.

———. *Landscapes of Promise: The Oregon Story, 1800–1940.* Seattle: University of Washington Press, 1997.

Rockie, William A. "Man's Effects on the Palouse." *The Geographical Review* 29, no. 1 (1939): 34–35.

———. "A Message to All Members of the Northwest Scientific Association." *Northwest Science* 9, no. 3 (1935): 3–4.

———. "Snowdrift Erosion in the Palouse." *Geographical Review* 41, no. 3 (July 1951): 461–463.

Rockie, William A., and Paul C. McGrew. "Erosive Effects of Heavy Summer Rains in Southeastern Washington." State College of Washington, Agricultural Experiment Station, Bulletin No. 271, 1932.

Rothstein, Morton. "West Coast Farmers and the Tyranny of Distance: Agriculture on the Fringes of the World Market." *Agricultural History* 49, no. 1 (1975): 272–283.

Rowalt, E. M. "Soil and Water Conservation in the Pacific Northwest." USDA Farmers' Bulletin No. 1773, 1937.

Roylance, Howard B., and K. H. Klages. "Winter Wheat Production." University of Idaho, Agricultural Experiment Station, Bulletin No. 314, 1959.

———. *A Guide to the Indian Tribes of the Pacific Northwest.* Norman: University of Oklahoma Press, 1986.

Rule, Glenn K. "Working Plans for Permanent Farms." USDA Miscellaneous Publication No. 411, 1940.

Russell, Edmund. *War and Nature: Fighting Humans and Insects with Chemicals from World War I to "Silent Spring."* New York: Cambridge University Press, 2001.

Santmire, H. Paul. *The Ambiguous Ecological Promise of Christian Theology*. Philadelphia: Fortress Press, 1985.

Scheinost, Pamela L. "Perennial Wheat: The Development of a Sustainable Cropping System for the US, Pacific Northwest." *American Journal of Alternative Agriculture* 16, no. 4 (2001): 147–151.

Scheuerman, Richard D. *Patterns of Settlement in the Palouse Country, 1860–1915*. N.p. Whitman County Historical Society, 1980.

Scheuerman, Richard, and Clifford Trafzer. "The First People of the Palouse Country." *Bunchgrass Historian* 8, no. 3 (1988): 3–18.

———, eds. "A Palouse Indian Speaks: Mary Jim Remembers." *Bunchgrass Historian* 8, no. 3 (1988): 20–23.

Schlebecker, John T. *Whereby We Thrive: A History of American Farming*. Ames: Iowa State University Press, 1975.

Schultz, Debra M. "Farmers' Perceptions of Soil Erosion and Soil Conservation in the Pleasant Valley Creek Watershed." Master's thesis, Washington State University, 1985.

Scobey, John. "Dairy Farming in Washington." State College of Washington, Agricultural Experiment Station, Bulletin No. 2, February 1892.

———. "Farm Dairying." State College of Washington, Agricultural Experiment Station, Bulletin No. 3, February 1982.

Section-by-Section Summary of Title II of the Farm Security and Rural Investment Act of 2002. USDA, Natural Resources Conservation Service, 2002.

SEPA Guidelines. State of Washington, Council on Environmental Policy, 1975.

Severence, George. "Field Peas on a Palouse Wheat Farm." State College of Washington, Agricultural Experiment Station, Bulletin No. 36, 1911.

Shepherd, James F. "The Development of Wheat Production in the Pacific Northwest." *Agricultural History* 49, no. 1 (1975): 258–271.

———. "Soil Conservation in the Pacific Northwest Wheat-Producing Areas: Conservation in a Hilly Terrain." *Agricultural History* 59, no. 4 (1985): 229–245.

Shepard, Ward. *Food or Famine: The Challenge of Erosion*. New York: Macmillan, 1945.

Sievers, Frederick J., and Henry F. Holtz. "The Fertility of Washington Soils." State College of Washington, Agricultural Experiment Station, Bulletin No. 189, 1924.

———. "The Maintenance of Crop Production on Semi-Arid Soil." State College of Washington, Agricultural Experiment Station, Popular Bulletin No. 138, 1927.

———. "The Silt Loam Soils of Eastern Washington and Their Management." State College of Washington, Agricultural Experiment Station, Bulletin No. 166, 1922.

Simms, D. Harper. *The Soil Conservation Service*. New York: Praeger Publishers, 1970.

Sixth and Seventh Annual Eastern Washington Fertilizer and Pesticide Conference, 2 and 3 February 1970, 1 and 2 February 1971. Washington State University Cooperative Extension Service and College of Agriculture, n.d.

Smalley, E. V. "In the Palouse Country." *Northwest Magazine*, September 1892.

Smith, Henry W., S. C. Vandecaveye, and L. T. Kardos. "Wheat Production and Properties of Palouse Silt Loam as Affected by Organic Residues and Fertilizers." State College of Washington, Agricultural Experiment Stations, Bulletin No. 476, 1946.

Soil and Water Conservation: An Introduction to the Problem and Its Control. Spokane, WA: Soil Conservation Service, 1942.

Soil Conservation in Outline. Northwest Regional Council, 1940.

Soil Survey of Whitman County, Washington. USDA, Soil Conservation Service, 1980.

Steiner, Frederick R. *The Productive and Erosive Palouse Environment*. Washington State University, Cooperative Extension, USDA, 1987.

——. *Soil Conservation in the United States: Policy and Planning*. Baltimore, MD: Johns Hopkins University Press, 1990.

Steiner, Michael P., and Gerald Marousek. *Food for Freedom: On the Causes of War and the Conditions for Peace*. Moscow: University of Idaho Press, 1967.

Stephens, David E. *Conservation Practices on Wheat Lands of the Pacific Northwest*. USDA, Soil Conservation Service, 1944.

St. John, Harold. *Flora of Southeastern Washington and of Adjacent Idaho*. Escondido, CA: Outdoor Pictures, 1963.

Stoll, Steven. *Larding the Lean Earth: Soil and Society in Nineteenth-Century America*. New York: Hill and Wang, 2002.

Stratton, David H., ed. *Spokane and the Inland Empire: An Interior Pacific Northwest Anthology*. Pullman: Washington State University Press, 1991.

Taylor, Maurice C., and Vernon W. Baker. "Economic Aspects of Soil Conservation in the Palouse Wheat-Pea Area." State College of Washington, Agricultural Experiment Station, Bulletin No. 494, 1947.

Thatcher, R. W. "The Nitrogen and Humus Problem in Dry Farming." State College of Washington, Agricultural Experiment Station, Bulletin No. 105, June 1912.

Thompson, Albert W. "The Early History of the Palouse River and Its Names." *Pacific Northwest Quarterly* 62, no. 2 (1971): 69–76.

Thompson, David. *Columbia Journals*. Edited by Barbara Belyea. Montreal, PQ: McGill-Queens University Press, 1994.

"Timely Economic Information for Washington Farmers." State College of Washington, Extension Service, 1931–1945.

Tisdale, E. W. "Ecologic Changes in the Palouse." *Northwest Science* 35, no. 4 (1961): 134–137.

Trafzer, Clifford E., and Richard D. Scheuerman. "The First People of the Palouse Country." *Bunchgrass Historian* 8, no. 3 (1988): 3–23.

———. *Renegade Tribe: The Palouse Indians and the Invasion of the Inland Pacific Northwest.* Pullman: Washington State University Press, 1986.

"Trends in Agriculture in Washington, 1900–1930." State College of Washington, Agricultural Experiment Station, Bulletin No. 300, 1931.

Tukey, H. B. "Historical Changes in Bindweed and Sowthistle Following Applications of 2,4-D in Herbicidal Concentrations." *Botany Gazette* 107 (1945): 62–73.

US Comptroller General. *To Protect Tomorrow's Food Supply—Soil Conservation Needs Priority Attention.* Washington, DC: GPO, 1977.

USGS. Land Use History of North America, August 15, 2000, http://biology.usgs.gov /luhna (accessed 12 October 2000).

Victor, Earl. "Some Effects of Cultivation Upon Stream History and Upon the Topography of the Palouse Region." *Northwest Science* 9, no. 3 (1935): 18–19.

Vogel, O. A., S. P. Swenson, and C. S. Holton. "Brevor and Elmar—Two New Wheats for Washington." State College of Washington, Agricultural Experiment Station, Bulletin No. 525, 1951.

Walker, Deward E., ed. *Handbook of North American Indians.* Vol. 12. Washington, DC: Smithsonian Institution, 1998.

Washington—Our Soil, Our Water: 1960–1964 Annual Report. USDA, Agricultural Stabilization and Conservation Service, n.d.

Washington Pest Control Handbook. Washington State University, Washington State Department of Agriculture, 1971.

Water Pollution as Related to Agriculture. Columbia Plateau Resources Council, 1967.

Water Quality Status Report No. WQ-46: South Fork of the Palouse River/Paradise Creek. Idaho Department of Health and Welfare, Division of Environment, 1981.

Weaver, J. E. *A Study of the Vegetation of Southeastern Washington and Adjacent Idaho.* Lincoln: University of Nebraska, 1917.

Webster, R. L. "New Insecticides: Their Use, Limitations, and Hazards to Human Health." State College of Washington, Agricultural Experiment Station, Circular No. 64, 1951.

Weddell, Bertie J. "Changing Perceptions in Nineteenth Century Written Descriptions of Palouse and Canyon Grasslands." Idaho Bureau of Land Management, Technical Bulletin No. 01–13, August 2001.

———. "Restoring Palouse and Canyon Grasslands: Putting Back the Missing Pieces." Bureau of Land Management, Technical Bulletin No. 01–15, August 2001.

Weis, Paul L., and William L. Newman. *The Channeled Scablands of Eastern Washington.* US Department of Interior, Eastern Washington University, 1989.

West, Elliott. *The Way to the West: Essays on the Great Plains.* Albuquerque: University of New Mexico Press, 1995.

"What if Pesticide Use Stopped?" *Farmer's Journal* 34, no. 3 (1970): 29–32.

Wheeting, L. C. "The Significance of Natural Erosion." *Northwest Science* 14, no. 1 (1940): 11–13.

Where the Buffalo Roamed. Phillips Petroleum, 1956.

White, Richard, and John M. Findlay, eds. *Power and Place in the North American West.* Seattle: University of Washington Press, 1999.

Whorton, James. *Before Silent Spring: Pesticides and Public Health in Pre-DDT America.* Princeton, NJ: Princeton University Press, 1974.

Williams, Hill. *The Restless Northwest: A Geological Story.* Pullman: Washington State University Press, 2002.

Williams, Keith Roy. "The Agricultural History of Latah County and the Palouse: An Overview and Three Case Studies." Master's thesis, Washington State University, 1984.

———. "Hills of Gold: A History of Wheat Production Technologies in the Palouse Region of Washington and Idaho." PhD dissertation, Washington State University, 1991.

Williamson, Alex K., et al. *Water Quality in the Central Columbia Plateau: Washington and Idaho, 1992–1995.* Tacoma: USGS, 1998.

Wilson, John A. "Water Pollution by Sediments in the Columbia Plateau Resources Area." N.p, 1967, Verle G. Kaiser Papers, 1932–1982, Washington State University, Manuscripts, Archives, and Special Collections.

Windbreak/Shelterbelt. USDA, Natural Resources Conservation Service, January 1998.

Worobec, Mary Devine. *Toxic Substances Controls Primer,* 2nd ed. Washington, DC: Bureau of National Affairs, 1986.

Worster, Donald. *Dust Bowl: The Southern Plains in the 1930s.* New York: Oxford University Press, 1979.

———. *Under Western Skies: Nature and History in the American West.* New York: Oxford University Press, 1992.

The Yearbook of Agriculture, 1954. Washington, DC: GPO, 1954.

Yoder, Fred R. *Stories of Early Pioneers in Whitman County, Washington.* N.p., 1938.

Yoder, Fred R., and A. A. Smick. "Migration of Farm Population and Flow of Farm Wealth." State College of Washington, Agricultural Experiment Station, Bulletin No. 315, 1935.

Young, Douglas L., et al. "Yields and Profitability of Conservation Tillage in the Eastern Palouse." Washington State University, Agricultural Research Center, Research Bulletin XB 0941, 1984.

Young, Douglas L., and David Walker. "Technical Progress in Yields—No Substitute for Soil Conservation." University of Idaho, College of Agriculture, Current Information Series No. 671, 1982.

Young, Gladwin E. "Water for Peace." *Soil Conservation* 32, no. 10 (May 1967): 220–221.

Zinn, Jeffrey. "How Are Soil Erosion Control Programs Working?" *Journal of Soil and Water Conservation* 48 (July–August 1993): 257.

INDEX

agrarianism, 8, 33, 43, 54–56, 88, 103, 117–19, 166

agrarian liberal, 14, 33, 54–56, 72, 75, 94, 100–1, 129, 145, 148, 162, 165; defined, 8–9

Agricultural Adjustment Act (1933), 80, 87, 93

Agricultural Improvement and Reform Act, a.k.a. the "Freedom to Farm Act" (1996), 155–56, 160–61

Agricultural Trade Development and Assistance Act, a.k.a. Public Law 480 and the "Food for Peace bill" (1954), 121

agriculture: chemicals, 102–4, 107, 110–15, 124, 126, 129–30, 134, 157–60, 169; conservation farming, 74–75, 82, 97, 120–26, 131–33, 140–41, 145, 149, 155; "diversified," 69–71, 77; dryland, 36, 40, 51; ethics (including steward-ship), 88–90, 103, 116–20, 123–26, 144–46, 162, 168–70; fruit, 46–47; "golden age" of, 56–57, 73, 151; labor, 46, 57; land consolidation, 61–62, 75, 95, 108; land retirement, 95, 120–22, 132, 140, 150–52, 154–56, 166–68; legumes (including alfalfa, clover, lentils, and peas), 46, 67–71, 81, 87, 93, 97–98, 108, 141; livestock, 30, 34–35, 38–40, 43–44, 70–71, 77, 94, 168, 193n64; New Deal, 74–75, 80–96, 100–101, 118, 120–21, 150–51; no-till, 146–47, 155; organic, 119, 169; subsis-tence, 33, 44, 70–79; sustainability, 11–13, 74, 88, 147–48, 167–70, technol-ogy, 5, 8, 34, 45, 59–60, 64–65, 90–92, 102, 107–8, 146–47, 155, 158–60, 169–70. *See also* erosion; fertilizers, artificial; herbicides; insecticides; loess; specific congressional acts

Almota, WA, 34, 40

Anthon, E.W., 130

WEYERHAEUSER ENVIRONMENTAL
BOOKS

*The Natural History of Puget Sound
Country* by Arthur R. Kruckeberg

*Forest Dreams, Forest Nightmares:
The Paradox of Old Growth in the
Inland West* by Nancy Langston

*Landscapes of Promise: The Oregon
Story, 1800–1940*
by William G. Robbins

*The Dawn of Conservation Diplomacy:
U.S.-Canadian Wildlife Protection
Treaties in the Progressive Era* by
Kurkpatrick Dorsey

*Irrigated Eden: The Making of an
Agricultural Landscape in the
American West* by Mark Fiege

*Making Salmon: An Environmental
History of the Northwest Fisheries
Crisis* by Joseph E. Taylor III

*George Perkins Marsh, Prophet of
Conservation* by David Lowenthal

*Driven Wild: How the Fight against
Automobiles Launched the Modern
Wilderness Movement* by Paul S. Sutter

*The Rhine: An Eco-Biography,
1815–2000* by Mark Cioc

*Where Land and Water Meet:
A Western Landscape Transformed*
by Nancy Langston

*The Nature of Gold: An Environmental
History of the Alaska/Yukon Gold
Rush* by Kathryn Morse

*Faith in Nature: Environmentalism as
Religious Quest* by Thomas R. Dunlap

*Landscapes of Conflict: The Oregon
Story, 1940–2000*
by William G. Robbins

The Lost Wolves of Japan
by Brett L. Walker

*Wilderness Forever: Howard Zahniser
and the Path to the Wilderness Act*
by Mark Harvey

*On the Road Again: Montana's
Changing Landscape*
by William Wyckoff

*Public Power, Private Dams: The Hells
Canyon High Dam Controversy* by
Karl Boyd Brooks

*Windshield Wilderness: Cars, Roads,
and Nature in Washington's National
Parks* by David Louter

*Native Seattle: Histories from the
Crossing-Over Place* by Coll Thrush

The Country in the City: The Greening of the San Francisco Bay Area by Richard Walker

Drawing Lines in the Forest: Creating Wilderness Areas in the Pacific Northwest by Kevin R. Marsh

Plowed Under: Agriculture and Environment in the Palouse by Andrew P. Duffin

Making Mountains: New York City and the Catskills by David Stradling

WEYERHAEUSER ENVIRONMENTAL CLASSICS

The Great Columbia Plain: A Historical Geography, 1805–1910 by D. W. Meinig

Mountain Gloom and Mountain Glory: The Development of the Aesthetics of the Infinite by Marjorie Hope Nicolson

Tutira: The Story of a New Zealand Sheep Station by Herbert Guthrie-Smith

A Symbol of Wilderness: Echo Park and the American Conservation Movement by Mark W. T. Harvey

Man and Nature: Or, Physical Geography as Modified by Human Action by George Perkins Marsh; edited and annotated by David Lowenthal

Conservation in the Progressive Era: Classic Texts edited by David Stradling

CYCLE OF FIRE
BY STEPHEN J. PYNE

Fire: A Brief History

World Fire: The Culture of Fire on Earth

Vestal Fire: An Environmental History, Told through Fire, of Europe and Europe's Encounter with the World

Fire in America: A Cultural History of Wildland and Rural Fire

Burning Bush: A Fire History of Australia

The Ice: A Journey to Antarctica

Breinigsville, PA USA
04 February 2010
231888BV00001B/7/P